LEGAL REASONING AND OBJECTIVE WRITING

Editorial Advisors

Erwin Chemerinsky
Dean and Distinguished Professor of Law
Raymond Pryke Professor of First Amendment Law
University of California, Irvine School of Law

Richard A. Epstein
Laurence A. Tisch Professor of Law
New York University School of Law
Peter and Kirsten Bedford Senior Fellow
The Hoover Institution
Senior Lecturer in Law
The University of Chicago

Ronald J. Gilson
Charles J. Meyers Professor of Law and Business
Stanford University
Marc and Eva Stern Professor of Law and Business
Columbia Law School

James E. Krier
Earl Warren DeLano Professor of Law
The University of Michigan Law School

Richard K. Neumann, Jr.
Professor of Law
Maurice A. Deane School of Law at Hofstra University

Robert H. Sitkoff
John L. Gray Professor of Law
Harvard Law School

David Alan Sklansky
Stanley Morrison Professor of Law, Stanford Law School
Faculty Co-Director, Stanford Criminal Justice Center

ASPEN COURSEBOOK SERIES

LEGAL REASONING AND OBJECTIVE WRITING:

A Comprehensive Approach

Daniel L. Barnett
Professor of Law
Director of Legal Writing
William S. Richardson School of Law
University of Hawai'i

Jane Kent Gionfriddo
Professor of Legal
Reasoning, Research & Writing
Boston College Law School

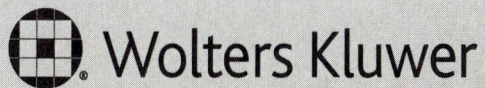

Copyright © 2016 CCH Incorporated.

Published by Wolters Kluwer in New York.

Wolters Kluwer Legal & Regulatory Solutions U.S. serves customers worldwide with CCH, Aspen Publishers, and Kluwer Law International products. (www.WKLegaledu.com)

No part of this publication may be reproduced or transmitted in any form or by any means, electronic or mechanical, including photocopy, recording, or utilized by any information storage or retrieval system, without written permission from the publisher. For information about permissions or to request permissions online, visit us at www.WKLegaledu.com, or a written request may be faxed to our permissions department at 212-771-0803.

To contact Customer Service, e-mail customer.service@wolterskluwer.com, call 1-800-234-1660, fax 1-800-901-9075, or mail correspondence to:

> Wolters Kluwer
> Attn: Order Department
> PO Box 990
> Frederick, MD 21705

Printed in the United States of America.

1 2 3 4 5 6 7 8 9 0

ISBN 978-1-4548-5897-3

Library of Congress Cataloging-in-Publication Data

Names: Barnett, Daniel L., author. | Gionfriddo, Jane Kent, author.
Title: Legal reasoning and objective writing : a comprehensive approach / Daniel L. Barnett, Professor of Law, Director of Legal Writing, William S. Richardson School of Law, University of Hawaii, Jane Kent Gionfriddo, Professor of Legal, Reasoning, Research & Writing, Boston College Law School.
Description: New York : Wolters Kluwer, [2016]
Identifiers: LCCN 2015049824 | ISBN 9781454858973
Subjects: LCSH: Law—United States—Methodology. | Law—United States—Language. | Legal composition.
Classification: LCC KF250 .B373 2016 | DDC 808.06/634—dc23
LC record available at http://lccn.loc.gov/2015049824

About Wolters Kluwer Legal & Regulatory Solutions U.S.

Wolters Kluwer Legal & Regulatory Solutions U.S. delivers expert content and solutions in the areas of law, corporate compliance, health compliance, reimbursement, and legal education. Its practical solutions help customers successfully navigate the demands of a changing environment to drive their daily activities, enhance decision quality and inspire confident outcomes.

Serving customers worldwide, its legal and regulatory solutions portfolio includes products under the Aspen Publishers, CCH Incorporated, Kluwer Law International, ftwilliam.com and MediRegs names. They are regarded as exceptional and trusted resources for general legal and practice-specific knowledge, compliance and risk management, dynamic workflow solutions, and expert commentary.

To all of my teachers, whose support, encouragement, and example continue to inspire me, especially: Miss Bluett, Coach Cave, Mr. Cole, Mr. Coyne, Mme. Darcy, Miss Herndandez, Mr. Jacobsen, Mr. Jacobson, Dr. Kinney, Mrs. Monson, Dr. Raitt, Mr. Robinson, Sal Salas, Mr. Schneider, Mrs. Vaught, and Ms. White.

D.L.B.

To Michael and Catherine, the loves of my life.
To Sally (1955-2015), who's missed.
To Sharon, who's inspired and supported me every step of the way.
To my students, who've taught me more than they know.

J.K.G.

Summary of Contents

Contents	xi
Acknowledgements	xxvii
Preface	xxix

PART I
INTRODUCTION TO LAW PRACTICE WRITING — 1

CHAPTER 1
The Basics of Objective Writing — 3

CHAPTER 2
The Stages of Objective Writing — 11

PART II
OBJECTIVE ANALYSIS OF LEGAL PROBLEMS — 27

CHAPTER 3
Sources of Law and Their Relationship — 29

CHAPTER 4
Statutory Analysis—A Basic Process — 39

CHAPTER 5
Statutory Analysis—Additional Steps — 53

CHAPTER 6
Analysis of Individual Judicial Opinions — 73

CHAPTER 7
Synthesis of Judicial Opinions — 95

CHAPTER 8
Synthesis of Judicial Opinions in Complex Analyses — 125

CHAPTER 9
Questions of First Impression — 137

CHAPTER 10
Analytical Foundation of Predictions — 145

PART III
THE DISCUSSION SECTION OF AN OBJECTIVE MEMO — 155

CHAPTER 11
Effective Overall Organization — 157

CHAPTER 12
Analyses of the Law: Effective Structure — 171

CHAPTER 13
Application-Predictions: Effective Structure — 203

CHAPTER 14
Citation to Legal Authority — 225

PART IV
THE FINAL STEPS TO COMPLETE AN OBJECTIVE MEMO — 235

CHAPTER 15
Beyond the Discussion Section: Adding the Facts, Conclusion, Question Presented, and Brief Answer Sections — 237

CHAPTER 16
Presentational Considerations — 253

PART V
OTHER FORMS OF OBJECTIVE WRITING — 273

CHAPTER 17
Informal Internal Office Communications: Shorthand Memos and Emails — 275

APPENDICES

APPENDIX I
Sample of a Formal Objective Memorandum — 283

APPENDIX II
Sample Email to Supervisor — 295

Index — 297

Contents

Acknowledgements	xxvii
Preface	xxix

PART I
INTRODUCTION TO LAW PRACTICE WRITING   1

CHAPTER 1
The Basics of Objective Writing   3

A. Introduction	3
B. Audience and Purpose of an Objective Memorandum	3
1. Audience: Who are your readers?	4
a. Another lawyer with little prior knowledge of your memo's content	4
b. A lawyer who is very busy	4
c. A lawyer who will take action based on your memo's analysis	4
d. A supervisor who may be evaluating your written work for hiring or promotion	5
2. Purpose: What are you trying to accomplish for your readers?	5
C. An Overview of an Objective Memo	6
1. The Heading	7
2. The Question Presented and Brief Answer Sections	7
3. The Facts Section	7
4. The Discussion Section	8
5. The Conclusion Section	8
6. Addendum that includes the full text of a relevant constitutional provision, statute, or regulation	8
7. Sample of a formal objective memo	9
Checklist	9

CHAPTER 2
The Stages of Objective Writing   11

A. Introduction	11
B. The Brainstorming Stage: Generating and Developing Ideas	12
1. Develop effective note-taking techniques to document your research and analysis	13

2. Determine what law is relevant to your legal problem	13
3. Be prepared for the kinds of legal issues you'll likely encounter as a first-year law student	14
a. Legal issues where the relevant legal authority provides a clear answer	14
b. Legal issues requiring in-depth interpretation of the relevant legal authority	14
c. Legal issues that are questions of first impression	14
C. The Preliminary Drafting Stage: Moving from Generating Ideas to Presenting Them	15
1. Writing to yourself as the author as you develop the analysis	15
a. Developing an analysis of the current status of the law	16
b. Predicting the outcome that a future court will reach on a client's facts	16
2. Shifting to convey your analysis effectively to your readers	17
3. Understanding your own process of writing about legal analysis	18
a. Using the process of writing itself	18
b. Using outlines	19
c. Using techniques such as diagrams, charts, or pictures that represent ideas visually	20
d. Using a combination of techniques	20
4. Keeping track of ideas that need further exploration or problems that need to be solved	21
5. Dealing with "writer's block"	21
a. Using "free writing"	22
b. Working with a paper copy of your memo	23
c. Explaining ideas verbally	23
d. Using methods other than ones that come most naturally	23
D. The Final Presentational Stage: Conveying the Analysis Effectively to Your Readers	23
1. Moving to the final presentational aspects of your memo at the right time	24
2. Following a two-step process	24
Checklist	24

PART II
OBJECTIVE ANALYSIS OF LEGAL PROBLEMS   27

CHAPTER 3
Sources of Law and Their Relationship   29

A. Introduction	29
B. The Sources of Law in the United States	29

C. The Relationship Among Sources of Law	30
1. The concept of jurisdiction	30
2. The hierarchy among sources of law	31
D. The Courts' Role Under *Stare Decisis*	32
1. When must a court follow the decision of another court in the same jurisdiction?	33
2. Must a highest appeals court follow its own prior decisions?	35
3. Must courts from one jurisdiction follow decisions of courts from another jurisdiction?	35
E. How the Course of Litigation Results in Written Judicial Opinions	36
F. Primary Legal Authority Versus Secondary Authority	37
Checklist	38

CHAPTER 4
Statutory Analysis — A Basic Process   39

A. Introduction	39
B. Understanding the Role of Statutes	39
1. Statutes as a source of law	39
2. The relationship between courts and statutes	40
C. Using a Code to Begin Your Analysis of a Statute	40
1. Using a code to locate the complete statute	40
2. Using a code's topical organization to put the statute in context	42
3. Using an annotated code for editorial features	43
D. Confirming the Statute's Applicability to Your Client's Situation	43
1. Checking the effective date	43
2. Verifying that the statute regulates activities or conduct related to the client's situation	44
E. Working with Statutory Text: The First Steps	45
1. Skimming the statute to gain an overall sense of its content	45
2. Rereading the statute to break down its content	45
3. Exploring actively what you understand and what you do not	47
a. Narrative writing — using the process of writing itself	48
b. Outlines	48
c. Diagrams or pictures	48
4. Summarizing your understanding of the statute in a tangible form	49
F. Further Developing Statutory Analysis	49
1. Using statutory definitions	49
2. Using relevant regulations	50
3. Using court interpretations	50

    4. Using canons of statutory construction when no court has applied the statute   50
G. Expressing Statutory Analysis in Your Memo   51
Checklist   51

CHAPTER 5
Statutory Analysis — Additional Steps   53

A. Introduction   53
B. Re-evaluate the Statute's Organization   53
    1. Identify the overall structure used by the legislature   54
    2. Break down the statute further using the overall structure   55
        a. Separate out each specific piece   55
        b. Identify the distinct role of each specific piece   56
           i. Addressing the substantive focus of the statute   57
           ii. Creating an exception to what the statute covers   58
           iii. Indicating a cause and a result   58
           iv. Providing a restriction   58
           v. Identifying a test   59
        c. Identify the relationship between the specific pieces of the statute and their roles   60
           i. Common transitions   60
           ii. Transitions that connect one idea by referring to a prior idea   62
        d. Consider taking notes on your process of analyzing a statute   62
    3. Break down each specific piece of the statute into its individual terms   64
        a. Separate out each term   64
        b. Determine the distinct role that each term plays in the statute   65
        c. Determine the relationship between or among terms   66
C. Check That You Understand How All the Pieces Fit Back Together Again   68
D. Develop the Statutory Analysis Further   70
Checklist   70

CHAPTER 6
Analysis of Individual Judicial Opinions   73

A. Introduction   73
B. Compare the Legislative Process with Judicial Decision Making   73
C. Understand the Different Purposes for Analyzing a Judicial Opinion   74
    1. Analyzing cases to determine the law of a jurisdiction   74
    2. Analyzing cases to learn the doctrine of a specific subject area   74

D. Read a Case Actively	75
1. Skim for overall sense of the case's content	75
2. Distinguish between the court's text and editorial features	75
3. Reread the court's text to actively engage with its content	76
a. Narrative writing—using the process of writing itself	77
b. Outlines	78
c. Diagrams or pictures	78
4. Summarize your understanding of the case in some tangible form	79
E. Analyze the Majority Opinion Thoroughly	79
1. Determine the procedural history of the case	80
2. Distinguish between relevant and irrelevant issues	80
F. Analyze All Important Aspects of the Court's Analysis for Each Relevant Legal Issue	81
1. The decisions the court reached	81
a. Procedural results	81
b. Substantive decisions	82
2. The facts relevant to the court's decision(s)	83
a. Locate background facts and legally significant facts	83
b. Describe facts accurately	84
3. The analysis the court used to reach its decision(s)	85
a. Track the court's analysis	85
i. Determine the court's interpretation of the law	85
ii. Determine the court's application of that law to the controversy before it	86
b. Rely on the correct parts of the court's discussion	87
i. Distinguish between the court's discussion that is analysis in support of its decision and analysis that it considers but rejects	87
ii. Distinguish between the parts of the court's analysis that are relevant to your legal issue and those that are not	87
c. Evaluate the weight of any dicta	88
G. Distinguish Between the Court's Actual Analysis and Your Opinion About That Analysis	89
H. Analyze any Concurring or Dissenting Opinion	91
I. Use the Court's Language to Describe Important Ideas in the Analysis	91
Checklist	92

CHAPTER 7
Synthesis of Judicial Opinions — 95

- A. Introduction — 95
- B. Understanding the Process of Synthesizing Cases: An Overview — 95
- C. Understanding Different Types of Tests — 96
  1. Bright-line tests — 97
  2. Balancing tests — 97
  3. Totality tests — 98
  4. Checklists — series of requirements — 99
  5. Threshold tests — 100
- D. Identifying the Courts' Overall Test and Its Components — 100
  1. Determine the courts' overall test and the courts' reasons for that test — 101
     a. Use a thorough process as you read the group of cases — 102
        i. Choose a first case to get started — 102
        ii. Proceed with the rest of the cases — 103
     b. Reevaluate the courts' overall test as you determine the courts' analysis of the components — 104
  2. Develop an analysis of each component of the courts' overall test — 104
     a. Determine a "label" for the component — 104
     b. Determine the component's role in the courts' overall test — 105
     c. Determine an explanation of the courts' analysis for the component — 105
     d. Determine the courts' reasoning for the component — 106
- E. Working with Explicit and Implicit Ideas to Develop the Analysis — 107
  1. Begin with the courts' explicitly articulated ideas — 107
     a. Ideas that are explicit in all relevant cases — 108
     b. Ideas that are explicit in some cases but only implicit in others — 109
  2. Work with courts' implicit ideas, if necessary — 109
     a. Begin by brainstorming descriptions of the implicit ideas — 110
     b. Test the descriptions back on the cases — 111
     c. Revise or discard descriptions that are inconsistent with the cases — 112
     d. Be ready to cycle through this process several times — 113
  3. Use your client's facts to determine the necessary level of detail for the explanation of the courts' analysis — 113
- F. Keeping Track of Ideas as You Synthesize Cases — 114
  1. Consider using a diagram to refine the courts' overall test — 114
  2. Consider using a chart to synthesize cases as you develop the analysis of components — 115

a. Setting up the chart	115
i. Include basic information for each case	115
ii. Include the facts of each case relevant to the particular component	115
iii. Include the decision that each court reached on the component	115
iv. Include any explicit language relevant to the component	116
v. Include any necessary implicit analysis relevant to the component	116
b. Using the chart to synthesize ideas	116
G. Describing the Results of Your Synthesis	117
1. Using general principles	117
2. Using verbatim language or paraphrasing	118
a. Choosing between using the courts' verbatim language or your own words	118
b. Deciding when to use quotation marks around verbatim language	119
H. Illustrations of Synthesizing Cases	119
Checklist	122

CHAPTER 8
Synthesis of Judicial Opinions in Complex Analyses   125

A. Introduction	125
B. Synthesizing Cases That Indicate a Consistent but Undeveloped Approach	126
C. Synthesizing Cases That Indicate Contradictory Approaches	127
1. Contradictory approaches in highest appeals court cases	127
a. Determine the contradictory approaches	128
b. Predict how the highest appeals court would likely resolve the conflict	129
2. Contradictory approaches in intermediate appeals court cases	130
D. Excluding Unique or Wrongly Decided Cases	131
1. Cases based on unique facts	131
2. Incorrectly decided cases	133
a. Intermediate appeals court's decisions that contradict the analysis of the highest appeals court	133
b. Highest appeals court's decisions that apply incorrect analysis	133
E. Using Cases from Other Jurisdictions to Guide Your Synthesis	135
Checklist	136

CHAPTER 9
Questions of First Impression 137

A. Introduction 137
B. Legal Issues Governed by Uninterpreted Constitutional or Statutory Provisions 137
   1. Textual evaluation 138
   2. Textual context 139
   3. External sources 140
      a. Sources of law from other jurisdictions 141
      b. A jurisdiction's common law related to the same subject matter 141
      c. Secondary authority 141
      d. Historical context of the provision 141
C. Situations Where the Court Must Consider a New Approach to the Jurisdiction's Common Law 141
   1. Analogous law in its own jurisdiction 142
   2. Cases from other jurisdictions 142
   3. Secondary sources 142
Checklist 143

CHAPTER 10
Analytical Foundation of Predictions 145

A. Introduction 145
B. Understanding the Purpose of Application-Predictions in an Objective Memo 146
C. Deciding when to Include Single or Alternative Possible Predictions 147
   1. Counter-predictions when the law is clear but the result is uncertain given the client's facts 148
   2. Counter-predictions because the law is unclear 149
D. Determining when Case Comparisons Are Necessary 150
   1. Comparing to precedent because the legal analysis is dependent upon facts 150
   2. Not comparing to precedent because specific facts are not relevant to the analysis 152
E. Moving from Making Predictions to Developing Arguments 153
Checklist 154

PART III
THE DISCUSSION SECTION OF AN OBJECTIVE MEMO   155

CHAPTER 11
Effective Overall Organization   157

A. Introduction   157
B. Overall Organization for Discussion Sections with More than One Legal Issue   158
C. Organization of Legal Issues That Do Not Involve a Question of First Impression   159
  1. Introductory paragraphs   159
    a. Introduce the legal authority   160
      i. Begin by introducing relevant statutory or constitutional provisions   160
      ii. Begin by introducing common law if it controls the legal issue   161
    b. Introduce the courts' analysis when relevant   162
    c. Organize the introduction to help your reader   163
  2. The discussion after the introduction   163
    a. Organize around relevant statutory or constitutional provisions   164
    b. Include an introduction to the courts' analysis   165
      i. Consider organizing around the components of the courts' overall test   165
      ii. Decide whether to break down the analysis of each component   166
    c. Separate analyses of the law from application-predictions   166
  3. Order of drafting the discussion   168
    a. Introductory paragraphs and the discussion that follows   168
    b. Abstract analysis of the law and application to the client's situation   168
D. Organization of Legal Issues That Are a Question of First Impression   169
Checklist   169

CHAPTER 12
Analyses of the Law: Effective Structure   171

A. Introduction   171
B. Basic Structure of an Analysis of the Law Based on Judicial Interpretations   171

	1. Use general principles to express your analysis	172
	2. Begin with the component's "label" and the component's role in the overall test	173
	3. Develop an explanation of the courts' analysis	174
	4. Describe the courts' reasoning	175
	5. Use cases to illustrate the courts' analysis when helpful	175
	a. Situations when the analysis depends on facts of cases	175
	b. Situations when the analysis does not depend on facts of cases	177
	6. Support your analysis with citation to legal authority	178
	7. Sample of memo with an analysis of the law based on judicial interpretations	178
C.	Effective Case Illustrations	178
	1. Choosing which cases to describe	179
	2. Using case illustrations in the text	179
	a. Place case illustrations in the text carefully	180
	b. Tailor the content of case illustrations in the text to the analysis	180
	i. Describe necessary aspects of a case	180
	ii. Begin by stating how the case relates to the preceding description of analysis	181
	iii. Use consistent content and phrasing	183
	c. Describe cases consistently with legal convention	184
	d. Identify explicit or implicit analysis	184
	e. Clarify the parties' relationship to the analysis	185
	f. Sample of memo with case illustrations in the text	185
	3. Using parenthetical illustrations	185
	a. Place parenthetical illustrations carefully	186
	b. Tailor the content of parenthetical illustrations to the analysis	186
	c. Construct concise parenthetical illustrations	189
	d. Make parenthetical illustrations easy to read	190
	e. Present a series of parenthetical illustrations consistently	191
	f. Sample of memo with parenthetical case illustrations	192
	4. Using illustrations in the text and parenthetical illustrations together	192
	5. Choosing one form of illustration for an individual case	193
	6. Organizing illustrations by the court's result	195
D.	Additional Organizational Techniques	196
	1. Evaluate transitions	196
	a. Choosing accurate transitions	196
	b. Verifying that transitions connect ideas precisely	198

2. Construct topic-transition sentences carefully	199
3. Evaluate paragraph development	200
4. Consider summary sentences or paragraphs	200
5. Use headings	201
Checklist	201

CHAPTER 13
Application-Predictions: Effective Structure — 203

A. Introduction	203
B. Placement of Application-Predictions	204
C. Structure of an Application-Prediction with a Single Prediction	205
1. Begin with the predicted outcome	205
2. Apply your explanation from the analysis of the law to support the predicted outcome	206
3. Include case comparisons	206
4. Consider ending with a summary of how the courts' reasoning supports the predicted outcome	208
5. Support the application-prediction with citation to legal authority	209
6. Sample of an application-prediction in a memo	209
D. Effective Case Comparisons	209
1. Choose precedent that a future court would likely use	210
2. Include comparisons to similar and dissimilar precedent when possible	211
3. Provide the information a court would use to compare the client's facts to precedent	211
a. The legally significant facts of the client's situation	212
b. The legally significant facts of precedent	212
c. Your explanation from the analysis of the law	213
E. Structure of Application-Predictions with Predictions and Counter-Predictions	214
1. Begin with a statement that the outcome is unclear	215
2. Develop the prediction and counter-predictions separately	215
3. Develop the prediction and counter-predictions fully	216
4. Decide on the order of the prediction and counter-predictions	216
5. Sample of an application-prediction based on a prediction and counter-prediction	217
F. Additional Organizational Techniques	217
1. Summaries	218
a. Beginning "roadmap" paragraph or sentence	218
b. Ending summary sentence or paragraph	218
2. Transitions	218

3. Topic-transition sentences — 219
4. Paragraph development — 219
G. Structure of Complex Application-Predictions — 219
   1. Placing an application-prediction when the analysis does not indicate a clear organizational choice — 220
   2. Structuring a prediction or counter-prediction based on complex analysis — 221
   3. Placing comparisons in a prediction or counter-prediction that is based on complex analysis — 222
Checklist — 224

CHAPTER 14
Citation to Legal Authority — 225

A. Introduction — 225
B. Analytical Decisions — 225
   1. Choosing the legal authority — 225
      a. Cite to mandatory primary authority — 226
      b. Cite to the "best" mandatory primary authority — 226
         i. Constitutions, statutes, or regulations — 226
         ii. Court decisions — 226
   2. Citing sufficient legal authority — 227
      a. Analyses of the law — 228
         i. Providing sufficient support for a description of analysis — 228
         ii. Providing sufficient support for case illustrations — 228
      b. Application-predictions — 228
   3. Using citation signals — 229
      a. No signal as compared to the "see" signal — 229
      b. Some additional citation signals: "see also," "e.g.," and "compare . . . with . . . ." — 230
C. Techniques to Incorporate Citation During Drafting — 230
D. Plagiarism Considerations — 231
   1. Secondary authority — 231
   2. Primary authority — 232
      a. Authors' viewpoint — 232
      b. Contrary viewpoint — 232
Checklist — 233

PART IV
THE FINAL STEPS TO COMPLETE AN OBJECTIVE MEMO   235

CHAPTER 15
Beyond the Discussion Section: Adding the Facts, Conclusion, Question Presented, and Brief Answer Sections   237

A. Introduction   237
B. The Facts Section   237
   1. Understanding the information to include   238
      a. Include all legally significant facts   238
      b. Include necessary background facts   238
      c. Include the procedural history of your client's case, if applicable   239
      d. Exclude irrelevant facts   239
      e. Exclude legal conclusions   239
   2. Describing the information   240
      a. Describe facts accurately   240
      b. Make the relationship of all people or entities to the legal issue clear   240
   3. Organizing the section   240
      a. Overall organization   241
         i. Chronological organization   241
         ii. Topical organization   241
         iii. Combination of chronological and topical organization   241
      b. Statement of context   241
C. The Conclusion Section   242
   1. Understanding the information to include   242
      a. Base the summary on the application-predictions   242
      b. Be sure the summary is consistent with the analysis in the Discussion Section   243
      c. Do not include new analysis that was not explored in the Discussion Section   243
      d. Communicate all ideas in a manner that adequately informs readers   243
      e. Do not include citation to legal authority   244
   2. Organizing the section   244
      a. Organize the summary consistently with the Discussion Section   244
      b. Begin with your overall prediction for your client   245

c. Summarize how you reached all predicted outcomes by ordering ideas from general to specific	245
d. Summarize all predictions and counter-predictions	245
e. Use precise transitions	246
D. The Question Presented and Brief Answer Sections	246
1. The Question Presented Section	246
a. Include the central issue and the client's facts relevant to that issue	246
b. Make the question consistent with the analysis in all other sections	247
c. Draft the question so it can be answered by a "yes" or "no" answer	247
d. Make the relationship of all people or entities to the legal issue clear	247
e. Order ideas from general to specific	247
2. The Brief Answer Section	247
a. Include a "yes" or "no" answer to the Question Presented and state how you reached that conclusion	248
b. Be sure the Brief Answer Section is consistent with the analysis in all other sections	248
c. Do not include citation to legal authority	248
d. Organizing this section	248
i. Organize this summary consistently with the Question Presented	248
ii. Begin this summary with your overall prediction for your client	249
iii. Summarize how you reached that prediction by ordering ideas from general to specific	249
3. More than one Question Presented and Brief Answer	249
E. The Timing to Draft the Discussion Section and the Other Sections	249
1. Try beginning with the Discussion Section	249
2. Consider starting with sections other than the Discussion Section	250
3. Ensure consistency among all sections	250
Checklist	251

CHAPTER 16
Presentational Considerations   253

A. Introduction	253
B. Decide Between Quoting or Paraphrasing Legal Authority	253
C. Precision	253
D. Consistency	255

	1. The introductory paragraphs and the rest of the Discussion Section	256
	2. Descriptions of the courts' analysis and case illustrations	256
	3. Analysis of the law and the corresponding application-prediction	257
	4. The Discussion Section and other sections of the memo	257
E.	Concision	257
	1. Evaluate the organization	257
	2. Consider all summaries	258
	3. Revise passages with unnecessary repetition	258
	4. Reduce use of repetitive transitions	258
	5. Delete unnecessary statements	259
	6. Remove unnecessary introductory phrases	260
F.	Clarity	261
	1. Evaluate paragraph length	261
	2. Consider sentence length	261
	3. Clarify "who does what to whom"	262
	a. Consider using active verbs instead of passive verbs	262
	i. Using an active verb when the analysis focuses on the actor	262
	ii. Using passive verbs when the analysis focuses on the action	263
	b. Question use of "there is"	263
	c. Avoid turning active verbs into nouns	264
	d. Modify the correct idea in the sentence	264
	e. Correct problems with pronouns	265
	f. Avoid too much separation between a subject and its verb	266
	4. Edit and proofread	267
G.	A Professional Tone	267
	1. Use third-party neutral tone	267
	2. Avoid archaic and informal language	268
	a. Avoid "legalese"	268
	b. Avoid informal language	269
	3. Describe parties with appropriate formality	269
H.	Gender-Neutral Language	270
	1. Use plurals	270
	2. Repeat nouns	271
Checklist		271

PART V
OTHER FORMS OF OBJECTIVE WRITING 273

CHAPTER 17
Informal Internal Office Communications: Shorthand Memos and Emails 275

A. Introduction 275
B. Analytical Foundation 275
C. Format 276
D. Structure 277
E. Professionalism 277
F. Email – Some Special Issues 278
   1. Draft emails off-line 278
   2. Keep emails at an appropriate length 278
   3. Use a precise subject-matter reference 278
   4. Use an appropriately formal tone 278
   5. Consider waiting to react to email about important matters 279
   6. Pay special attention to confidential emails 280
Checklist 280

APPENDICES

APPENDIX I
Sample of a Formal Objective Memorandum 283

APPENDIX II
Sample Email to Supervisor 295

Index 297

Acknowledgements

I would like to thank my research assistants, Alana Bryant and Letani Peltier, for their hard work on this book. I would like to gratefully acknowledge the financial support of the University of Hawai'i William S. Richardson School of Law and Lewis & Clark Law School. I would also like to express my appreciation to Aspen Publishers for permission to use the following book, which is the basis for parts of this textbook: Daniel L. Barnett, *Putting Skills Into Practice: Legal Problem Solving and Writing for New Lawyers* (Aspen Publishers 2014). Finally, I would like to express my deep gratitude to my students, whose enthusiasm and energy motivated me to undertake this project.

—Daniel L. Barnett

I would like to thank my research assistants who provided valuable insights and editing help on drafts of this book: Brian Bieschke, Natalia Cabrera, Melissa Dess, Minh Le, Mark Potash, Jennifer St. Mary, and Tulia VanDunk. I am also very grateful to Boston College and Boston College Law School for their financial support for this project. Finally, I would like to express my appreciation to Texas Tech Law Review for publishing the following article, which is the basis for parts of Chapter 7 of this textbook: Jane Kent Gionfriddo, *Thinking Like a Lawyer: The Heuristics of Case Synthesis*, 40 Tex. Tech L. Rev. 1, 1-16 (2007).

—Jane Kent Gionfriddo

We want to thank our editors and publishers at Wolters Kluwer Law & Business for their invaluable assistance.

—Daniel L. Barnett and Jane Kent Gionfriddo

Preface

If you are reading this preface, you are probably preparing for the first week of law school. Welcome to your new profession! You'll quickly learn that the law is fun, exciting, and demanding because lawyers spend much of their time using legal concepts creatively. As you begin your first year of law school, you are embarking on a new kind of educational experience designed to teach you the critical reasoning skills you need as a creative legal thinker. The learning curve can feel steep, and therefore challenging. But those challenges make the study of law rewarding and interesting. Soon, many of the fundamental ideas that you'll struggle to understand in the first few weeks of law school will become second nature, and you'll wonder why you had such a hard time grasping them. Those basic concepts will be replaced by more complex ideas, that, in turn, you'll master as well. With perseverance and guidance from your professors, you will soon realize how fun and satisfying the law can be.

As you begin law school, you'll quickly recognize that all of the first-year classes are designed to help you acquire the critical reasoning skills lawyers use to analyze legal problems. In the subject matter courses—like contracts and torts—you will refine those analytical skills by learning concepts relevant to different areas of the law. In your legal writing course, you'll develop analytical skills by learning to prepare the basic type of documents lawyers write in practice. This legal writing text and related materials are designed to teach you the methodology to analyze and write about legal issues so that you'll eventually be able to apply those skills to even the most complicated legal questions. Through that process, you will soon have a good grasp of how to "think like a lawyer" and how to write like one, too!

Let's get started!

PART I

INTRODUCTION TO LAW PRACTICE WRITING

CHAPTER 1

The Basics of Objective Writing

A. INTRODUCTION

As a first-year law student, you've likely arrived in your legal writing class as an accomplished writer from prior school and employment experiences. You may have written a thesis in college or graduate school; done technical writing in a field such as medicine or architecture or engineering; written for a newspaper or a magazine; published short stories or poetry or novels; or written memos or legal documents in a business environment. In such prior situations, you will have developed an intimate understanding of the overall context within which you were writing and, in particular, a sense of your readers, why you were writing to them, and what they needed from your writing.

Now that you are in your legal writing class, you'll need to translate this prior understanding of audience and purpose into a new context. From this point on, you'll be writing to someone in law practice who'll need ideas conveyed in ways that may be quite different from what was required in your previous experiences, which you'll learn about in the sections below.

B. AUDIENCE AND PURPOSE OF AN OBJECTIVE MEMORANDUM

In law practice, junior lawyers are often asked to locate and analyze the legal authority relevant to a client's situation and then write up that analysis in a memorandum for other lawyers in the office. These lawyers then use the memo's analysis as the basis to give the client advice and take additional steps to represent the client. To communicate analysis effectively in this kind of memo, you'll need to fully understand your audience—these other lawyers you'll be writing to and who'll be reading your memo—and exactly what this memo must accomplish for them.

1. Audience: Who are your readers?

a. Another lawyer with little prior knowledge of your memo's content

The primary person reading your memo will be your supervising attorney—someone who understands our legal system and legal analysis but who probably has little knowledge about the content of your memo. The fact that your audience doesn't know much about the substance of your memo makes sense if you think about the division of labor in a law practice work place. Your supervisor will be a senior attorney with many responsibilities. To free up her time, she will ask you as the junior attorney to analyze the client's legal problem and then write up your ideas in memo form. Your supervisor is therefore unlikely herself to read the relevant legal authority; analyze what the legal authority indicates about the area of law; and figure out what that analysis means for the client's situation. Instead, she will rely completely on your memo's analysis to be fully informed.

In addition, you may be working with a team of lawyers in your office or even with another firm's attorney who is somehow associated with the case. Just like your supervising attorney, these lawyers will also rely on your memo's analysis. If you think about the fact that "time is money" in a law practice context, it makes sense that each lawyer on a team will play a specific role on a case: If one team member is assigned to analyze and write a legal memo on part of that case, no other lawyer on the team will replicate that work.

b. A lawyer who is very busy

Your supervising attorney will likely be very busy, given the fast-paced environment of law practice, and therefore often will need to read your memo quickly and understand your analysis easily. Imagine that you hand your memo to your supervising attorney and she skims it for the first time as she walks down the hall to meet with the client. To prepare for that meeting, your supervisor will need to effortlessly grasp your ideas. Later on, she will study your memo in more depth: Even at this point, though, she will need a memo that conveys complex information clearly and efficiently.

c. A lawyer who will take action based on your memo's analysis

Your supervisor will use your memo as the basis to advise the client or take other steps to represent the client, such as filing a complaint or preparing an agreement. Given these possibilities, your memo must include the important aspects of the analysis and convey all those ideas accurately and precisely.

Memos that are incomplete, inaccurate, or cumbersome to read do not prepare your supervisor well to represent the client. Most importantly, they risk she will take action based on incorrect analysis, resulting in serious consequences for the client.

d. A supervisor who may be evaluating your written work for hiring or promotion

Your written work will play an important role in your being hired initially for a job in law practice, rehired after summer employment, or retained as a junior lawyer. An impressive writing sample will give you a considerable edge in applying for jobs, whether during or after law school. In addition, as a summer employee or as a junior lawyer, you will be judged to a significant degree on your written work — how sophisticated your analysis is and how well you've conveyed those ideas in writing. All in all, writing impressive memos will have a direct effect on your success throughout your career.

2. Purpose: What are you trying to accomplish for your readers?

Your supervising attorney will count on you to achieve two important goals in a formal objective memo. First, she will want an objective analysis of the current status of the law relevant to your client's situation. To achieve this goal, you'll need to develop a reasonable interpretation of the legal authority relevant to your client's issue, an interpretation that is neutral and therefore isn't slanted for the client. Second, your supervisor will expect you to apply that interpretation of the law to your client's facts to neutrally predict how a future court would likely use the law to reach a decision. Here, you'll need to include all reasonably possible decisions by the future court even if they are not helpful for the client. If you provide your supervisor with this kind of objective analysis, she will be in a much stronger position to accurately evaluate the client's case and consequently give the client sound advice or take other action that will represent the client effectively.

The following two examples illustrate this concept of an objective evaluation of the law and what that law indicates for the client.

> **Example of objective evaluation of liability for dog-bite injury**
>
> Imagine the situation where a senior supervising attorney interviews a client who has been seriously injured when he was bitten by a neighbor's dog in Florida. The client wants to sue the dog owner to recover for his injuries. While the supervising attorney might vaguely

remember encountering this legal issue in law school, she probably has little actual knowledge about a dog owner's responsibilities under Florida law in the client's situation. She therefore would ask a junior lawyer to analyze the relevant law and write a memo based on that law and what it indicates for the client.

At this stage, this memo would need to present analysis that was neutral, and not slanted to the outcome most desirable for the client, because the supervisor would need to give the client an accurate indication of his chances to succeed in suing the dog owner. Is it likely? Unlikely? Or unclear, given the law at this point in time in Florida? On the basis of the junior attorney's conclusions about the likelihood of success, the supervisor and client will discuss whether the client can proceed, and, if so, should proceed, given the cost of litigation. If the decision is to go forward, then the supervisor will use the memo's analysis as the basis to draft the complaint and so forth.

Example of objective evaluation of liability waiver

Imagine the situation where a property owner hires a senior attorney in the state of Nebraska to draft a provision in a commercial lease that waives the property owner's liability to his tenants in certain circumstances. Before crafting the language, the supervisor will need to understand what an objective analysis of the current status of the law in Nebraska indicates about property owners' waiver of liability in this type of lease. Does Nebraska law allow property owners to waive their liability in this situation? If so, are there circumstances that are excluded as a matter of public policy? How specific does the language have to be? The junior attorney's analysis in an objective memo will be the foundation for this particular provision of the lease: The supervising attorney will want to draft the waiver to protect the property owner as much as possible, yet not unduly risk that the provision will be unenforceable under Nebraska law.

C. AN OVERVIEW OF AN OBJECTIVE MEMO

The discussion below will give you a fundamental sense of the different possible sections of an objective memo and the purpose they serve for your potential readers. Don't forget, though, that any particular work place will have their own variation of this kind of memo that might be different from the descriptions below and the Sample of a Formal Objective Memorandum in Appendix I. For instance, the majority of work places are likely to use a form that includes a Heading, Facts Section, Discussion Section, and Conclusion Section. The Question Presented and Brief Answer sections, however, are not always included. In addition, lawyers are increasingly using short informal memos or emails rather than formal objective memos, and drafting successful written documents in this situation is discussed in Chapter 17.

1. The Heading

Your supervising attorney—and other readers—need some types of basic information in a Heading. Therefore, this beginning section of an objective memo identifies the main audience of the memo in the "To" line; the author in the "From" line; the date of the memo in the "Date" line; and the client's name as well as the general subject matter of the memo in the "Re" line.

How all of this information helps your supervisor is obvious, except for one aspect of the "Re" line. That line's identification of the subject matter has a dual purpose. First, your current supervising attorney will need to quickly understand the overall subject of the memo. Second, many work places arrange memos in a central file by subject matter. This file, then, provides lawyers at a later point in time with a "jump-start" on their analysis, which saves time and money.

2. The Question Presented and Brief Answer Sections

At the beginning of the memo, after the Heading, your supervisor may want you to include two sections that will provide her with an initial overview of the memo's analysis: A Question Presented Section and a Brief Answer Section. The Question Presented identifies the legal issue (or issues) in terms of the client's facts, framed as a question. The Brief Answer then "answers" this question in a very concise manner—usually one or two sentences that spell out the result for the client even more concisely than the Conclusion Section, which is discussed in Section 5 below.

Chapter 15 discusses in detail how to draft these sections successfully.

3. The Facts Section

Your supervisor needs to be prepared for your analysis in the Discussion Section—see Section 4 below—and therefore will find it very helpful to read through a Facts Section beforehand that describes the "story" of the client's situation. First, and most important, your supervisor needs to understand all legally significant facts. These facts are the basis for your prediction in the Discussion Section as to what the law indicates objectively for your client. Second, your supervisor will need any background facts that help her understand how the client's legal issue arose, even if those facts are not legally significant.

Chapter 15 discusses in detail how to draft the Facts Section successfully.

4. The Discussion Section

The Discussion Section is the heart of an objective memorandum. Your supervising attorney will count on you to achieve two important goals in this section. First, she will want an objective analysis of the current status of the law. To achieve this goal, you'll need to come up with a reasonable analysis of the legal authority relevant to your client's issue—an analysis that is neutral and isn't slanted one way or the other for the client. Chapters 2 through 9 discuss this process. Second, your supervisor will expect an explanation of what that law indicates objectively on the facts of your client's situation. Here, you'll need to use the law to predict a result for your client—a prediction that is neutral and includes possible outcomes even if they are not helpful for the client. Chapter 10 discusses this process.

Chapters 11 through 14 discuss in detail how to structure and communicate the analysis effectively in the Discussion Section.

5. The Conclusion Section

Your supervising attorney will not always be able to read your entire memo right away, given time constraints in law practice. When this occurs, she will need a Conclusion Section that sets out a complete, but very concise, executive summary of the Discussion Section's analysis as this may be the only section of your memo she has time to read.

Chapter 15 discusses in detail how to draft the Conclusion Section successfully.

6. Addendum that includes the full text of a relevant constitutional provision, statute, or regulation

Your supervising attorney will want a relevant constitutional provision, statute, or regulation described or quoted to some degree in the Discussion Section's analysis since the precise language of such a piece of legal authority will govern the client's situation. For that very reason, she will also want the full text of such a provision included at some point in the memo.

A supervisor might want the full text included in a separate section placed before the Discussion Section. In the alternative, she might want the full text in a footnote at the appropriate point in the Discussion Section or in an appendix at the end of the memo.

7. Sample of a formal objective memo

Please see Appendix I for the Sample of a Formal Objective Memorandum. Just spend a few minutes reviewing the sample to gain a sense of the form of this kind of memo.

CHECKLIST

☐ Know that the audience of your memo will be lawyers who:

- Will likely have little prior knowledge of your memo's content;
- Are very busy;
- Will take action based on your memo's analysis; and
- May evaluate your written work for hiring or promotion.

☐ Understand that the purpose of your memo is to:

- Present an objective analysis of the current status of the law relevant to your client's situation; and
- Provide a prediction of what the law indicates neutrally for your client's situation.

☐ Quickly review the parts of an Objective Memo:

- The Heading, which includes the main audience of the memo, the author, the date of the memo, the client's name, and the general subject matter of the memo;
- The Question Presented Section, which identifies the particular legal issue(s) addressed in the memo, phrased as a question in terms of the client's facts;
- The Brief Answer Section, which answers the Question Presented concisely in one or two sentences;
- The Facts Section, which describes the "story" of the client's situation in a neutral manner, including all legally significant facts as well as relevant background facts;
- The Discussion Section, which:
  - Presents an objective analysis of the current status of the relevant law; and

- Provides a prediction of what the law indicates for the client's situation, conveyed in a neutral manner;
- The Conclusion Section, which provides a complete and concise summary of the Discussion Section's analysis; and
- Possible addendum, which could include the full text of a relevant constitutional provision, statute, or regulation.

CHAPTER 2

The Stages of Objective Writing

A. INTRODUCTION

In Chapter 1, you learned about the audience and purpose of an objective memorandum and gained a general understanding of its different parts. In this chapter, you'll learn about the stages of drafting an objective memo to set out a neutral analysis of the current status of the law and what that law indicates for the client's situation. This overall drafting process, in conjunction with the specific analytical, organizational, and communication skills discussed in subsequent chapters, will help you write effective memos in law practice.

As you draft a memo, you are likely to use writing in some manner during all of the following stages of your process: The brainstorming stage; the preliminary drafting stage; and the final presentational stage. To begin with, you'll likely use writing as you generate the ideas that will become the foundation of your memo. During this early brainstorming stage, discussed in Section B below, you'll be locating and beginning to analyze the relevant legal authority.

You'll then move on to a preliminary drafting stage, discussed in Section C. At that point, you'll be working on what will become the final document, although initial drafts may not be very presentable. During these initial drafts, you'll be writing to yourself as author as you continue to develop your own understanding of the analysis. Refining your analysis is critical since you must fully grasp all ideas yourself in order to convey them completely and accurately to others.

As you deepen your understanding, you'll naturally begin to shift from writing to yourself to presenting the ideas to your readers. At this point, you'll begin to work on the organization of the Discussion Section and to fine-tune all ideas.

Eventually, you'll move to the final presentational stage when you'll polish your writing and finalize your citation form. This stage is discussed in Section D.

The dividing line between these different stages isn't always clear, however, since your writing process will likely be recursive. For instance, as you attempt to finalize the memo, thinking that you are finishing up with editing, you may realize that you have not fully worked out an important concept. At that point, you will need to stop and work through that idea, before returning to polishing your writing and finalizing your citation form.

B. THE BRAINSTORMING STAGE: GENERATING AND DEVELOPING IDEAS

In the first stage, you'll brainstorm about the ideas that will ultimately be the analytical foundation for the memo. As soon as you learn about a client's situation, you'll begin to consider the potential legal issues and possible avenues to resolve those issues. You'll then move on to locating and analyzing the relevant legal authority in order to figure out the current status of the law and what that law indicates for the client.

During this brainstorming stage, you may feel somewhat overwhelmed with all the possibilities, even if the supervising lawyer or someone else has identified the precise legal issue. The more you learn about the issue, the more questions you'll uncover. For each new question, you'll often identify several new avenues to explore. Since you won't have any experience with the law, you may feel intimidated with all of the ideas that you generate. Fortunately, this stage of your process doesn't last very long. As you'll learn during your research instruction, once your research leads you to the relevant legal authority, you'll begin evaluating which avenues of inquiry you should discard and which you should explore further.

Before beginning this initial brainstorming stage, you need to grasp a few basics about handling legal writing projects. You must:

- Develop careful note-taking methods to be sure you effectively document the progression of your research and analysis, which is discussed in Section 1 below;
- Understand the hierarchy of the legal authority that governs your question, which is discussed in Section 2; and
- Be prepared to encounter different kinds of legal issues, and the analysis each requires, which is discussed in Section 3.

1. Develop effective note-taking techniques to document your research and analysis

During the initial stage of brainstorming, you must document the progression of your research and analysis with some form of note-taking, such as quick narrative summaries, outlines, charts, or diagrams. Continue with methods you've used effectively in your experience before law school, but also experiment with ones that are new.

As you prepare these notes, you'll be keeping a record of your research and early analysis as you distinguish between relevant and irrelevant legal authority. Once you've determined which pieces of authority are relevant, you'll be documenting what each piece adds to your emerging analysis. In particular, you'll be keeping track of the ideas you've considered and found relevant, and those that you've considered and eliminated.

As you work from the legal authority to your own written observations, and back again, you'll test and refine the range of ideas that you've generated. Through this process, you'll develop a more focused understanding of the legal authority and what it indicates about the law and your client's situation. Ultimately, this understanding will become the analytical foundation of your memo.

Your notes will play other important roles as well. First, they need to be detailed enough to provide a road map of your research path and preliminary analysis. At times during this process, you'll explore ideas that lead nowhere and need to retrace your steps to find more productive ideas to explore. You might also need to use these notes to locate a piece of authority that you had initially discarded but later concluded was relevant to the analysis.

Second, your notes need to be detailed enough that, when interrupted for periods of time, you'll be able to jump back into your research and analysis without having to repeat portions of prior work. Given the many demands of law school, and law practice, you'll find careful note-taking essential to managing your time economically.

2. Determine what law is relevant to your legal problem

As you begin to generate ideas about a legal problem, you must determine what sources of law are relevant. First, you'll need an accurate understanding of basic sources of law and their relationship. Next, using that knowledge, you'll need to determine which sources of law in the relevant jurisdiction actually govern your client's legal problem.

Working with these sources of law, you'll be able to develop an analysis of the current status of the law and what that law indicates for your client's situation, which will be the foundation of your memo. Chapter 3 discusses the sources of law and how they interrelate.

3. Be prepared for the kinds of legal issues you'll likely encounter as a first-year law student

You'll also find it helpful to have a basic sense about the kinds of legal issues that you might encounter, and the analysis each requires, which are discussed in the sections below.

a. Legal issues where the relevant legal authority provides a clear answer

You may encounter some legal problems where the relevant source or sources of law clearly set out an answer—either to an abstract legal question or to a particular client's legal issue. When this occurs, your analysis will likely be relatively straightforward.

> **Example of legal question with clear answer**
>
> Imagine that your supervisor asks you to research whether your jurisdiction allows parental immunity when a parent is sued by the parent's minor child because of physical injuries received from the parent's negligent driving. You locate no relevant statute. Moving on to case law, you locate only one relevant case in your jurisdiction, which is a recent case by the highest appeals court. In its opinion, the court states unequivocally that a child may not sue a parent in this circumstance. In this situation, you would take a definitive answer to your supervising attorney.

b. Legal issues requiring in-depth interpretation of the relevant legal authority

While you might encounter legal issues where the authority provides a clear answer, you will most likely be working on projects that require in-depth interpretation of one or more sources of law in your jurisdiction. You might need to interpret a complex statute by figuring out its overall analytical structure and analyzing all relevant parts and their relationship, as you'll learn about in Chapters 4 and 5. Instead, you might be working with a group of cases where the courts are either interpreting a statute that was unclear or interpreting their own common law. In this situation, you would need to analyze what the cases indicated together about the law, as you'll learn about in Chapters 7 and 8.

c. Legal issues that are questions of first impression

Although much less likely as a first-year law student or even as a young lawyer, you might be assigned a problem based on a question of first impression, which might arise in the following two situations. First, a problem might be based on a relevant statute that was unclear either in the abstract or as applied to a client's situation, and no court in the jurisdiction has yet interpreted what the legislature intended. Second, a problem might be based on a state common law question that had not yet been raised in the jurisdiction. When dealing with questions of first impression, you would need to work through a complex series of analytical steps, using a range of sophisticated sources, as is discussed in Chapter 9.

C. THE PRELIMINARY DRAFTING STAGE: MOVING FROM GENERATING IDEAS TO PRESENTING THEM

Once you've gone through the initial brainstorming stage, you'll be ready to move on to the preliminary drafting stage. At this point, you'll begin to draft the actual memo where you'll describe the analysis of the current status of the law and what that law indicates in the client's situation.

You'll now begin to work with all the ideas in your rough notes and to translate them into written analysis in narrative form in the memo. As explained in Section 1 below, when you work with these early drafts, you'll move from a basic understanding of the analysis to one that is complete and accurate. As your understanding of the analysis deepens—as you'll read about in Section 2—you'll naturally begin to shift the focus of your writing from working out ideas for yourself as author to expressing those ideas for busy law practice readers.

While an experienced lawyer will have developed strategies to use the drafting stage efficiently, you will need to develop your own approach as a new legal writer. You should therefore think about your own individual process for developing and conveying analysis, which is discussed in Section 3. In addition, you'll need to develop strategies to use as you draft to keep track of ideas that need further exploration or problems that need to be solved, which is discussed in Section 4. Finally, you should be prepared with techniques to work through analytical roadblocks that you might encounter, which is discussed in Section 5.

1. Writing to yourself as the author as you develop the analysis

During the preliminary drafting stage, you'll likely use a series of early drafts to work out many of the analytical subtleties necessary to lay the foundation for the memo. As discussed in Section 3 below, if you work primarily from outlines, you may use writing less often in these early drafts than someone who uses the process of writing itself to explore ideas. However, almost everyone will use writing in some manner to develop a complete and accurate analysis of the current status of the law.

a. Developing an analysis of the current status of the law

When you first begin drafting an analysis of the current status of the law, you'll be using your writing to actively engage with the ideas in the legal authority. In essence, you'll be writing to yourself as author. You'll be free to go off on tangents to explore possible ways of thinking through and articulating the overall analytical structure and its components. You'll be free to ask questions and spend some time working out answers in any kind of rambling, repetitious manner that is helpful to your own process of figuring out the analysis. You won't need, therefore, to worry about whether your readers will be able to follow your train of thought easily, quickly, and accurately. In fact, you won't want to be distracted by the purely presentational aspects of your memo that you'll deal with during the final stage of your process, which is discussed in Section D below.

> **Example of using narrative writing to develop analysis**
>
> Imagine that you are analyzing a statute, which is a piece of legal authority that you'll learn about in more detail in Chapters 3 through 5. As you struggle to figure out how one part of the statute relates to another, you might use narrative writing to engage actively with the ideas. Using writing in this manner, you might work back and forth between two provisions, comparing and contrasting wording to work out the precise relationship between the provisions. That writing might be extremely valuable for you as author, since the comparisons over and over might ultimately spark an understanding that you would not have gained by simply reading the statute more passively. In contrast, this type of writing would be very unproductive for your busy readers who would need a direct, concise statement of the end result of your analysis, as discussed in Section 2 below.

b. Predicting the outcome that a future court will reach on a client's facts

In addition to developing an analysis of the current status of the law, you'll need to figure out a complete and accurate analysis of what that law indicates for your client, which is discussed in Chapter 10. In this textbook, this step is called an "application-prediction" because you'll be applying the law to your client's situation and predicting the outcome before a future court. As you develop this aspect of your analysis, you might use writing to explore whether the future court could reasonably reach only one outcome or alternative outcomes. You might also use writing to explore exactly how the future court would reason to any possible outcome, including how it might view precedent as similar or not to your client's situation.

As you develop an application-prediction, you might intuitively write from the point of view of being a lawyer making arguments instead of a lawyer presenting an objective analysis. Alternatively, you might write from the point of view of how you would resolve the issue if you were the future judge deciding the question. Writing from these perspectives, you might present arguments and relevant responses, and then counterarguments. Without worrying about any ultimate reader's ability to follow your train of thought, you might explore aspects of your analysis by bouncing back and forth between different points of view and the strengths and weaknesses of each. Through this open-ended process, you would slowly begin to develop the in-depth analysis needed by your readers to fully understand the outcome, or potential outcomes, for the client.

2. Shifting to convey your analysis effectively to your readers

As you become more convinced of the analysis, you'll naturally begin to shift the focus of your writing from communicating to yourself as author, as discussed above, to communicating to someone else. This shift is critical since the way in which you'll use writing to work out the subtleties of the analysis for yourself will not be helpful to your law practice readers. As you know from Chapter 1, these readers are busy and do not bring the same level of knowledge to the writing as you do as author. They therefore need you to convey a complete and accurate analysis in a highly structured, precise, and concise manner.

You must, therefore, bring order to your early drafts. First, you must structure your analysis effectively by using the principles of good organization that you'll learn about in Chapters 11 through 13. Second, you must begin to focus on whether you've expressed all ideas precisely and consistently, which you'll learn more about in Chapter 16. Finally, you should begin work on citing to legal authority to support your analysis, which you'll learn about in Chapter 14. Keep in mind, however, that you'll likely wait to polish your writing and finalize citation form until the final presentational stage, discussed in Section D below.

As you begin to focus on the structure and presentation of your analysis, however, you must be prepared to encounter times when you realize that you don't fully grasp an important idea. When this occurs, you'll need to shift back to developing that idea, possibly undertaking more research, and rereading the relevant legal authority. Once you've figured out that aspect of the analysis, you'll be able to return to drafting your memo.

The bottom line is that you should not view these three stages — brainstorming, preliminary drafting, and final presentation — as ones that are completely separate from each other. You won't necessarily work through each and never return to it, therefore. Instead, you may need to stop at times and return to an earlier point in the process.

3. Understanding your own process of writing about legal analysis

During the preliminary drafting stage, you'll need to develop strategies to transition from generating analysis to conveying analysis effectively to busy law practice readers. In order to develop these strategies, you first need to identify your own preferred process for writing about legal analysis. You must then evaluate the strengths and potential challenges of using that process. Finally, you need to be open to using strategies that are not those that you prefer during those times when you get "stuck" in drafting your memo.

a. Using the process of writing itself

You may be someone who favors using writing itself to develop ideas in early drafts of your memo. Rather than outlining your ideas before drafting the document, you will let the ideas flow onto the page however they come out as you write. Through writing in this manner, you'll generate and develop ideas as well as determine the logic of how you should order and connect those ideas.

You must be careful, however, that you don't get fooled into submitting a memo that does not communicate your analysis in a manner helpful to law practice readers. When you use writing to yourself to develop your analysis, you may end up with pages of writing that appear as if they are in fairly final form. In fact, however, these pages of writing in early drafts may explore ideas in a repetitious, rambling, and even incomplete manner. With a piece of writing in this form, you'll need to go through several subsequent drafts to ensure that you've structured and conveyed your analysis in the polished manner needed by readers in the busy environment of law practice.

To avoid submitting a memo that would be unhelpful to readers, you might consider taking the following two steps. First, if possible, you should set aside your memo and come back to it after some reasonable interval of time. After this time period, you'll be better able to read the memo from the point of view of readers. Remember that these readers do not bring the same level of knowledge to the ideas as you have as author and also will be reading quickly because they are working under time constraints.

As you read your memo from your readers' point of view and not from your own as the author, evaluate the following. Did you have any reasonable question about the substance that wasn't answered by what was actually on the page of the document? Did you find that important concepts were there but out of order, leaving you to figure out how ideas related? Were you unable to follow along easily, quickly grasping each idea and its relationship to other ideas? Did you encounter repetitious passages that were difficult to understand? If the answer is "yes" to any of these questions, then you know you have some work to do to turn your memo into the final form needed by readers.

In addition to leaving your memo for a period of time, try outlining parts of your memo in the following manner. For instance, for a Discussion Section, run a quick draft where you include any beginning introductory paragraphs and the first sentence of each subsequent paragraph. From the point of view of your readers, skim the outline to see if you can easily follow the ideas. Are some crucial ideas missing? Are those ideas out of order or not precisely connected? Do you see the same ideas discussed repeatedly but can't see any reason for that repetition?

If you get "stopped," then you've uncovered either analytical or structural problems that you must fix. At that point, you might have to work out additional ideas, develop certain aspects of the analysis in more depth and more precisely, restructure certain passages, reorder ideas, edit repetitious places, or simply revise carefully to express ideas more precisely.

b. Using outlines

You may be someone who generally outlines before you begin writing. Like many writers who outline, you may feel — or subconsciously expect — that you must have a complete understanding of all ideas before being comfortable conveying these ideas in narrative writing. If you tend to use outlines to draft memos, you may therefore do much of the difficult conceptual work mentally as you translate your rough notes into your outline.

Working with an outline in this manner may be very efficient. If your outline spells out a complete and final writing plan, you may need to go through only a few drafts to finalize your memo.

However, your normal process of working out everything mentally, and only then creating an outline, will not always sufficiently help you generate the necessary depth of analysis. For instance, the outline might skip an important idea, merge ideas that need to be separated, fail to order ideas logically, and so forth. In these situations, therefore, you would need to use additional strategies to address and correct these problems in the analysis.

You might view the outline not just as a reporting mechanism for your analysis but as a "living document" that helps you figure out ideas and their relationship. Using an outline in this manner, you would move ideas around in conjunction with revisiting your notes and the relevant legal authority.

You might also annotate the outline by expanding parts with quick narrative explanations of ideas in rough paragraph form. When developing these annotations, you would not necessarily work through the outline in chronological order. Instead, you might skip over parts that you understood less well and focus on developing narrative explanations for parts that you did. Using this approach, you would develop a foundation for at least some part of the analysis and therefore gain more confidence to confront the problem areas.

After working with an outline in this manner, you would have a much better chance to develop analysis that you could use to draft your memo. Your outline would set out ideas in logical order, connect those ideas precisely, and include a beginning development of these ideas in narrative form. In some instances, you would even be able to use whole paragraphs from the outline as a beginning foundation for your memo.

c. Using techniques such as diagrams, charts, or pictures that represent ideas visually

You may be someone who benefits from creating visual representations of ideas, using techniques such as diagrams, charts, or pictures. These techniques may therefore help you figure out relationships among ideas more easily than narrative writing or outlining. In addition, certain kinds of substance, by their very nature, may be captured more clearly in images than in verbal descriptions.

Be prepared, however, to spend a period of time translating the visual images into the narrative writing that will convey your analysis in the Discussion Section of your memo. To help yourself make that transition, you might include some narrative descriptions of the ideas represented visually on the diagram, chart, or picture. With some added description in writing, you'll be able to move more easily from the visual representation to writing about those ideas and their relationship. In addition, or in the alternative, you might use the ideas from your diagram, chart, or picture as the basis for developing an outline or using writing to yourself to further develop your analysis.

d. Using a combination of techniques

You may be someone who uses a combination of all of the techniques discussed above to complete your writing projects. As someone who uses a combination, you will intuitively move back and forth from outline to narrative writing to some form of visual representation of ideas. You'll work with different techniques at different times to develop the analysis and determine the most effective organization to express that analysis.

Even as someone who uses a combination, however, you should review the strategies for each kind of approach discussed in the sections above. You will use each approach more effectively if you've thought about its strengths and limitations.

4. Keeping track of ideas that need further exploration or problems that need to be solved

As you draft your memo, regardless of the writing strategies that you use to develop the analysis, you will likely need to keep track of new ideas that you need to explore further, or analytical or structural problems that you need to solve. On the one hand, you might need to stop writing your memo and deal with such an issue right away in the situation where you couldn't otherwise proceed. In this circumstance, you might put aside the draft of your memo and begin a separate document. In this document, you would use techniques that were purely focused on figuring out the analysis and not at all focused on conveying analysis to readers. To come at the analysis in a different manner, you would choose a technique different from any you had worked with previously. For instance, if you were working from an outline to draft your memo, you would try using the free writing techniques discussed in Section 5 below or developing a visual representation of ideas, as discussed in Section 3 above.

On the other hand, you might not want to deal with a particular issue at a given point yet would need to keep track of it for a later time in your drafting process. In this circumstance, you might note the issue in a list at the end of the outline or in a separate document. In order not to lose your current insights, you would identify the particular issue in a phrase and summarize quickly your thoughts about it.

Instead of noting the issue at the end of the document or on a separate list, you could choose to include a notation right at the point in the body of your draft where you thought it was relevant. You could insert the notation in brackets and perhaps highlight it in color so that it would stand out. You could also use "track changes" in your word-processing program.

Later on, when it wouldn't interrupt your drafting process, you would revisit all the issues on the list or noted in brackets or tracked changes in the body of the draft. At that point, you might decide that what you thought was a problem actually wasn't one or that you had already fixed it in some other manner. You might decide that an idea you thought was important was not. You might conclude, however, that you needed to address a problem or new idea in order to convey a complete and accurate analysis.

5. Dealing with "writer's block"

Generally, we think about writer's block as applying only to writers who struggle to find inspiration in creative writing. However, as a legal writer, you could also encounter analytical roadblocks as you develop and attempt to convey the analysis. In fact, you should be prepared for times when you end up so puzzled about the ideas that you feel as if you'll never find any path out of the morass no matter how much you read and think about the underlying legal authority. In this situation, you'll need to turn to some or all of the techniques discussed below to help you work through your confusion.

a. Using "free writing"

You may find the technique of free writing helpful when you are struggling to understand an aspect of the analysis. Using free writing, you would just let ideas flow out in an unconstrained manner as you write.

To use this technique, you should begin by creating a new document that is separate from any outline or beginning draft of your memo. You must then be disciplined as you use this document to free write.

In general, you should write in a place where you'll be completely undisturbed for a predetermined about of time. Initially, you might just write for 10 to 15 minutes; later on, you could increase the time, if necessary.

During that period of time, you should not stop for any reason but should keep writing even if you feel confused and think you have nothing to say. So that you don't interrupt the flow of your writing, you should not focus on any presentational matters. Therefore, completely ignore paragraph development, sentence structure, word choice, spelling, correct punctuation, and correct citation form.

Although you should not attempt to control the ideas as you write, you should begin with a general sense of what you believe is the analytical or structural problem at that point in your analysis. Other than that general focus, you should simply write about any ideas that come to mind about the problem and how to solve it. Through this process, you may find that you actually understand more than you thought. You may also begin thinking you have one problem and learn through the writing that you actually have another.

After an initial free writing period or two, you may need to move on to other sessions. You might want to write about a new idea that you generated during an initial session. You might then use that more specific idea to check your understanding of broader issues in the analysis. Similarly, you could use a later free writing session to focus on how to break down a part of your analysis into logical pieces.

Whatever the focus of your free writing, you may intuitively identify the flaws or gaps in your analysis when you are forced to write about the different ideas from different perspectives and without any constraints. Once you've identified these flaws or gaps, you'll be better able to use free writing or other techniques to develop solutions to the problem.

b. Working with a paper copy of your memo

At certain discrete points in your drafting process, you might print your entire memo or some parts of the memo. While using a computer is efficient at most points during the drafting process, working with a paper copy may help you solve a particular analytical or structural problem.

In a complex and difficult analysis, for instance, your early drafts will likely be repetitious and rambling. You may find it more difficult to follow and unravel tangled-up ideas as they appear and reappear on multiple screens on a computer than to work with the more tangible pages of a paper copy. In addition, you might find it valuable to write out suggestions to yourself in the margins of a paper copy. The very nature of writing by hand slows you down and might help you to see problems and solutions more easily.

c. Explaining ideas verbally

You might try explaining an idea verbally when you are having trouble explaining it in writing. You could try talking about the analysis with a colleague whom you trust or to yourself on a recording device. Through articulating your thoughts verbally in either of these ways, you might identify deficiencies in your thinking and therefore develop a more precise analysis.

d. Using methods other than ones that come most naturally

You should also try using techniques that are not the ones that you naturally prefer as you work on developing and conveying your analysis. As you can see from Section 3 above, your preferred approach not only will have strengths but will also present specific challenges. When you encounter an analytical roadblock using your preferred approach, therefore, you should turn to a different approach that may help you look at the analysis from a fresh perspective and therefore work through your confusion.

D. THE FINAL PRESENTATIONAL STAGE: CONVEYING THE ANALYSIS EFFECTIVELY TO YOUR READERS

During the preliminary drafting stage discussed above, you will generally use your writing to perfect your understanding of the relevant legal analysis, to structure that analysis well, and to begin to convey all important ideas precisely and consistently enough for busy law practice readers. At some point, you'll switch into the final presentational stage where you'll focus specifically on ensuring that you've communicated a complete and accurate analysis in the professional manner expected by your readers.

1. Moving to the final presentational aspects of your memo at the right time

You must be sure that you move on to these final editing steps at the very end of drafting your memo, or discrete portions of that memo, when you are fairly confident that you already have a good understanding of the analysis and have structured it effectively. A focus too soon on stylistic changes may interfere with developing a complete and accurate analysis.

You must also train yourself to recognize when the editing process provides you with clues that, even though you thought you were at the final editing phase, you are still struggling with an idea in the analysis. When this situation occurs, you must stop and work on that problem area before you continue with the presentational aspects of the document.

2. Following a two-step process

Once you begin the final presentational stage, you'll tend to go through two steps. During the first step, you'll reevaluate whether you've communicated a complete and accurate analysis effectively for law practice readers. This step tends to overlap with the end of the prior stage of preliminary drafting. You'll evaluate the overall structure of the Discussion Section and how you've organized each piece of the analysis. You'll check that you've included all important ideas and expressed, and connected, those ideas precisely and consistently.

Once you've verified that you have developed, and structured effectively, a complete and accurate analysis, you'll move on to the second step. At this point of your drafting process, you'll make sure that you've conveyed that analysis in a professional manner. You'll check that you've expressed all ideas concisely, clearly, grammatically, and with correct punctuation. You'll proofread carefully for errors in spelling and format. Finally, you'll finalize your citation form and be sure that it's consistent with professional rules on citation.

CHECKLIST

- ☐ Use the brainstorming stage to generate and develop ideas:
    - Develop effective note-taking techniques;
    - Determine the relevant law;
    - Understand different types of legal issues:
        - Legal issues where relevant authority provides clear answer;
        - Legal issues requiring in-depth interpretation of the relevant authority; and
        - Legal issues that are questions of first impression.

☐ **Develop and structure the analysis for your readers during the preliminary drafting stage:**
  - Write to yourself to:
    - Develop an analysis of the law; and
    - Develop a prediction of the outcome on your client's facts.
  - Shift to convey the analysis to your readers.
  - Experiment with your own writing process:
    - Writing to develop ideas;
    - Outlines; and
    - Visual aids.
  - Keep track of ideas that need more exploration.
  - Consider techniques to deal with "writer's block":
    - Use free writing;
    - Work with paper copy of memo; and
    - Explain ideas verbally.

☐ **Verify at the final presentation stage that you convey a complete and accurate analysis to your readers in a professional manner:**
  - Choose the timing of shifting to presentational stage carefully;
  - Develop techniques to verify the accuracy of your discussion; and
  - Use tools to check that your presentation is concise and well copyedited.

PART II

OBJECTIVE ANALYSIS OF LEGAL PROBLEMS

CHAPTER 3

Sources of Law and Their Relationship

A. INTRODUCTION

In our legal system, various sources of law set out the rules that govern our society. As a lawyer, you must have a basic knowledge of these sources in order to choose the legal authority that governs a client's situation. This authority is the foundation for your analysis in an objective memorandum.

Sections B through D provide an overview of the sources of law in our legal system and their relationship. Section E describes how the course of litigation results in written judicial opinions. Finally, the difference between primary sources of law—the law itself—and secondary sources that are either commentary on the law or legal research tools that help locate actual law is discussed in Section F.

B. THE SOURCES OF LAW IN THE UNITED STATES

In the United States, the basic sources of law that may apply to a legal problem are federal and state. In addition, certain native groups may also have the power to create law that could apply to the question. To understand the relationship among these different sources of law, you need to review some basics about our legal system.

The federal constitution identifies the fundamental personal rights of all citizens of the United States in the Bill of Rights. It also sets up our federal form of government by granting certain limited powers to the federal government and by leaving all other powers to the individual states.

The federal constitution also assigns different responsibilities to each of the three branches of the federal government—the executive, legislative, and judicial—and all these branches create law. Under the legislative branch of the federal government, elected legislators in Congress enact federal statutes that govern all citizens. The executive branch under the president administers and enforces these federal laws, including, among other things, overseeing the federal agencies that have been given authority under federal statutes to promulgate regulations and sometimes interpret and apply those regulations. The third branch, the judiciary, oversees the system of federal courts that decide cases arising under the federal constitution and under federal statutes. Federal courts also have jurisdiction over matters dealing with state law when the parties are citizens of different states or when state law issues are combined with federal issues.

Each state has a constitution that recognizes the fundamental personal rights of citizens of that state and may contain provisions relating to other state questions. The constitution also sets up the form of government for the state, and all states have the same three branches as the federal government. The state legislature enacts statutes that govern citizens of the state. The executive branch under the governor administers and enforces state laws, including, among other things, overseeing agencies created by the state legislature. And, finally, the judicial branch oversees the system of courts that hears cases concerning issues arising under state law.

In addition, certain groups of native people, such as Indian tribes, have sovereignty rights that allow them to establish their government. The types of those laws vary from group to group, but may include laws created by the different branches of government—executive, legislative, and judicial.

C. THE RELATIONSHIP AMONG SOURCES OF LAW

1. The concept of jurisdiction

To understand the relationship among sources of law, you must first be familiar with the general concept of jurisdiction. Black's Law Dictionary[1] defines this concept generally as "a government's general power to exercise authority over all persons and things within its territory." Therefore, a state, for instance, has the power through its legislature and its courts to create law that affects all citizens of the state. In addition, the federal government has the power through the federal legislature and the federal courts to affect

---

1. *Jurisdiction*, BLACK'S LAW DICTIONARY (10th ed. 2014).

citizens of the whole country. Finally, Indian tribes and other native groups may have power to create laws that affect their territory or members.

However, understanding the general concept of jurisdiction is just the first step. You must also understand the complex relationships among sources of law and the governmental entities that promulgate that law, which is discussed in the next section.

2. The hierarchy among sources of law

As a lawyer, you must understand the hierarchy of the sources of law—which kinds take precedence over other kinds—in order to determine the relevant legal authority for a client's situation. In particular, you must understand the relationship between federal and state law as well as the relationship among constitutions, statutes, regulatory law, and judicial opinions.

To begin with, under the federal constitution, there is a complex relationship between our federal jurisdiction—the federal government and the law it promulgates—and the governments of each of 50 states that also produce law—state jurisdictions. Federal law takes precedence over state law if they are conflicting; however, in some circumstances federal law works in concert with that of the state. Therefore, faced with a legal issue, you must first figure out what jurisdiction's law controls: Is the client's issue governed by federal law or a particular state's law or, in complex situations, by both? In other situations, you may need to determine if the law of a native group, such as an Indian tribe, would apply. Because this area is so specialized and complex, however, for the purposes of the rest of this discussion you should assume that the only possible sources of law that could apply are federal or state.

Once you answer this question, you must find the law of the relevant jurisdiction—federal or state or both—that governs the client's situation. In the federal and all state systems, sources of law include the constitution, statutes enacted by the legislature, regulations promulgated by an agency under the auspices of a statute, and judicial opinions. As to judicial opinions, judges create law in different ways as they reach a decision between the parties to a controversy. First, judges have the responsibility to interpret constitutions, statutes, and regulations that apply to the situation before the court. Second, when no constitution, statute, or regulation governs the legal issue, courts may develop and interpret their own law, otherwise known as common law. In both situations, courts explain their decisions in written opinions, also known as "cases."

A constitution is the highest authority of a jurisdiction. Therefore, you must always begin by determining whether a federal or state constitutional provision applies to a client's problem. If one does apply, then you need to determine whether the courts have interpreted that provision. A case that interprets the constitution is law; it continues to have the force of law unless a constitutional amendment undermines its authority or a later court overrules it.

Next, you must ascertain whether the jurisdiction's legislature has enacted any relevant statutory law. The citizens in a jurisdiction elect legislators. If these legislators "speak" for those citizens by enacting a statute, and it's constitutional, then that statute will govern the client's situation, even if it conflicts with the jurisdiction's judge-made common law.

To govern a client's situation, a statute must be constitutional—that is, it must not violate any provisions of any relevant constitution. A federal statute must not violate the federal constitution. A state statute must not violate the federal constitution as well as the constitution of its state.

The courts have the responsibility to determine whether statutes are constitutional. In a state jurisdiction, the highest appeals court of the state decides whether a statute is constitutional under the state constitution. The highest federal court, the United States Supreme Court, decides whether a federal statute is constitutional under the federal constitution. It must also decide if a state statute violates the federal constitution in any respect.

A statute found unconstitutional no longer has any effect. At that point, the relevant legislature may choose to amend the statute to remedy the problem.

If a constitutional statute applies, then you must determine whether the courts have interpreted the statute. If necessary to decide a controversy brought before them, courts have the responsibility to interpret a statute as they apply it to the situation before them. A judicial opinion that interprets a statute is law; it continues to have the force of law unless the legislature or a later court undermines its authority. For instance, the legislature might amend or repeal the statute that was the basis for the court's decision in the case, or a later court might overrule the case.

If a statute applies, and the legislature has given a regulatory agency the authority to promulgate rules under that statute, otherwise known as regulations, those regulations will have the effect of statutory law and may govern your client's situation. In this situation, too, courts have the responsibility to interpret the regulation. If authorized under the statute, an agency may have this responsibility also.

Finally, if no relevant constitutional provision, statute, or regulation applies, the question then becomes whether there is judicially created common law in the jurisdiction that applies to your client's situation. Here, the courts themselves develop and interpret their own law. There continue to be many areas of state law and a few areas of federal law that include this kind of purely judge-made law.

D. THE COURTS' ROLE UNDER *STARE DECISIS*

You must also understand the concept of *stare decisis* as you work with judicial opinions. As courts decide issues that come before them, they must adhere to the principle of *stare decisis*, a fundamental concept in our legal system that requires courts to "stand by things decided." In other words, in theory, courts must follow the analysis of prior judicial opinions — precedent — that have similar issues to those of the situation before the court. *Stare decisis* creates consistency, and therefore stability, in the law of a jurisdiction. Individuals feel fairly treated by the courts since "like cases are treated alike." The judicial system is more efficient since courts can rely on settled aspects of the law.

The question then becomes, in what circumstances under *stare decisis* must a court follow a prior judicial opinion in reaching its decision, and in what circumstances may a court choose to follow one or not? To answer this question, you must understand the hierarchy of relationships among courts from the same or different jurisdictions and therefore why some precedent is mandatory and thus binding on a court, and some is merely persuasive. As a lawyer, this distinction is very important: Judicial decisions that are mandatory, and therefore ones that a court must consider, bring much more weight to an analysis than ones that are persuasive and therefore may be ignored.

1. When must a court follow the decision of another court in the same jurisdiction?

You must first understand the basic structure of both the federal and state court systems. Then you must understand the hierarchy of courts in these systems to determine when one court must follow the decision of another court.

The federal court system and most state court systems include a highest appeals court, an intermediate appeals court, and one or more trial courts. Some trial courts hear most civil and criminal cases. Other trial courts may be limited to hearing cases on certain subjects or cases claiming only a limited amount of damages.

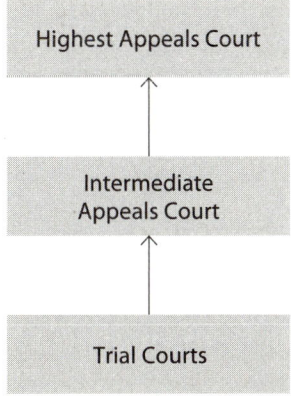

The highest appeals court is the final arbiter of the law of its jurisdiction and, under *stare decisis*, lower courts of that jurisdiction must therefore follow its decisions. Similarly, intermediate appeals court decisions are binding on trial courts within their jurisdiction. Courts on the same level, however, do not have authority over each other and therefore do not have to follow each other's decisions, although they may find them persuasive. For example, a decision by one trial court is not binding on a decision by another trial court.

Some court systems are more complex, however, since they include a highest appeals court that oversees lower courts that are divided into separate geographical areas, often called "circuits," each of which includes an intermediate appeals court and trial courts. In each "circuit," the decisions of the intermediate appeals court are binding on the trial courts of that circuit but may not be binding on the intermediate appeals court and trial courts of any other circuit.

For instance, in the federal system, the highest appeals court is the United States Supreme Court. This court oversees a system that divides the country geographically into 13 separate circuits, each of which includes an intermediate appeals court — a United States Court of Appeals for that circuit; trial courts that hear most civil and criminal matters — United States District Courts; and trial courts limited to certain kinds of cases.

In this system, decisions by the United States Supreme Court must be followed by all lower courts in the federal system, which includes the intermediate-level United States Courts of Appeal and all United States District Courts and other trial-level courts. However, a decision by a court of appeals in one circuit is not mandatory authority for a court of appeals sitting in another circuit. Similarly, a court of appeals decision in one circuit is not even binding on a trial court in another circuit.

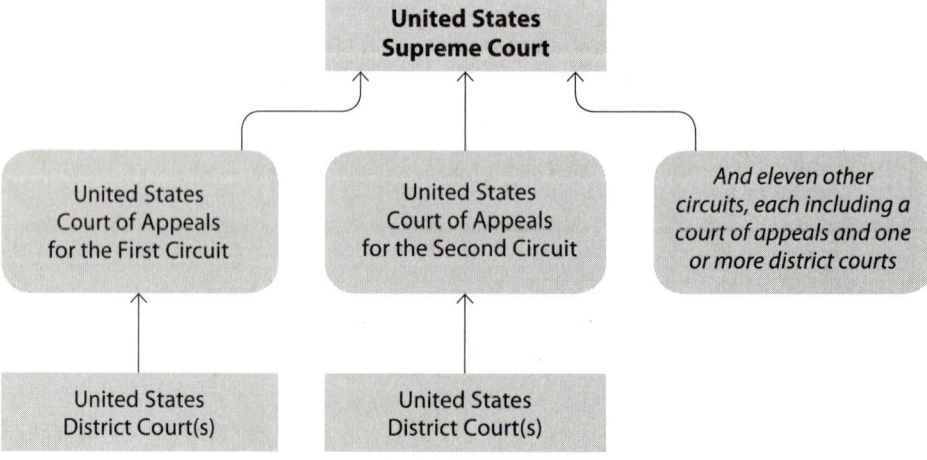

2. Must a highest appeals court follow its own prior decisions?

In theory, highest appeals courts in both the federal and state systems are required to follow their own prior decisions under *stare decisis*. In practice, however, these courts retain a great deal of flexibility in dealing with their own precedent because even technically "binding" cases almost never have identical facts to the situation before the court. On one hand, the court may choose to view the facts of a prior decision as similar and therefore use the decision's analysis to decide the controversy before the court. On the other hand, the court may distinguish precedent as factually dissimilar and adopt a different approach to decide the case before it.

In fact, even after deciding a prior decision is similar to the case before the court, a highest appeals court may overrule that decision so that it no longer has the force of law in the jurisdiction. Although relatively rare, a court is likely to do so, for instance, when it becomes convinced that the analysis supporting a prior decision's approach is no longer consistent with prevalent social values and a new approach will serve the jurisdiction better.

3. Must courts from one jurisdiction follow decisions of courts from another jurisdiction?

Given that courts have the power to make or interpret law only in their own jurisdictions, courts of one jurisdiction are not required to take into account the analysis from judicial decisions from another, although ideas from other courts may persuade them.

Example of a state court using cases from other states as persuasive authority

A decision by the highest appeals court in Utah, for instance, is not binding on the courts of Massachusetts under *stare decisis*. However, the courts of Massachusetts could choose to adopt the Utah court's approach to a legal issue if they found it compelling.

Example of a state court using federal cases as persuasive authority

A federal court sitting in diversity jurisdiction—again, when the litigants are citizens of two different states—must apply relevant state law. However, the federal court's decision based on this law is not binding on the courts of that state, although it could be quite persuasive.

> **Example of a state court using a United States Supreme Court case as persuasive authority**
>
> The highest appeals court of each state is the final arbiter of the common law of that jurisdiction. Therefore, the courts of that state need not follow a decision by even the United States Supreme Court on a purely state law issue.

E. HOW THE COURSE OF LITIGATION RESULTS IN WRITTEN JUDICIAL OPINIONS

You need to be familiar with how litigation begins with a client seeking advice from a lawyer and then proceeds through arriving at court and progressing up through the court system on appeal. This is the process that results in written judicial opinions.

Imagine that a client comes into your office and speaks with your supervising attorney about a dispute over terms in a contract. As the junior lawyer, you locate and analyze legal authority in the jurisdiction relevant to your client's situation and then write an objective memo. On the basis of your memo's objective analysis, your supervisor advises the client concerning the next step.

This next step could be negotiating with the opponent's attorney to settle the dispute. If the parties do not settle, one of the parties could file an action at the trial court to get the desired relief from the opponent. Once a party files the action, the parties would probably ask the court to consider a variety of pretrial motions, including some to end the action in their favor. At this point, the losing party of such a motion would have the right to appeal the trial court's decision to the intermediate appellate court in the jurisdiction.

Assuming that the action is not decided on this kind of pretrial motion, your client's contract issue will go to trial as a civil action, which is a dispute between two parties where one party is claiming damages or other kinds of relief.

A judge will preside over the trial. The judge will be the factfinder unless there is a jury. The parties will present testimony and submit evidence. When the trial concludes, the factfinder will reach a verdict by applying the relevant law to the evidence that different parties presented.

After the trial, the losing party usually has the right to appeal the verdict to the intermediate appellate court of the jurisdiction.

In handling appeals, including appeals of pretrial motions or verdicts, an appeals court will not hear new evidence or testimony in most circumstances. Instead, it will simply evaluate whether the trial court applied the correct law—and applied it correctly—to the evidence at trial, and then either affirm or reverse the lower court's decision.

The party who loses at the intermediate appellate level may then attempt to appeal to the highest appellate court in the jurisdiction. Although there are exceptions, generally the highest appellate court is not required to hear an appeal and will decide whether to take the appeal based on its sense of the importance of the legal issue presented.

In a criminal action, representatives of the government—a federal, state, or other governmental entity—bring a complaint against an individual or entity to enforce the criminal laws of the jurisdiction. Once the trial ends, generally only the defendant may appeal to higher-level courts.

Throughout the course of litigation, judges will need to interpret and apply the relevant law to the situation before the court as they reason to various decisions at different stages, including decisions on motions, the trial itself, and any appeals. For each of these decisions, the judge may write a formal judicial opinion, although a judge is more likely to do so for questions on appeal than at the trial court level. These judicial opinions, or "cases," then become part of the jurisdiction's law.

F. PRIMARY LEGAL AUTHORITY VERSUS SECONDARY AUTHORITY

You must understand what sources are law and what sources are not law. To make this distinction, many people use the terms *primary legal authority* and *secondary authority*. By this point in this chapter, you should have a good understanding of primary legal authority since it includes the "law" of constitutions, statutes, agency regulations, and judicial decisions, all of which are discussed in Sections B through D above.

In contrast, secondary authority is not law at all, but either commentary on the law or a legal research tool that will help you as a lawyer to understand and locate law. For instance, a law professor might write an article identifying weaknesses in a federal statute and discussing why Congress should have crafted certain provisions more beneficially. This article might be very helpful to other legal scholars; those who enact statutes—legislators; those who interpret statutes—courts; or lawyers who are analyzing a client's legal problem. The article is not law, however, since the law professor, unlike the legislature, had no authority under our legal system to change the statute itself and could only criticize its content and hope to influence the legislature.

In addition to the type of secondary authority that provides commentary on primary legal authority, many legal publishers publish research aids that help lawyers do research. These sources often provide helpful introductions to complex areas of law and citations to the primary authority that may answer a client's legal question. These research tools, however, are not law themselves and therefore have no legal authority whatsoever.

CHECKLIST

☐ Review the sources of law in the United States.

☐ Consider the relationship among sources of law:
- The concept of jurisdiction; and
- Hierarchy of sources of law.

☐ Know the court's role under *stare decisis*:
- When a court must follow the decision of another court;
- When a highest appeals court must follow its own decisions; and
- How courts from one jurisdiction follow decisions of courts from other jurisdictions.

☐ Understand how the course of litigation results in written judicial opinions.

☐ Learn the difference between primary legal authority and secondary authority.

CHAPTER 4

Statutory Analysis—A Basic Process

A. INTRODUCTION

To analyze a statute in your jurisdiction that appears relevant to your client's situation, you'll need to follow a basic process. You might begin by reviewing the role of a statute as a source of law and the relationship between courts and statutes, as discussed in Section B. To take a first step in understanding the statute's meaning, you'll work with the complete current statute in its code version and determine the role it plays within the context of related statutes—as explained in Section C. At that point, as discussed in Section D, you'll confirm the statute's applicability to your client's situation. Once you've confirmed that applicability, you'll move on to analyze the statute's text in more depth, using the techniques explained in Section E.

When you've completed these steps, you'll decide whether you have a solid understanding of the statute, as discussed in Section F. If you do, you'll be ready to move on to analyze legal authority that interprets the statute, such as judicial opinions. If you remain unsure about the statute's meaning, you'll need to explore the text of the statute more critically, using the process set out in Chapter 5, before analyzing additional authority.

Once you've analyzed the statute, you'll need to consider how to express the ideas in your memo, as discussed in Section G.

B. UNDERSTANDING THE ROLE OF STATUTES

1. Statutes as a source of law

A legislature may enact a statute to address prospectively any issue that it views as important to govern the citizens of its jurisdiction, as long as that statute is constitutional. The legislature may amend or repeal a statute at any time it believes changing the law is necessary.

A statute that is constitutional is mandatory authority in its jurisdiction. It will supersede any conflicting judicial opinions of that jurisdiction, even when decided by the highest appeals court.

However, a statute has no binding authority beyond the boundaries of its own jurisdiction. For instance, a statute of one state is not mandatory when the law of another state governs the client's situation, though courts may use statutes from other jurisdictions as persuasive authority.

2. The relationship between courts and statutes

While the legislature has the authority to enact statutes, courts still play an important role. Courts have the authority to determine whether a statute is constitutional. If it is, the statute is mandatory authority that supersedes conflicting common law developed by the courts. Furthermore, courts must apply and therefore interpret statutes.

First, courts have the responsibility to determine whether statutes are constitutional. In a state jurisdiction, the highest appeals court has the final authority to decide if a state statute is constitutional under the state constitution. The highest federal court, the United States Supreme Court, has the authority to decide if a federal statute is constitutional under the federal constitution. It also can decide if a state statute violates the federal constitution.

Second, when a statute is relevant to controversies brought before them, courts must apply the statute. To do so, they often need to interpret its language. When taking that step, courts are not free to decide what they would have legislated themselves but, instead, must determine what the statutory language means.

C. USING A CODE TO BEGIN YOUR ANALYSIS OF A STATUTE

In working with a statute that appears relevant to your client's situation, you'll likely use its code version. Given the organization of a code, you'll find the complete current statute in one place and be able to determine the statute's role in relation to other statutes. In addition, if you use a code that is annotated, you'll find editorial information in addition to the text of the statute.

1. Using a code to locate the complete statute

Lawyers generally work with statutes in their code form because codes allow lawyers to quickly locate in one place all current statutory law relevant to a particular subject. To fully appreciate the importance of using a code, however, you must understand the difference between statutes published in session law form and in code form.

Legislatures enact individual statutes during each legislative session and publish them in volumes called *session laws* that arrange all enacted legislation for a given legislative session in chronological order. Each individual statute enacted during a legislative session does not necessarily set out the legislature's complete approach to the subject addressed, however. For instance, a recent statute in its session law form might add new content to a prior statute but might not republish the prior statute with the new content incorporated.

In contrast, the publisher of a code does not arrange statutes chronologically like sessions laws, but by subject. To do so, the publisher compiles in one place all relevant session laws that have been enacted over time relating to the same subject. The publisher organizes all of these statutes into general subject categories that reflect all areas of law addressed by the legislature. As the legislature changes its statutes, the publisher continually updates the code by adding new statutes; deleting repealed statutes; and editing the text of statutes by adding, deleting, or changing language to match the most recently amended version.

Example of why lawyers work with statutes in a code and not in their session law form

Imagine that the legislature enacted the following legislation regarding driving laws for turning right on a red light:

Individual statutes published in session laws:

- In 1960, the legislature enacts a statute that requires drivers to stop at a red light, making a violation subject to a fine of not less than $25 and not more than $100.
- In 2000, the legislature enacts a statute that allows drivers to turn right at a red light after stopping, unless a posted sign prohibits that action. Legislature makes a violation of either of these actions subject to a fine of not less than $35 and not more than $300.
- In 2015, the legislature changes the fine to not less than $50 and not more than $500.

Rather than searching over many years of session laws to locate all relevant statutory provisions, the lawyer would use a code. There, the lawyer would have instant access to the legislature's current approach to this subject:

Current code section:

> **Driving on a roadway: Stopping at red light; turning right after stopping**
> A driver must stop at a red light. A driver may, however, turn right after stopping, unless a posted sign prohibits that action. Any person who violates the provisions of this section shall be punished by a fine of not less than $50 and not more than $500.

2. Using a code's topical organization to put the statute in context

Codes are organized topically and that organization will often provide important contextual information as you analyze a statute. Publishers of codes use a breakdown of subject categories from the most general to the most specific. Within this breakdown, a publisher separates each general subject category into increasingly more specific aspects of that subject and assigns labels for each, such as "titles," "subtitles," "parts," "chapters," and "sections"—though the way in which the relevant code divides and labels the subject categories varies from jurisdiction to jurisdiction. You can use this organization to identify where a statute fits within the code's subject breakdown, and use that information to help determine the role the statute plays in relation to the surrounding sections in that part of the code.

> **Example of using a code's topical breakdown**
>
> Imagine that you had located Iowa Code Section 724.2, which addresses the "authority to possess offensive weapons." Turning to the topical breakdown for this part of the Iowa code, you would quickly see that this section is a criminal statute because it falls within the Title of "Criminal Law and Procedure" and then the Subtitle of "Crime Control and Criminal Acts." In particular, Section 724.2 is located in the Chapter of "Weapons" because it addresses "authority to possess offensive weapons." You would also be able to see that Section 724.2 relates to other surrounding sections that might be important to your analysis, such as "Unauthorized possession of offensive weapons."

> **Iowa Code**
>   Title XVI. Criminal Law and Procedure
>   Subtitle 1. Crime Control and Criminal Acts
>   Chapter 724. Weapons
>   Section 724.1 Offensive weapons
>   Section 724.2 Authority to possess offensive weapons
>   Section 724.2A Peace officer defined
>   Section 724.3 Unauthorized possession of offensive weapons
>   Section 724.4 Carrying weapons

3. Using an annotated code for editorial features

Many publishers "annotate" codes by adding their own editorial features to help lawyers as they research and analyze statutes rather than only providing the text of the statutes as enacted by the legislature—the law itself. For instance, an annotated code will include references to quick descriptions and citations to court decisions interpreting aspects of the statute, secondary authority that provides commentary on the statute, and other research aids.

When using an annotated code, you must distinguish between the actual "law"—the text of the statute enacted by the legislature—and any editorial features written by the publisher. Editorial features written by publishers have no legal authority, and therefore you may not base your analysis on them. While making this distinction will become second nature with experience, you must be careful the first few times you work with a statute as a first-year law student.

D. CONFIRMING THE STATUTE'S APPLICABILITY TO YOUR CLIENT'S SITUATION

Before you spend too much time analyzing a statute in depth, you must confirm that the statute does appear to control your client's situation. At this point, you should check the statute's effective date and verify that the statute regulates activities or conduct related to your client.

1. Checking the effective date

You should check the statute's effective date to ensure it actually applies to your client's situation. At the time of enacting a statute, the legislature mandates the date when the statute becomes effective and governs situations that fall within its purview. In order for a statute to be relevant to your analysis, therefore, the statute must be effective at the time of your client's situation, unless the legislature has made clear that the statute applies retroactively or a court has so construed the intent of the legislature.

2. Verifying that the statute regulates activities or conduct related to the client's situation

You should also skim the statute to verify that it includes operative language related to your client's situation. Such language authorizes, mandates, or prohibits certain activities, or provides the related consequences. Statutory sections that merely provide definitions or set out the legislature's policy concerns do not do so.

Of course, statutes that play these other roles may be helpful to your analysis in other ways. For instance, while a definitions section does not explain the consequences of actions relevant to your question, it may interpret terms in a section that do.

> **Example of comparing a code section that explains consequences of actions to a code section that only provides definitions**
>
> The following two code sections from Iowa demonstrate the difference between a statute that directly affects the outcome for a client by addressing whether an activity is authorized or not, and one that merely provides definitions.
>
> The first section, 724.2, would directly affect the outcome for a client since it authorizes the activity of possessing an offensive weapon in certain circumstances.
>
>> 724.2 Authority to possess offensive weapons
>> 1. Any of the following persons or entities is ***authorized to possess*** an offensive weapon when the person's or entity's duties or lawful activities require or permit such possession [*emphasis added*]:
>> a. Any peace officer.
>> b. Any member of the armed forces of the United States or of the national guard.
>> [*subsections c through i are omitted*]. . . .
>
> In contrast, Section 724.1 below defines "an offensive weapon," rather than addressing the classes of those authorized to possess this type of weapon and under what circumstances. The legislature used no words that addressed whether an activity was allowed or not.

> **724.1 Offensive weapons**
> *An offensive weapon is any device* or instrumentality of the following types:
> 1. A machine gun. A machine gun is a firearm which shoots or is designed to shoot more than one shot, without manual reloading, by a single function of the trigger.
> 2. A short-barreled rifle or short-barreled shotgun. A short-barreled rifle or short-barreled shot-gun is a [*full definition is omitted*]. . . . [*emphasis added*]

E. WORKING WITH STATUTORY TEXT: THE FIRST STEPS

Once you've located a statute in its current, complete form in a code and gained an overview of its content using the code's organization—as described in the previous sections—you are ready to analyze the text in depth. When you are first learning to analyze statutes, you should experiment with the methods discussed below. As you gain experience and confidence, you'll be able to choose a process that is best for you.

1. Skimming the statute to gain an overall sense of its content

Begin by skimming the text of a statute to gain an overall sense of its content. As you read through, try not to get bogged down when you don't fully understand an idea. Instead, make quick notes about any questions you need to answer or passages you need to come back to. Only stop to figure something out when you must absolutely understand it to move to the next idea.

2. Rereading the statute to break down its content

When rereading a statute, you need to break it down into its different pieces. You'll sometimes encounter statutes that organize these pieces in a checklist format and therefore this step will be fairly straightforward. However, you'll also encounter statutes that are densely written in long, cumbersome sentences and paragraphs. In either circumstance, however, you should begin by reading the text to identify the following types of questions that generally help determine how the statute governs the outcome in a client's situation and often will help you break down the statutory text into its relevant pieces:

- What kinds of activities are covered?
- Are certain activities authorized? Mandated? Prohibited?

- What are the consequences of engaging in prohibited activity or failing to engage in mandated activity? What are the possible results or actions allowed from engaging in authorized activity?
- What classes of individuals or entities are covered?
- Are there exceptions to the kinds of activities or classes of individuals or entities that are covered?

Of course, this list cannot include all conceivable issues addressed in every federal or state statute that you might encounter, given the increasing areas of law that are statutory. Therefore, you should always be prepared to encounter issues that are not included in the list above, based on the substantive focus of a particular statute.

> **Example of comparing two statutes with similar content presented differently**
>
> **Massachusetts General Laws Chapter 266 § 14:**
>
> > **§ 14. Burglary; armed; assault on occupants; weapons; punishment** Whoever breaks and enters a dwelling house in the night time, with intent to commit a felony, or whoever, after having entered with such intent, breaks such dwelling house in the night time, any person being then lawfully therein, and the offender being armed with a dangerous weapon at the time of such breaking or entry, or so arming himself in such house, or making an actual assault on a person lawfully therein, shall be punished by imprisonment in the state prison for life or for any term of not less than ten years.
>
> Quickly skimming this statute, you'll immediately realize that a lot of information is packed into this paragraph. Look again, and you'll see that the paragraph is one very long sentence. Many statutory provisions — even fairly simple statutes — are often written in this fashion. When faced with this type of statutory text — as explained above — you would likely begin by breaking down the language into its separate ideas. By doing so with the above statute, you would end up with the following:
>
> - *Whoever breaks and enters*
> - *a dwelling house*
> - *in the night time,*
> - *with intent to commit a felony,*
> - *or whoever, after having entered with such intent, breaks such dwelling house in the night time,*
> - *any person being then lawfully therein,*

> - *and the offender being armed with a dangerous weapon at the time of such breaking or entry,*
> - *or so arming himself in such house,*
> - *or making an actual assault on a person lawfully therein,*
> - *shall be punished by imprisonment in the state prison for life or for any term of not less than ten years.*
>
> Now consider another burglary statute where the legislature has used formatting that helps identify the different ideas:
>
> **Hawaii Revised Statutes Section 708-810:**
>
> **§ 708-810. Burglary in the first degree**
> (1) A person commits the offense of burglary in the first degree if the person intentionally enters or remains unlawfully in a building, with intent to commit therein a crime against a person or against property rights, and:
> (a) The person is armed with a dangerous instrument in the course of committing the offense; or
> (b) The person intentionally, knowingly, or recklessly inflicts or attempts to inflict bodily injury on anyone in the course of committing the offense; or
> (c) The person recklessly disregards a risk that the building is the dwelling of another, and the building is such a dwelling.
> (2) An act occurs "in the course of committing the offense" if it occurs in effecting entry or while in the building or in immediate flight therefrom.
> (3) Burglary in the first degree is a class B felony.
>
> Here, the Hawaii legislature wrote and formatted the statutory text in a way that would help you more quickly identify the different pieces, a step that you were required to do yourself in breaking down the Massachusetts statute. You might still want to further break down each paragraph in the Hawaii statute to fully identify all the different, more specific ideas, but the legislature's own formatting would be a good first step.

3. Exploring actively what you understand and what you do not

Once you've skimmed the statute to gain a sense of its overall content and tried to break it down, read the text again slowly and carefully to fully engage with the ideas. This time, question what you think you do understand and don't be afraid to admit what you do not. Readers who make quick assumptions, and don't challenge those assumptions, will likely reach only a superficial understanding. They therefore may miss critical aspects of the substance, especially at points where the legislature was unclear or ideas were complex.

As you read the language again, experiment with the techniques discussed below to help you engage with the relevant ideas. Eventually you'll be able to choose the techniques that are most appropriate given the substance of any particular statute or the one that is best for your own learning style.

a. Narrative writing — using the process of writing itself

As you learned in Chapter 2, you might use narrative writing to work with the text of a statute. By using the process of writing itself to explore ideas and how they relate to each other, you may connect more intimately with the language and move beyond passively summarizing a general sense of the content. For instance, as you struggle to understand a particular aspect of the analysis, you might pose a question and then attempt to work out an answer as you write.

Using narrative writing to explore the substance of a statute is very different, therefore, from underlining or highlighting ideas in the text. These more passive techniques merely identify ideas and require little thought about what those ideas actually mean. While you might find these techniques somewhat effective to hold your attention during your first quick read of a statute, you'll find them much less effective to engage actively with its content.

b. Outlines

Instead of narrative writing, you might try outlining the statute, as was first discussed in Chapter 2. Creating an outline, you must engage actively in figuring out ideas and their relationships. Begin by drafting an initial outline. Go back and read the statute to challenge the way you've organized ideas and their relationship to one another. Take any new insights back to the outline and move ideas around to represent the content more accurately.

c. Diagrams or pictures

You might also, or instead, use a diagram or picture to actively engage with text, as was discussed in Chapter 2. Especially if you benefit from creating some kind of visual representation of ideas, these techniques may help you "see" relationships among ideas more easily than narrative writing or outlining. In addition, certain kinds of substance by their very nature may be captured more clearly in images rather than described in words.

Begin by creating the diagram or picture. Go back and read the statute to challenge the way you've visually represented the ideas and their relationship. Take any new insights back and move ideas around to more accurately represent the content.

4. Summarizing your understanding of the statute in a tangible form

After you have actively worked with the text of the statute, you will need to summarize your understanding in a tangible form to provide a foundation for the next steps in your analytical process. To summarize your understanding, you could use the same techniques explained in Section 3 above, including narrative writing, an outline, or a diagram. In whatever form you choose, you should include any questions you still have and any areas in the analysis about which you remain unsure.

F. FURTHER DEVELOPING STATUTORY ANALYSIS

After taking the steps outlined above, you must determine the next step in your analytical process. If, after working with the statute, you are fairly confident that you understand the statutory text, you are ready to continue the process by adding additional legal authority. At that point, you might need to analyze other related statutory provisions, such as a definitions section as explained in Section 1 below or regulations as discussed in Section 2. In addition to related statutes or regulations, you would need to determine whether the courts of the jurisdiction had applied the statute, as explained in Section 3. Section 4 discusses how to proceed when the courts have not interpreted the relevant statute.

If after using the initial steps discussed in this chapter, you do not have a sufficient understanding of the statutory text, you would need to work with that language in more depth, using the techniques described in Chapter 5. Once you understand the language, you would then be prepared to analyze additional legal authority, as discussed in the sections below.

1. Using statutory definitions

Once you understand the relevant statutory text, you need to determine whether the legislature defined any of the relevant terms, either in the section itself or in a related definitions section. To analyze additional statutory provisions, you would use the steps discussed in the sections of this chapter above.

> **Example of using a definitional section**
>
> Imagine that your client, a member of the National Guard, wanted to know if she could possess a machine gun. Working with Section 724.2(1) of the Iowa Code—see Section D2 above—you would not be able to figure out from the phrase "offensive weapon" whether that term includes a machine gun or not.
>
> Once you had checked the definitions, Section 724.1, however, you would determine that a machine gun was considered an "offensive weapon" under Section 724.2(1). Section 724.1 states unequivocally that "An offensive weapon is any device or instrumentality of the following types: 1. A machine gun. . . ."

2. Using relevant regulations

You would also determine if any regulations further explained the statutory provision. In advanced law school classes, you'll learn how to analyze statutes where the legislature has authorized an agency to promulgate regulations to give effect to part or all of a statute and may also have authorized an agency to decide certain controversies arising under those regulations. While you are much less likely to encounter this kind of legal problem as a first-year law student, you will often do so as a lawyer.

3. Using court interpretations

You would then look to judicial opinions where the courts of the jurisdiction have applied the statute. If so, you would need to analyze those cases using the steps discussed in Chapters 6 through 8, to complete your statutory analysis.

4. Using canons of statutory construction when no court has applied the statute

In some situations, you may encounter a statute that the courts of the jurisdiction have not yet applied and therefore have not clarified its meaning. In this type of legal problem, you must anticipate how a future court would determine the meaning of the statutory text using legislative intent. In Chapter 9, you'll learn how to determine the intent of the legislature by using the jurisdiction's canons of statutory construction.

G. EXPRESSING STATUTORY ANALYSIS IN YOUR MEMO

At some point, you will need to decide whether you should use the exact language of the statute or whether you should paraphrase that language in your memo. In general, you should use the exact words of the statute when you are focusing on specific language that is relevant to your client's legal issue. That specific language used by the legislature is the anchor for the rest of your analysis. You should also use quotation marks in this situation because that is conventional for this type of law in law practice.

In contrast, you would likely paraphrase the statute when you are summarizing the overall gist of the statute to provide a context for the specific language relevant to your client. Especially when dealing with authority that is very complex, summarizing in this manner will be more concise, and therefore more helpful to your readers, than setting out a long quotation.

CHECKLIST

☐ Review the role of statutes and their relationship to courts.

☐ Begin your analysis by locating the complete current statute in an annotated code:
  • Use the code's topical organization to put the statute in context; and
  • Consider the editorial features of an annotated code.

☐ Confirm the statute's applicability to your client's situation:
  • Check the statute's effective date; and
  • Verify that the statute governs activities or conduct related to your client's situation.

☐ Use initial steps to work with the statutory text:
  • Skim the statute to gain an overall sense of its content;
  • Reread the statute to break it down:
    • What kinds of activities are covered?
    • Are certain activities authorized? Mandated? Prohibited?
    • What are the consequences of engaging in prohibited activity or failing to engage in mandated activity?
    • What are the possible results or actions allowed from engaging in authorized activity?
    • What classes of individuals or entities are covered? and
    • Are there exceptions to the kinds of activities or classes of individuals or entities that are covered?

- Actively explore what you understand and what you do not:
  - Narrative writing;
  - Outlines; and
  - Diagrams or pictures.
- Summarize your understanding of the statute in tangible form.

☐ **Further develop statutory analysis:**
- Statutory definitions;
- Relevant regulations;
- Court interpretations; and
- Canons of statutory construction when no court has interpreted the statute.

☐ **Decide whether to use the exact language of the statute or to paraphrase that language in your memo.**

CHAPTER 5

Statutory Analysis—Additional Steps

A. INTRODUCTION

After you've gained an overall sense of a statute's substance, as discussed in Chapter 4, you still may not fully understand that substance when the statute is complex and densely written. In this chapter, you'll learn additional steps to help you work with the statutory text in that situation.

B. RE-EVALUATE THE STATUTE'S ORGANIZATION

When working with a complex statute, you'll find it helpful to continue to break down its content into pieces, from general to more specific, after you've gained an overall sense of the statute. To break down a complex statute, use the following process:

- Identify the overall structure that the legislature used to organize the statute;
- Based on that structure, break down each subsection (or each paragraph or sentence) into its specific pieces, each of which plays a distinct role in the statute; and
- Break down each of those pieces into its individual terms, each of which expresses a specific idea.

However, you should not view these steps as a linear checklist that you necessarily work through only once in the same order each time that you analyze a complex statute. Instead, you may need to vary the order depending upon what you encounter in the text of any particular statute. In addition, you may find that your process is recursive, requiring you to move back and forth between different steps several times. Finally, given any particular statute, you may find that in completing one step you'll have completed aspects or all of another. Therefore, you should use these three steps as a beginning framework but tailor that framework as you analyze a particular statute to solve a client's legal problem.

1. Identify the overall structure used by the legislature

In some statutes, the legislature will have set out the ideas in one sentence or in one paragraph of two or more sentences. In these situations, you would continue your analysis by breaking down that paragraph or sentence into its specific pieces that each play a distinct role in conveying the substance of the statute, as discussed in Section 2 below. See, for example, the Massachusetts statute set out in Chapter 4, Section E2.

In other statutes, the legislature will have organized the content by initially breaking it down into two or more subsections of numbered paragraphs in outline form or of unnumbered paragraphs. When you encounter this kind of structure, you should continue your analysis by evaluating each subsection to gain a general overview of the substantive role it plays in the overall statute, as well as its relationship to other subsections. You should then proceed to analyze each subsection by breaking it down further into its specific pieces, as discussed in Section 2 below. See the Hawaii statute set out in Chapter 4, Section E2, and the following example from the state of Iowa.

> **Example of identifying the overall structure of a statute**
>
> The following is the criminal statute enacted by the Iowa legislature that you first encountered in Chapter 4:
>
> 724.2 Authority to possess offensive weapons
> 1. Any of the following persons or entities is authorized to possess an offensive weapon when the person's or entity's duties or lawful activities require or permit such possession:
> a. Any peace officer.
> b. Any member of the armed forces of the United States or of the national guard.
> [subsections c through i are omitted]. . . .
> 2. Notwithstanding subsection 1, a person is not authorized to possess in this state a shotshell or cartridge intended to project a flame or fireball of the type described in section 724.1.
>
> The Iowa legislature organized the content of Section 724.2 around two subsections. In Subsection 1, the legislature identified the people

> the statute covers as well as the fact that the statute permits the activity of possessing an offensive weapon in certain circumstances. In Subsection 2, the legislature identified an exception to what was permitted in Subsection 1. In particular, note the phrase of ***notwithstanding*** subsection 1, a person is not authorized. . . ." [*emphasis added*]
>
> After dealing with this first step in your analysis, you would have gained a general understanding of the substance of the statute, but you would still need to verify that understanding by analyzing each subsection in depth. You would therefore take the next steps of breaking each subsection down into its more specific pieces, as discussed in Section 2 below, and then breaking each of those pieces down into its individual terms, as discussed in Section 3.

2. Break down the statute further using the overall structure

After identifying the overall structure the legislature used to organize the content, as was discussed above in Section 1, you would be prepared to move on to the next step. Here, you would break down each subsection (or each paragraph or sentence) into its more specific pieces by:

- Separating out each specific piece, discussed in Section a below;
- Identifying the distinct role that each specific piece plays in the statute, discussed in Section b; and
- Determining the relationship among the specific pieces and their roles, discussed in Section c.

Remember that, as you break down a statute into its logical pieces, you should keep track of your progress with some type of note-taking technique, as demonstrated in Section d.

a. Separate out each specific piece

To break down a subsection into its more specific pieces, you need to determine where each piece begins and ends. Unfortunately, no easy formula exists that will work for all of the different statutes that you'll come across. Instead, as you read a subsection (or a paragraph or sentence), you must evaluate the wording of that part of the statute to locate the logical divisions between important but separate ideas in the statute. While these ideas could be expressed in one word only, at this level of generality you'll more likely encounter phrases that are based on a series of ideas that combine to express an overall important idea in the substance. To keep a record of this step of your analysis as you read, you should consider using visual techniques such as brackets around, and indentations of, each separate specific piece of the statute.

As you work through the subsection and separate out these specific pieces, you'll likely begin thinking about the distinct role that each piece plays. In some statutes, you'll get far with this as you separate out the pieces; in others, you will not. In either situation, however, you'll need to spend time verifying the distinct role that each specific piece plays, which is discussed in more depth in Section b below.

> **Example of breaking down a statute into relevant pieces**
>
> As discussed in Section 1 above, you had already determined that the Iowa legislature organized the content of Section 724.2 around two subsections. In focusing on the overall structure, you would probably have already begun to gain a general sense of the content of this statute. To check that step, however, you would still need to break each of these subsections down into its separate specific pieces.
>
> To begin with, you would read the wording of each subsection and look for the logical divisions between important but separate ideas in the statute. You could note these divisions for yourself by using the following visual techniques that would indicate where you thought each piece began and ended. First, you could use brackets around phrases (or words). Second, you could also indent each separate piece.
>
> Using these techniques as you worked through Subsection 1 of Section 724.2, you would end up with a visual representation of ideas that looked like the following:
>
> > [Any of the following persons or entities]
> >   [is authorized] [to possess an offensive weapon]
> >   [when the person's or entity's duties or lawful activities
> >   require or permit such possession]. . . .
>
> For each separate piece that you had bracketed, you would go on to identify the significance of its role. You would probably already have a general sense about some or all of these roles at this point in your analysis, but you would need to verify that your initial understanding was accurate and complete, which is discussed in Section b below.

b. Identify the distinct role of each specific piece

Once you had begun the process of separating out the pieces, as discussed in Section a above, you would move on to verify the distinct role that each piece plays. To provide you with a foundation for this aspect of your analysis, the sections below describe some of the most common roles that you'll encounter:

- Addressing generally the substantive focus of the statute, discussed in Section i;
- Creating an exception to what the statute covers, discussed in Section ii;
- Indicating a cause and result, discussed in Section iii;
- Providing a restriction, discussed in Section iv; and
- Identifying a test, discussed in Section v.

i. Addressing the substantive focus of the statute

Some specific pieces will address the substantive focus of the statute in terms of one or more of the following:

- What kinds of activities are covered?
- Does the statute authorize certain activity? Mandate certain activity? Prohibit certain activity?
- What are the consequences of engaging in prohibited activity or failing to engage in mandated activity? What are the possible results or actions allowed from engaging in authorized activity?
- What classes of individuals or entities are covered?

For instance, a specific piece of the statute might play the role of identifying certain activities and whether they are authorized, mandated, or prohibited. To figure out whether the legislature was authorizing an activity, look for words such as "may," "authorize," "permit," or "allow." To figure out whether the legislature was mandating an activity, look for words such as "shall," "require," or "must." When the legislature has prohibited an activity, the legislature may use such words as "prohibit," "not allowed," "may not," or "must not."

Example of identifying the substantive focus of a statute

If you were analyzing the statutory language below, you would need to identify its substantive focus as follows:

> **Code section:** A grandparent may be granted visitation rights with an adopted or biological grandchild.
>
> *Substantive role of a specific piece — permitted class*: a grandparent
>
> *Substantive role of a specific piece — permitting a certain activity*: may be granted visitation rights with an adopted or biological grandchild

ii. Creating an exception to what the statute covers

A specific piece may play the role of providing an exception to what is covered by the statute. To identify an exception, you should look for words such as "except," "unless," or "notwithstanding."

> **Example of identifying an exception**
>
> If you were analyzing the statutory language below, you would need to identify the exception as follows:
>
> **Code section:** A grandparent may be granted visitation rights with an adopted or biological grandchild unless that grandparent has been convicted of an aggravated misdemeanor or a felony.
>
> *Substantive role of a specific piece — permitting activity*: may be granted visitation rights with an adopted or biological grandchild
>
> *Role of a specific piece — exception*: unless the grandparent has been convicted of an aggravated misdemeanor or a felony

iii. Indicating a cause and a result

Some specific pieces of the statute may indicate a causal relationship where one piece is the "cause" that leads to another piece that is the "result." To indicate this relationship, the legislature may use "if" followed by "then" (either an explicit "then" or an implicit "then").

> **Example of identifying statutory language that indicates a cause and result**
>
> If you were analyzing the following statutory language, you would need to identify the cause and result as follows:
>
> **Code section:** If the following test is met, the court may then grant a grandparent the right of visitation with a grandchild: . . . .
>
> *Role of a specific piece — the "cause"*: If the following test is met
>
> *Role of a specific piece — the "result"*: the court may then grant a grandparent the right of visitation with a grandchild

iv. Providing a restriction

A piece may play the role of restricting some other aspect of the statute. To introduce one idea that restricts another, the legislature may use a word such as "when" or "if."

> **Example of identifying a restriction**
>
> If you were analyzing the statutory language below, you would need to identify the restriction as follows:
>
> **Code section:** A grandparent may be granted visitation rights with a biological or adopted grandchild when the grandparent has had substantial prior contact with the child.
>
> *Substantive role of a specific piece—permitting activity*: may be granted visitation rights with a biological or adopted grandchild
>
> *Role of a specific piece—restriction*: when the grandparent has had substantial prior contact with the child

Note that a specific piece of the statute that restricts another piece is generally just another way of setting out a requirement—something that must be satisfied. Therefore, in the example above, the requirement is implicit: A grandparent may be granted visitation rights with a biological or adopted grandchild [when the grandparent **meets the requirement of** having had substantial prior contact with the child].

v. Identifying a test

A specific piece of the statute may play the role of identifying a test that must be satisfied for the statute to take effect. While such a test could take a variety of forms, it often includes a requirement or a series of requirements.

As discussed in Section iv) above, a piece of the statute that plays the role of restricting some other aspect of the statute is often actually setting out an implicit requirement. However, it could also explicitly set out a test based on requirements.

> **Example of identifying a test based on requirements**
>
> In the statute set out below, the legislature used a test based on a series of three requirements, each of which must be satisfied for a court to conclude that a grandparent should have visitation rights with a grandchild. The legislature explicitly conveyed the idea of "requirement" by using "must find" in conjunction with the way it phrased each of the substantive ideas that followed:
>
> **Code section:** To decide whether a grandparent should have visitation rights with a grandchild, a court **must find** that the grandparents' prior interaction with the child was long-standing and beneficial [*one requirement*]; that the grandparents' prior

> interaction with each of the parents was amicable [*one requirement*]; and that visitation would be beneficial for the child [*one requirement*].

In addition to tests based on requirements, legislatures also use tests based on factors that are not individually required but play some role together in determining whether a statute is met.

> **Example of identifying a test based on factors**
>
> In contrast to the example above, the legislature could have chosen to use a series of factors that were discretionary. The following statute, therefore, requires a court to "assess" three factors in reaching a decision that a particular grandparent should have visitation rights with a grandchild. However, the statute allows the court a great deal of discretion as to how to use the factors in reaching that decision:
>
>> **Code section:** To decide whether a grandparent should have visitation rights with a grandchild, a court *shall assess the following factors*: The nature of the grandparents' prior interaction with the child [*one factor*]; the nature of the grandparents' prior interaction with each of the parents [*one factor*]; the benefits to the child of visitation [*one factor*]; and any other factor the court believes necessary to figure out the best interests of the child [*one factor*].

c. Identify the relationship between the specific pieces of the statute and their roles

At this point in analyzing a statute, you are focused on breaking each subsection (or each paragraph or sentence) into its more specific pieces. You will have already separated out each piece, discussed in Section a above, and identified the distinct role that it plays in the statute, which was discussed in Section b.

You now need to figure out the relationship among those specific pieces, and the roles they play, to fully understand how all aspects of the subsection join together to convey the substance at this point in the statute. To figure out this relationship, you would evaluate the transitional words or phrases that the legislature used to connect ideas.

i. Common transitions

In some circumstances, you'll recognize transitions that are commonly used in all writing to connect ideas, such as:

- "and": indicates that the ideas before and after have equal status.
- "or"/"either": indicates that only one of the ideas before and after must be present.

> **Example of "and" linking two specific pieces of a statute**
>
> In this example, the legislature has provided two restrictions to when a grandparent may be granted visitation rights. By connecting them with the transition of "and," the legislature has indicated that both restrictions have equal status as requirements. Therefore, both must be met before a grandparent may be granted visitation.
>
> **Code section:** A grandparent may be granted visitation rights with a biological or adopted grandchild when the grandparent has had substantial prior contact with the child and that contact has been beneficial to the child.
>
> *Substantive role of a specific piece—permitting activity*: may be granted visitation rights with a biological or adopted grandchild
>
> *Restricting phrases that have equal status because they are joined by the transition of "and"*: *when* the grandparent has had substantial prior contact with the child *and* [*when*] that contact has been beneficial to the child

> **Example of "or" linking two pieces of a statute**
>
> In this example, the legislature has provided alternative restrictions to when a grandparent may be granted visitation rights. The transition of "or" between the two restricting phrases indicates that only one must be met in order for a grandparent to be granted visitation.
>
> **Code section:** A grandparent may be granted visitation rights with a biological or adopted grandchild when the grandparent has had substantial prior contact with the child or the prior contact was not substantial but was greatly beneficial to the child.
>
> *Substantive role of a specific piece—permitting activity*: may be granted visitation rights with a biological or adopted grandchild
>
> *Restricting phrases that are alternatives because they are joined by the transition of "or"*: *when* the grandparent has had substantial prior contact with the child *or* [*when*] the prior contact was not substantial but was greatly beneficial to the child

ii. Transitions that connect one idea by referring to a prior idea

In other circumstances, you'll need to recognize transitions that connect one idea by referring back to a prior idea.

> **Example of a transition that links pieces of a statute**
>
> In the example below, the transition "that contact" indicates that the "contact" later on in the sentence is the same "substantial prior contact with the child" that is set out earlier in the sentence:
>
> > Code section: A grandparent may be granted visitation rights with a biological or adopted grandchild when the grandparent has had *substantial prior contact* with the child and *that contact* has been beneficial to the child.

d. Consider taking notes on your process of analyzing a statute

You should consider taking some kind of notes to keep track of your analysis of a statute so that you don't get lost. At different points, therefore, you should stop and think about—and perhaps keep notes on—what you've already done and what you should do next.

> **Example of taking notes on a statute**
>
> This example demonstrates how you might have used your notes to describe in narrative form your analysis of Iowa Code Section 724.2 to this point in the process. First, you would have identified the overall structure the legislature used to organize the statute—an organization based on two subsections. Second, you would have broken down each subsection into its specific pieces, including separating out the different pieces, identifying the distinct role that each played in the statute, and identifying the relationship among those pieces and their roles.
>
> **Language of statute you are analyzing:**
>
> > 724.2 Authority to possess offensive weapons
> > 1. Any of the following persons or entities is authorized to possess an offensive weapon when the person's or entity's duties or lawful activities require or permit such possession:
> > a. Any peace officer.
> > b. Any member of the armed forces of the United States or of the national guard.
> > [subsections c through i are omitted]. . . .

2. Notwithstanding subsection 1, a person is not authorized to possess in this state a shotshell or cartridge intended to project a flame or fireball of the type described in section 724.1.

Your possible notes that describe your analysis of the statute as a narrative:

Subsection 1:

<u>*Role in conveying substantive focus of subsection* by identifying class covered</u>: The legislature identified the class of those covered by the statute by using the phrase of "any of the *following* persons or entities [emphasis and bold added]" in conjunction with the later list of specific classes set out in a through i.

The <u>transitional word</u> "following" linked up the generic "any of the persons or entities" with the later specific list of classes set out in a through i.

<u>*Role in conveying substantive focus of subsection* by identifying that a specific activity is permitted</u>: The legislature identified the specific activity, and made clear that that activity was permitted, by using the phrasing of "[authorized] [to possess an offensive weapon]."

<u>*Role in conveying a restriction* as to when the activity is authorized</u>: The legislature added a restriction as to when someone might lawfully possess an offensive weapon with the phrase "when the person's or entity's duties or lawful activities require or permit such possession." The legislature's use of the word "when" to introduce this phrase indicates that "being authorized to possess an offensive weapon" is restricted by the phrase "the person's or entity's duties or lawful activities require or permit such possession." In other words, the words following "when" must be satisfied in order for any of the enumerated individuals to lawfully possess an offensive weapon.

Subsection 2:

<u>*Role providing an exception* to the activity allowed under Subsection 1</u>: The legislature indicated that Subsection 2 provided an exception to the activity allowed in Subsection 1 with the <u>transitional phrase</u> of "notwithstanding Subsection 1."

<u>*Role in conveying substantive focus of subsection* by identifying activity not authorized</u>: The legislature identified the particular activity, and made clear that it was not permitted, by using the phrasing of "[is not authorized to] [possess in this state a shotshell or cartridge intended to project a flame or fireball of the type described in section 724.1]."

3. Break down each specific piece of the statute into its individual terms

As you move to the third step, you should again stop and think about where you are in the overall process of breaking down the content of a statute into logical pieces, from general to more specific. You would have already completed the first step of identifying the overall structure that the legislature used to organize that content, which was discussed in Section 1 above. Based on that overall structure, you would have completed the second step of breaking down each subsection (or paragraph or sentence) into its more specific pieces. For each piece, you would have identified the distinct role that it played in the statute and the relationship among those pieces and their roles, which were discussed above in Section 2.

Your third step, therefore, would be to break down each piece into its individual ideas that were expressed in a word or short phrase, which are called *terms*. To take this final step, you would follow the same general process that you used in Section 2 above and would:

- Separate out each term;
- Determine the distinct role that each term plays in conveying the substance; and
- Determine the relationship between or among terms.

While conceptually the idea of analyzing each individual term as a final step in your process that moves from general to more specific may seem helpful, in practice that process may be less effective. In some statutes, you might logically need to begin this process sooner because some of the specific pieces of the statute discussed in Section 2 above will be individual terms of a word or short phrase instead of a long phrase based on a series of individual ideas. In other statutes, however, you will first need to break down any subsection (or paragraph or sentence) into its specific pieces and then break each of those pieces down into its individual terms to come to a complete and accurate understanding of the statute.

a. Separate out each term

You should read a specific piece of the statute slowly and carefully to begin the process of separating out each of its terms—a word or short phrase that expresses a specific idea. As you read, place brackets around words or short phrases that appear to be discussing separate ideas. You might also use the additional visual technique of indenting each term in the series of ideas. You may or may not at this point begin identifying the distinct role that each term plays in the statute at that point in the statute, which is discussed in Section b below.

> **Example of techniques to separate terms in a statute**
>
> The following are two examples of how you could report the end result of separating out each term within the specific piece of Section 724.2(1) that plays a restricting role.
>
> ... [when] [the person's or entity's] [duties or lawful activities] [require or permit] [such possession]. ...
>
> ... when
>   the person's or
>   entity's
>   duties or
>   lawful activities
>   require or
>   permit
>   such possession. ...

b. Determine the distinct role that each term plays in the statute

In general, once you've separated out the terms, their precise roles will be fairly obvious, unless, as is discussed in Section D below, the meaning of the term isn't clear from the words the legislature used, either in the abstract or as applied to the facts of a client.

> **Example of identifying the role of each term in a statute**
>
> In the specific piece of the statute of Subsection 1 in the example above, the terms "person" and "entity" refer back to other aspects of the subsection that make clear exactly who these people or entities must be.

However, you may struggle at times to figure out when individual terms are requirements that must be satisfied for the statute to take effect. In some circumstances, a legislature will communicate that idea clearly by using explicit words such as "must" or "require." In other circumstances, you'll need to recognize that a term is required when that idea is implicit.

For instance, when you are analyzing a specific piece that plays a restricting role, and is therefore a requirement, all terms within that piece of the statute will be separate requirements.

> **Example of recognizing separate requirements in a statute**
>
> Any of the following persons or entities is authorized to possess an offensive weapon *when the person's or entity's duties or lawful activities require or permit such possession.*
>
> In the excerpt from Section 724.2(1) above, the bolded phrase plays a restricting role. While the legislature did not use any words such as "must" or "require," the idea of "must" is implicit in the fact that this piece of the statute is a restriction. Given that the phrase plays this particular role, the idea of "must" is also implicit in the relationships among all of the individual terms included in that phrase. One way to report this relationship would be as follows:
>
> To be able to lawfully possess an offensive weapon under Section 724.2(1),
>
> >   the person or
> >   entity
> >   [*must have*]
> >   duties or
> >   lawful activities
> >   [*that must*]
> >   require or
> >   permit
> >   such possession.

c. Determine the relationship between or among terms

Just as you must determine the relationship between or among separate specific pieces of the statute, as discussed in Section 2c above, you must also determine the relationship between or among separate terms within that specific piece. To begin with, you may have already figured out one kind of relationship by determining that they are requirements that must each be satisfied for the statute to take effect.

To figure out other relationships, you must evaluate the language the legislature used to connect the separate words or short phrases. In some circumstances, you'll just need to recognize transitions that are commonly used in all writing to connect ideas, such as:

- "and": indicates that the ideas before and after have equal status.
- "or"/"either": indicates that only one of the ideas before and after must be present.

In other circumstances, you'll need to recognize transitions that connect one idea by referring back to a prior idea.

> **Example of using transitions to understand the relationships between ideas in a statute**
>
> Any of the following persons or entities is authorized to possess an offensive weapon when the person's or entity's duties or lawful activities require or permit such possession. . . .
>
> In the following phrase from the excerpt from Iowa Code Section 724.2(1) above, the legislature used two different kinds of transitions. First, it used the transition "or" in three different places to provide alternatives. Second, it used the transition "such" to refer back to the specific idea of "possess offensive weapon" earlier in the sentence.
>
> . . . when
>   the person's *or*
>   entity's
>   duties *or*
>   lawful activities
>   require *or*
>   permit
>   *such* possession. . . .
>
> Given the transitions used by the legislature, you would analyze the relationship among the terms, and therefore the overall substance of this specific piece of 724.2(1), as follows: Someone must engage in either a "duty" or a "lawful activity," and one of those must either "require" or "permit" possession of an "offensive weapon."

C. CHECK THAT YOU UNDERSTAND HOW ALL THE PIECES FIT BACK TOGETHER AGAIN

Once you think you've completed the process of analyzing the statute by breaking it down as discussed in Section B above, you must check that you understand how all those pieces fit back together again. If you haven't been working with the ideas in a tangible form up to this point, such as narrative writing, an outline, or a diagram, pick one form now and use it to describe your analysis of the statute. Once you've done so, challenge yourself to justify why the language and structure of the statute verify the way in which you've described the ideas and their relationship. Be sure that you've included any next steps you need to take, such as going to court decisions that interpret vague or ambiguous terms.

If you find at any point that you can't explain an aspect of the statute, then you must go back through some or all of the prior steps of analysis. As discussed at the beginning of Section B, the process of breaking down a statute into its logical pieces is not necessarily linear and therefore you may not be able to go through each step once and check it off as "done." Instead, you may need to go through some of the steps several times, especially when a statute's substance and structure are complex.

The examples below demonstrate how you might have used a diagram and an outline to set out your analysis of Iowa Code Section 724.2 instead of using a narrative list as set out in Section B2d. Here is the language of the section:

> **724.2 Authority to possess offensive weapons.**
> 1. Any of the following persons or entities is authorized to possess an offensive weapon when the person's or entity's duties or lawful activities require or permit such possession:
> a. Any peace officer.
> b. Any member of the armed forces of the United States or of the national guard.
> [*subsections c through i are omitted*]. . . .
> 2. Notwithstanding subsection 1, a person is not authorized to possess in this state a shotshell or cartridge intended to project a flame or fireball of the type described in section 724.1.

Example of a diagram of Iowa Code Section 724.2

Iowa Code Section 724.2(1)

conveys substantive focus

by identifying permitted classes
- peace officer
- member of the armed forces of the United States or of the national guard

[*subsections c through i*]

by identifying permitted activity
- possess offensive weapon

conveys a restriction

on when activity is permitted
- when duties or lawful activities require or permit such possession

Iowa Code Section 724.2(2)

provides an exception

to activity authorized under Subsection 1

conveys substantive focus

by identifying activity not permitted
- possess shotshell or cartridge intended to project a flame or fireball of the type described in Section 724.1

> **Example of an outline of Iowa Code Section 724.2:**
>
> Iowa Code 724.2 Authority to possess offensive weapons
>
> A. *Subsection 1*:
>   1. <u>Activity covered</u>:
>   a. Identifies activity: "possess offensive weapon"
>   b. Identifies activity is permitted: "is authorized"
>   c. Uses a restriction as to when someone is permitted to possess an offensive weapon: "when the person's or entity's duties or lawful activities require or permit such possession."
>   2. <u>Classes of those permitted</u>:
>   "Any of the following persons or entities . . .
>   a. Any peace officer.
>   b. Any member of the armed forces of the United States or of the national guard.
>   [*subsections c through i are omitted*]. . . ."
>
> B. *Subsection 2*: Provides an exception to the activity permitted in Subsection 1 with use of "notwithstanding subsection 1":
>   1. <u>Identifies activity</u>: "possess in this state a shotshell or cartridge intended to project a flame or fireball of the type described in section 724.1"
>   2. <u>Identifies activity is not permitted</u>: "not authorized"

D. DEVELOP THE STATUTORY ANALYSIS FURTHER

Once you have worked through the steps discussed in this chapter to understand the text of a complex statute, you are ready to take the next steps explained in Chapter 4, Section F, to add additional relevant primary authority or, in the absence of more authority, to use the jurisdiction's canons of statutory construction to further analyze the meaning of the statute, as is discussed in Chapter 9.

CHECKLIST

☐ For complex statutes, after using the process explained in Chapter 4, use the statute's organization to divide its content into pieces:
  • Identify the statute's overall structure:
    • Examine sentence and paragraph structure; and
    • Consider organization and numbering scheme of paragraphs.

- Separate each piece of the statute and determine its role:
  - What kinds of activities are covered?
  - Are certain activities authorized? Mandated? Prohibited?
  - What are the consequences of engaging in prohibited activity or failing to engage in mandated activity?
  - What are the possible results or actions allowed from engaging in authorized activity?
  - What classes of individuals or entities are covered?
  - Are there exceptions to the kinds of activities or classes of individuals or entities that are covered? and
  - Verify the relationship between specific pieces of the statute and the roles they play by checking transitions that connect one idea to another idea.
- Divide each specific piece of the statute into its individual terms:
  - Isolate each term;
  - Identify the distinct role that each term plays in conveying the substance; and
  - Determine the relationship between or among terms.

☐ **Check that you understand how all the pieces fit back together again.**

☐ **Develop the statutory analysis further.**
- Add additional relevant primary authority; and
- Consider using the jurisdiction's canons of statutory construction.

CHAPTER 6

Analysis of Individual Judicial Opinions

A. INTRODUCTION

As a law student and as a lawyer, you'll spend a great deal of time reading judicial opinions, or "cases." The following chapter is designed to help you learn to read and analyze an individual "case," a skill that is the foundation for learning how to synthesize ideas from a group of cases, which is discussed in Chapters 7 and 8. While as a new law student, you may find these skills somewhat daunting at first, you'll quickly master them with practice.

B. COMPARE THE LEGISLATIVE PROCESS WITH JUDICIAL DECISION MAKING

As a background for analyzing cases, you need to review how legislatures create law as compared with how courts create law. As you learned in Chapters 3 and 4, a legislature may enact a statute to address prospectively any issue that it views as important to govern the citizens of its jurisdiction, as long as that statute is constitutional. The legislature may amend or repeal that statute any time it believes changing the law is necessary.

In contrast, a court may not address any legal issue that it chooses but may only decide issues raised in controversies brought before it. If a court desires to change the law in light of evolving conditions in society, the court must wait for a case that raises that particular question.

In deciding each case, a court is bound by the concept of *stare decisis*, which you first learned about in Chapter 3. Under this concept, a court must follow prior judicial opinions that are mandatory authority when those opinions are similar to the factual situation in the controversy before it. While a court still has discretion because deciding "similarity" is often murky, a court is bound by prior precedent in a manner that a legislature is not bound by its prior enactments. While a court may overrule its own precedent and radically change its approach to the law, it will do so only in rare circumstances.

C. UNDERSTAND THE DIFFERENT PURPOSES FOR ANALYZING A JUDICIAL OPINION

As a law student, you must work with a judicial opinion differently depending upon the context. On the one hand, you may be reading and analyzing an opinion for your legal writing class. In that class, you'll likely be in the position of a lawyer who must figure out a specific jurisdiction's approach to an area of law in order to solve a client's legal problem. On the other hand, you may be reading and analyzing a case to prepare for class discussion in a course that focuses on the doctrine of a specific subject area, such as torts or contracts.

1. Analyzing cases to determine the law of a jurisdiction

In your legal writing class, you'll likely be working with cases as a lawyer does: You'll be analyzing a specific jurisdiction's approach to an area of law in order to solve a client's legal problem. You'll begin by reading and analyzing individual judicial opinions, as explained in this chapter. Once you've done so, however, you'll likely need to reevaluate your analysis of each individual case as you read and analyze the rest of the relevant cases from the jurisdiction, as explained in Chapters 7 and 8. Therefore, for each relevant case you will likely need to read the precedent cited by that court in support of its analysis. Once you have developed an analysis of the current status of the law based on the relevant case or cases in the jurisdiction, you will use that analysis to prepare an objective memorandum.

2. Analyzing cases to learn the doctrine of a specific subject area

In contrast to your legal writing class, in your other law school classes you'll learn a general approach to a particular subject area of the law rather than the law of any specific jurisdiction. In your casebooks for these classes, the editor will have chosen judicial opinions from different jurisdictions, not as representative of a particular jurisdiction's law but as illustrative of important concepts in understanding the general subject area. For this reason, the cases chosen will likely provide a complete explanation of the concept being illustrated. As you analyze individual cases for your doctrinal classes, therefore, you won't usually need to read the precedent the court cited to support its analysis.

Once you've analyzed that individual case on your own, your professor will facilitate a discussion about the subject matter in class. During the discussion, you'll be challenged to think about the concepts from that one case by applying those concepts to new situations through questions and possibly in-class hypotheticals.

D. READ A CASE ACTIVELY

As a first-year law student, you'll spend much of your time working with cases in all of your classes, especially during the first few months of law school. While you'll develop your own method to analyze cases as you gain experience and confidence, try using the following four-stage process as a beginner:

- Begin by skimming to gain an overall sense of a case's content;
- Distinguish between the court's text and any editorial features;
- Reread the court's text to actively engage with its content; and
- Summarize your understanding of the case in some tangible form.

1. Skim for overall sense of the case's content

Begin by skimming a case to gain an overall sense of its content. As you read the first time, try not to get bogged down when you don't fully understand an idea. Instead, make quick notes about any questions you need to answer or passages you need to review. Only stop to figure something out when you must absolutely do so to move to the next idea.

As part of your quick notes, jot down any helpful background information. For instance, note the level of the deciding court — either the highest appeals court, intermediate appeals court, or trial court; the date of the court's decision; and whether the case is a civil action between two parties or a criminal action brought by the state against a defendant.

2. Distinguish between the court's text and editorial features

You must distinguish between the text written by the court, which usually begins right after the name of the judge who authored the opinion, and any editorial features that the publisher has added. Such editorial features are located at the beginning of the case and generally include headnotes that summarize individual points of law in the court's analysis and a synopsis that summarizes the court's decision and the analysis it used to reach that decision. Although these features are helpful during your research process, they are not part of the court's opinion and therefore have no authoritative value. They should therefore never be the foundation for your analysis or be cited to in a memo.

3. Reread the court's text to actively engage with its content

Once you've gained a sense of the overall content, read through the court's language again slowly and carefully to fully engage with the ideas. This time through, question what you think you do understand and don't be afraid to admit what you do not, just as you learned to do with statutes in Chapter 4. Readers who make quick assumptions, and don't challenge those assumptions, will likely reach only a superficial understanding. They will therefore miss critical aspects of the substance, especially at points where the court was unclear or the ideas were complex.

You should also stop and try to understand the technical meanings of unfamiliar words or concepts. You might turn to a legal dictionary for a definition of a particular word or a secondary source like a hornbook for a discussion of a concept that you don't understand.

As you learned in Chapter 4 when dealing with statutes, as you reread, try to use some tangible way to represent your understanding of the ideas. You'll be more likely to reach an accurate and sophisticated analysis of a piece of legal authority if you actively work with its content. Experimenting with many of the same techniques you might use to actively engage with the content of a statute—such as narrative writing, outlines, and diagrams—may help you as you are first learning to analyze cases. You'll eventually be able to choose the technique that is most appropriate given the particular substance of a case or the form that is best for your own learning style. For instance, you might be most comfortable using some form of narrative writing or outlining because you are someone who benefits from engaging with ideas verbally. In the alternative, you might find engaging with ideas visually to be most effective and therefore you might choose to use diagrams or pictures to engage with the ideas.

To use these techniques well, be sure to distinguish between using them actively to engage with ideas and using them simply to summarize the end result of your analysis, which is discussed below in Section 4. While you might use some of the same techniques at either stage, how you use them will be different. When you are working actively with a piece of legal authority, you must view these techniques as fluid representations of ideas that will likely change over a period of time. In contrast, reporting the end result of your analysis is a more static step where you simply summarize what you understand about a statute or case at a particular point.

a. Narrative writing — using the process of writing itself

As you learned in Chapter 2, you might naturally use narrative writing to work with the content of a judicial opinion. By using the process of writing itself to explore ideas and how they relate to each other, you'll connect more intimately with the text and move beyond passively summarizing a general sense of the content. For instance, as you struggle to understand a particular aspect of the analysis in a case, you might pose a question and then attempt to answer it as you write.

> **Example of using narrative writing to think through an aspect of a case**
>
> Imagine that in your legal writing class you are reading a case where the court evaluated three different factors in order to reach a conclusion on the legal issue before it. Skimming through the case the first time, you think you fully understand the court's analysis of these factors. Reading the case actively a second time, however, you realize that you are not at all clear as to how the court used these factors to reach its decision.
>
> Therefore, you decide to use narrative writing to explore this aspect of the court's analysis. As you write, you pose a question and then work actively with the ideas in the text of the case as you attempt to answer that question. During this process, you describe what you understand but also confront directly what you do not. At the end, you reach the best conclusion you can at that point in time. Here's what that narrative writing process might look like:
>
> *The court used the word "factors" for these ideas, and originally I thought, OK, I get that. But, while rereading the case, I wondered, well, what does a court **do** with these "factors"? Does each factor have to be satisfied? I mean, are they requirements? Checking the court's language, I don't see the word "require" or "requirement."*
>
> *I did notice that, in applying these factors to the facts, the court used the word "overall" when it reached the decision that two of the factors were enough to be sufficient even though the third factor was not present at all. Does the word "overall" indicate that the court evaluates these factors "all together" but not all factors have to be present? That seems to be what the court was doing since the third factor wasn't present, yet the court found that the other two were sufficient together. If these factors were requirements, I think that all three would have to be present and the court wouldn't view them in an "overall" manner.*

> <u>Conclusion</u>: *My best guess is that the court meant that the factors should be used in some sort of combination instead of each factor being required. But I'll need to check the other relevant cases in the jurisdiction.*

Using narrative writing to explore the substance of a case can often be more helpful to develop a deeper understanding of the language than simply highlighting or underlining text. These more passive techniques merely identify ideas and require little thought about what those ideas mean. While you might find underlining or highlighting holds your attention during your first quick read, they would be much less effective to actively engage with the language of a case.

Remember, however, that this type of narrative writing is different from more formal writing where your goal is to convey your understanding of the analysis—for example, in an objective memo in your legal writing class. In more formal memo writing, you are not exploring ideas for yourself but, instead, presenting the end result of that process for your readers.

b. Outlines

Instead of narrative writing, you might prefer using outlines, as was first discussed in Chapter 2. You might begin by drafting an initial outline of the major ideas from the case. You would then reread the case and, as you read, challenge the way in which you have organized the outline. Through this process, you might reach a new understanding of the court's analysis—an understanding that would require you to reassess how you had initially described ideas and their relationship.

c. Diagrams or pictures

You might benefit from the use of a diagram or picture of a case—either instead of, or in addition to, another technique, as was explained in Chapter 2. A visual presentation of ideas may be more helpful than narrative writing or outlining because certain analyses may be captured more clearly in images than in words.

Again, be willing to revise your diagrams or pictures. Start by creating one based on your initial reading of the case. Then, read the case again to verify that you've visually represented the ideas and their relationship accurately. Be willing to change your initial picture or diagram based on any new insights gained from rereading the case.

> **Example of using a visual presentation of a court's analysis**
>
> Imagine that you are reading a judicial opinion where, to figure out whether an individual could easily walk between two locations, the court evaluated the physical obstacles on the route. In that case, to walk between the two locations, an individual had to cross a stream that was 20 feet wide by walking on boulders; climb over 2 wooden fences that were 5 feet high; and walk around a large pasture that was gated by an electric fence. The court reached the decision that these particular physical obstacles did prevent an individual from easily walking from one location to the other.
>
> By just reading the court's description of the facts concerning the specific physical obstacles, some individuals would easily understand the analysis the court used to reach its decision. Others, however, would first need a visual representation of these facts and would therefore sketch out a picture of the particular obstacles an individual would encounter when walking between the two locations.

4. Summarize your understanding of the case in some tangible form

At some point, you should summarize your analysis in a tangible form to provide a foundation for the next steps in your analytical process. In your legal writing class, you'll often need to summarize your analysis of an individual case to move on to synthesizing the ideas in that case with the ideas in other relevant cases, as discussed in Chapters 7 and 8. In other classes, you'll need a summary for class discussion.

To summarize your analysis of a case, you could use narrative writing, an outline, or a diagram in much the same way as you used them to actively engage with the case's content, as explained in the previous section. In the alternative, you could choose to use the traditional form of a "case brief." A case brief describes each important aspect of the court's analysis in separate sections, which are discussed in Section F below. In whatever form you choose to summarize your analysis, don't forget to include any questions you still have.

E. ANALYZE THE MAJORITY OPINION THOROUGHLY

The majority opinion written by the court is the "law" and is therefore the basis for your analysis of the case. To analyze the majority opinion thoroughly and accurately, you should determine the overall procedural history that describes why the case is before the court and distinguish relevant from irrelevant issues to your question.

1. Determine the procedural history of the case

You'll need to understand the procedural history that describes how the case ended up before the court. Begin by identifying the level of the court that decided the case. Then figure out how the case reached that court by answering the following questions. Which party prevailed at the trial court? Why? Did the losing party then appeal to an intermediate appeals court? Which party prevailed at the intermediate appeals court level? Why? Did the losing party then appeal to the highest appeals court?

2. Distinguish between relevant and irrelevant issues

As a lawyer determining the law for a particular jurisdiction, you'll often analyze cases based on multiple legal issues arising from the same controversy. In this situation, you'll need to determine which parts of the case are relevant to your client's legal problem and which parts are not. In contrast, in your doctrinal courses you won't usually need to take this step. Your textbook typically will include only that portion of a case that is relevant to the text's focus at that particular point.

> **Example of determining which parts of a case are relevant to a client's legal problem**
>
> Imagine that you need to determine whether your client will be able to state a cause of action for negligent infliction of emotional distress. In one case, you find that the court examined whether the Plaintiff successfully stated three separate causes of action: A cause of action for negligent infliction of emotional distress, a cause of action for intentional infliction of emotional distress, and a cause of action for breach of warranty. Reading the case to determine the law of your jurisdiction regarding the negligent infliction question, you would focus your analysis on that part of the case where the court addressed the legal issue that was relevant to your client's situation. You would ignore the court's discussion of the other two causes of action since they would be irrelevant.

The difficulty of distinguishing between relevant and irrelevant legal issues will vary, however, depending upon how clearly the court has separated the different aspects of its analysis. In many judicial opinions the court will clearly distinguish between different issues by the way in which it organizes and conveys its analysis. For instance, the court may use headings for each legal issue and may clearly identify each legal issue at the beginning of the case or at the beginning of its discussion of each issue. In other situations, however, the court will not clearly separate different aspects of its analysis or clearly describe each legal issue, and therefore you may struggle to distinguish the relevant from the irrelevant portions of the opinion.

F. ANALYZE ALL IMPORTANT ASPECTS OF THE COURT'S ANALYSIS FOR EACH RELEVANT LEGAL ISSUE

You must analyze all important aspects of the court's analysis related to each relevant legal issue:

- The procedural results and substantive decisions the court reached;
- The facts that were relevant to the court's decision(s); and
- The court's analysis in reaching its decision(s).

1. The decisions the court reached

a. Procedural results

For each legal issue, a court will reach a procedural result, based on a substantive decision, as discussed below. That procedural result may include an order as to the next step in the case.

Example of identifying procedural results

A pretrial motion for summary judgment before a trial court:

Procedural result: Summary judgment granted on the basis that [*substantive decision*].
Order: Plaintiff's complaint dismissed.

Appeal of trial court's decision to intermediate appeals court:

Procedural result: Trial court's decision of summary judgment affirmed on the basis that [*substantive decision*].

Appeal of intermediate appeals court's decision to highest appeals court:

Procedural result: Judgment of intermediate appeals court affirming summary judgment reversed on the basis that [*substantive decision*].
Order: Case remanded for trial consistent with this opinion.

---

b. Substantive decisions

In complex cases, a court will likely reach a series of substantive decisions as it moves to an overall result for the parties before it. The court will reach an overall decision on each legal issue, and it may also reach decisions on component aspects of that legal issue. At each point, the court may reach a decision as to its interpretation of the relevant law and a decision as to what that law requires as applied to the parties. Determining a court's "decisions," therefore, is likely to be a complex endeavor, especially since courts do not always clearly state or explain the results they reach, even if they have in fact addressed that piece of the analysis.

Be careful not to be misled by the term "holding" in figuring out the range of substantive decisions that a court may reach in a particular case. The term "holding" is often used to describe a court's overall decision as to the entire case or as to a given legal issue that is before the court. It does not capture, however, the range of substantive decisions that a court might make—ones that you'll need to work with to understand the court's analysis.

> **Example of determining the range of a court's substantive decisions**
>
> Imagine that you are analyzing an opinion by the highest appeals court of the jurisdiction. While several legal issues were before the court, you are interested only in the court's analysis of the claim for aggravated sexual harassment, which is the issue relevant to your client's situation.
>
> You first determine how the case reached the highest appeals court. The trial court issued a judgment for the Defendant, granting the Defendant's Motion for Summary Judgment on the claim of aggravated sexual harassment. The court reached this procedural result on the substantive basis that both parties agreed that no physical contact had occurred between the Defendant and the Plaintiff, and physical contact was required to show aggravated sexual harassment.
>
> The Plaintiff then appealed the trial court's decision to the intermediate appeals court. That court agreed with the trial court and therefore affirmed the trial court's judgment on the basis that the Plaintiff had not satisfied the appealed requirement that was necessary to recover for aggravated sexual harassment. The Plaintiff then appealed the intermediate appeals court's decision to the state's highest appeals court, which is the court that decided the case that you are analyzing.
>
> In the highest appeals court's opinion, you find that the court reached the following procedural result as to the appeal on the aggravated sexual harassment claim: It overturned the intermediate appeals court's decision and therefore reversed the trial court's granting of the Defendant's Motion for Summary Judgment. The highest appeals court also ordered the next step in the case: "We remand the case to the trial court

for proceedings consistent with our opinion as to that part of the Plaintiff's complaint based on aggravated sexual harassment." After this order, the case would go back to the trial court to reconsider that claim.

You then determine that the highest appeals court reached that procedural result on the substantive basis that the Plaintiff was not required to show physical contact to prove aggravated sexual harassment. The court explained that, while physical contact is important, it is only one of several factors that must be used to determine aggravated sexual harassment. You would therefore have identified the highest appeals court's procedural result and substantive decisions relevant to aggravated sexual harassment, as outlined below:

- *Procedural result*: The trial court's granting of the Motion for Summary Judgment on the aggravated sexual harassment claim, as affirmed by the intermediate appeals court, is reversed. The case is remanded to the trial court for a new determination consistent with the analysis explained in the highest appeals court's opinion.
- *Substantive decisions:*
  - <u>As to the law relevant to the legal issue—is physical contact required for aggravated sexual harassment</u>? Although physical contact is an important consideration, a plaintiff is not required to show such conduct to prove a claim for aggravated sexual harassment.
  - <u>As to applying that law to the case before the court</u>: Defendant's motion for summary judgment is denied because it was based on the argument that the Plaintiff did not allege any physical contact and, on that basis alone, did not sufficiently allege aggravated sexual harassment. The highest appeals court could not determine whether the Defendant was liable since the trial court only based its decision on the lack of any physical contact and did not consider other factors. The highest appeals court therefore remanded the case back to the trial court so that the trial court could analyze the question based on other relevant factors.

2. The facts relevant to the court's decision(s)

a. Locate background facts and legally significant facts

You must locate two kinds of facts described by the court. First, look for any background facts that are necessary to understand what happened in the situation before the court. Second, and most importantly, locate all legally significant facts, which are those facts upon which the court based its decisions.

You must look for these facts in more than one place in a case. You'll locate some facts in the court's general overview of the situation before it, which usually comes at the very beginning of the opinion. An overview will likely include the background facts and may also include legally significant facts. In addition, you'll locate additional legally significant facts in those parts of the case where the court addresses, and reaches a decision on, each legal issue.

You must only rely on facts that you locate within the majority opinion itself because these are the facts used by the court in reaching its decision. Therefore, you may not base your analysis on facts that you may have found through investigating outside sources, such as the Internet.

b. Describe facts accurately

You must accurately describe facts relied on by a court. You must therefore transcribe all facts without making a mistake and not make assumptions about facts that the court has described imprecisely. Otherwise, you'll skew your description of the analysis the court used to reach its decision and end up with an inaccurate understanding of the case, with potentially dangerous or embarrassing consequences.

> **Example of describing facts accurately**
>
> Imagine that your supervisor is scheduled to argue a motion before a trial court. In preparation for her argument, she has asked you to analyze a legal issue that is based on knowing whether an individual is an adult or a minor child.
>
> You locate a group of potentially relevant cases in the jurisdiction and proceed to begin analyzing one where the court noted that an individual traveled on a plane that crashed. The court named the individual in its opinion but in no place addressed the individual's age. You assume that this person was an adult since he was traveling on a plane alone.
>
> However, that assumption could be incorrect since minor children can travel alone on a plane without an adult under certain circumstances. If you base your analysis on the fact that in this case the individual was an adult, you would have developed a faulty foundation for your analysis as to this particular case. What if your supervisor went into court on this legal issue and was asked the following question by the judge: "Why do you think that this case supports your argument, given that the court never makes clear whether the individual was an adult or a minor child?" You can only imagine the chagrin of your supervisor!
>
> Instead, you should have decided that the court was unclear about this fact and that you couldn't draw any conclusion one way or the other as to the individual's age. On that basis, you should have excluded the case from your analysis.

3. The analysis the court used to reach its decision(s)

You must understand thoroughly and accurately the analysis that the court used in reaching each decision on a legal issue relevant to your client's situation. To do so, you must:

- Track the analysis of the court, including its interpretation of the law and how it applied the law to the facts before the court, which is discussed in Section a;
- Rely on the correct parts of the court's analysis, which is discussed in Section b; and
- Evaluate the weight of any dicta, which is discussed in Section c.

a. Track the court's analysis

i. Determine the court's interpretation of the law

Use the following considerations to determine the court's interpretation of the law—law that is abstract in the sense that it is not specifically tied to the controversy before the court. Begin by evaluating the type of law that was the foundation for the court's analysis. Was the court interpreting a statutory term? Had that legislature included a statutory definition of the term or had prior courts interpreted it? In the alternative, was the court interpreting prior courts' analysis of a common law cause of action?

In addition, you must determine the court's overall approach to the legal issue under consideration, including the overall test that the court is using and the policy rationales that explain why the court uses that test. You must then determine answers to the following questions. What are the components of the test and why does the court use them to achieve its broader policy concerns? What is the relationship among those components? How does the court determine whether each component is satisfied, if a requirement, or how influential, if a factor? The answers to these questions are relevant when you analyze an individual judicial opinion, as discussed in this chapter, and when you are synthesizing a group of opinions, which is discussed in Chapter 7.

> **Example of determining a court's interpretation of the law**
>
> Imagine that you are working with an individual judicial opinion that is analyzing whether the Plaintiff satisfied one requirement for a cause of action for negligent infliction of emotional distress. You would need to determine each of the following steps in the court's interpretation of the law.
>
> <u>Type of law</u>: Common law cause of action where court was interpreting prior judicial opinions.

> Court's overall test and its components: In developing its approach to how a plaintiff will be able to successfully state a cause of action for negligent infliction of emotional distress, the court chose an overall test based on two requirements, one of which is that a plaintiff's emotional distress must result in serious physical or mental symptoms.
>
> Reasoning that connects the courts' overall test, and its components, to broader tort policy rationales: The court developed its overall test, including its components, to ensure that it is treating plaintiffs and negligent defendants fairly, an important policy goal in tort law. Using the "physical or mental symptom" requirement, for instance, the court is able to distinguish between plaintiffs who can provide objective verification that their emotional injury was severe, and therefore should be allowed into court, from plaintiffs who cannot and should be excluded.
>
> Court's analysis of the component that a plaintiff must have serious physical or mental symptoms: To determine whether a plaintiff had serious physical or mental symptoms, the court requires that the plaintiff's symptoms be permanent and substantially undermine the plaintiff's ability to function in personal or professional endeavors.

You may find that determining these aspects of the court's analytical process will vary in difficulty, depending upon how clearly the court has expressed itself in its opinion. You'll encounter some cases in which the court provides well-developed analysis that is clear from the court's language and the structure of the court's discussion, including headings, paragraph divisions, and connections between all ideas.

In other judicial opinions, you'll find that the court includes language that is not well developed or discussion that is not structured clearly. In these situations, you'll struggle to figure out exactly how the court reached its decision. For instance, in a situation where a later case is relying on earlier cases, the court may simply use citation to prior cases to take the place of actual discussion on the page of the case. When this occurs, you'll gain a complete understanding of the court's analysis only by reading the cited cases, as explained in Chapter 7.

> ii. *Determine the court's application of that law to the controversy before it*

You must also determine how the court used its abstract interpretation of the law to reach a result on the facts before it. First, figure out the result the court reached. Second, track how it used the law, step by step, to reach that result, including any comparisons of the situation before it to similar and dissimilar precedent.

You may find tracking the steps of the court's analysis tricky in some situations. Sometimes a court merges its abstract interpretation of the law with its application of that interpretation to the controversy before it. In this situation, you must separate these two steps to ensure that you completely understand the court's process, both in the abstract as to the law itself, as discussed in Section i) above, and as to how that law is being applied to the case before the court.

At other times, a court may develop an abstract analysis of the law that appears complete. However, the court may have fine-tuned that analysis by adding new ideas as it applied the law to the parties' situation. You must always be prepared, therefore, to combine ideas together in different parts of the court's opinion to develop a complete and accurate understanding of the case.

b. Rely on the correct parts of the court's discussion

i. Distinguish between the court's discussion that is analysis in support of its decision and analysis that it considers but rejects

You must distinguish between the following two situations to accurately figure out a court's analysis in support of its decision. When the court follows ideas from prior precedent, those ideas become the basis for the court's decision—and the basis for your understanding of the case. In contrast, the court may discuss prior precedent and reject those courts' approaches, which are often based on the losing party's argument. Rejected ideas cannot be the basis for the court's decision and therefore may not be the basis of your analysis.

ii. Distinguish between the parts of the court's analysis that are relevant to your legal issue and those that are not

You must carefully determine which parts of the court's analysis relate to each legal issue before the court. Remember that courts do not always distinguish clearly between separate legal issues as they develop their analysis, as discussed in Section E2 above. You must therefore avoid the analytical mistake of using the court's discussion in support of one legal issue as the basis of your analysis of another.

> **Example of carefully reading a case for a specific issue**
>
> Imagine that in the beginning of a case a court identified two legal issues that were before it: A cause of action based on loss of consortium and a bystander's cause of action based on negligent infliction of emotional distress. The court then proceeded to discuss its analysis of each legal issue. As it discussed both issues, the court addressed the "relationship" between the plaintiff and the direct victim of the negligent

> action by the defendant; however, its analysis of "relationship" was different as to each cause of action.
>
> In analyzing either cause of action, you would therefore need to take care that you were relying on the correct passages of the case. If you confused the two discussions of "relationship," you would end up with an incorrect analysis.

c. Evaluate the weight of any dicta

You may encounter "dicta," which is analysis that was not necessary for the court to reach its decision. In deciding whether to use dicta as the basis for your understanding of the case, you must decide whether that particular language is dicta that is authoritative or that is not.

One kind of dicta is authoritative, and lawyers rely on it all the time in developing an analysis of the current status of the law. In this situation, the court reaches a decision that it doesn't need to reach, given its analysis, but bases its discussion on the actual facts of the situation before it. This kind of dicta provides strong evidence of the court's thinking, even though technically it has less weight than analysis that directly supports a decision that the court must reach.

> **Example of authoritative dicta**
>
> Imagine that the court is using an analysis that is based on three requirements. The court reaches a decision that the Plaintiff's situation does not satisfy the first requirement. Given that all three requirements must be satisfied, the court does not need to go on to discuss whether the Plaintiff satisfied the next two requirements.
>
> If the court does go on to discuss that the Plaintiff did, or did not, satisfy the next two, it is technically "dicta" since the court didn't need to do so to decide the case. However, the court did come to an actual decision on the actual facts before it. This kind of dicta, therefore, could be very influential to future courts as representative of the thinking of a prior court, and a lawyer would likely rely on it in developing an analysis of the law.

In contrast, another kind of dicta is less authoritative and therefore less useful. Here, the court reaches a decision on *facts that are not before the court*. Since courts may only decide the controversy actually before them, this kind of hypothetical analysis in support of a hypothetical decision would be less likely to influence a future court, though it could be persuasive.

> **Example of dicta when the court analyzes hypothetical facts**
>
> Imagine that the court is using an analysis that is based on one requirement. The court reaches a decision that the Plaintiff's situation does not satisfy the requirement.
>
> If the court does go on to discuss that the Plaintiff would have satisfied the requirement if certain additional facts had been present, this part of the court's analysis is technically "dicta" since the court did not use those hypothetical facts to decide the case. This kind of dicta is less authoritative but could be influential to future courts as representative of the thinking of how a prior court would have decided a case with the hypothetical facts. Therefore, a lawyer would likely use it as guidance when developing an analysis of the law.

G. DISTINGUISH BETWEEN THE COURT'S ACTUAL ANALYSIS AND YOUR OPINION ABOUT THAT ANALYSIS

In analyzing a case as a lawyer, you must distinguish the court's actual decision, and why it reached that decision, from your own opinion about the logic and fairness of the court's analysis. In the former, you are figuring out what the judge in the actual case decided and the analysis that the judge actually used to reach that decision. In the latter, you are deciding what you would have decided as the judge and the analysis you would have used in support of your decision.

To understand the importance of this distinction, think about the analytical goal for the Discussion Section of an objective memo. In developing an analysis of the *current* status of the law, you must come up with a reasonable interpretation of the legal authority as it actually exists at that point in time. Only by analyzing the relevant authority in this manner are you able to accurately predict how a future court would apply that law and reach a conclusion in your client's situation.

As a lawyer, you are "stuck with" the law as it currently exists, so you must separate what you think the answer *will be* based on your objective understanding of the law from what you think the answer *should be* in an ideal world. Your own sense of what the law should be in an ideal world may be quite different from the analysis that opinion reflects. If you merge these two steps, you could end up with an incorrect understanding of the court's analysis and consequently an inaccurate prediction for your client.

Of course, as long as you keep these two steps separate, you will want to develop the skills to criticize judicial opinions. A sophisticated lawyer always thinks about the ways in which the law should develop to promote good outcomes for society in general and between the individual parties to a case. In fact, throughout your legal career, you'll have opportunities to influence the law in the ways in which you choose your clients and how you make arguments to a court. Never forget, however, that you must understand the law as it currently exists to effectively argue how that law should change.

> **Example of distinguishing the court's analysis from your own opinion**
>
> Imagine that you are analyzing whether your client will be able to state a cause of action for intentional infliction of emotional distress. You find that only one case in the jurisdiction addresses this cause of action, and that the highest appeals court decided the case within the last year. In this case, the court made explicitly clear that, to successfully state this cause of action, a plaintiff must satisfy three required factors. While you understand the court's analysis, you disagree with it. You believe that a better analysis would be a totality test where the court would evaluate the overall combination of the three factors.
>
> Given the clarity of the court's discussion in this recent case, however, you would be "stuck with" an analysis based on the three requirements. You would need to use the court's actual analysis as the foundation for your analysis of the current status of the law as to this cause of action and not your own belief that a better analysis would be one based on a totality test.
>
> To understand the importance of this distinction, you need to imagine the potentially dangerous result if you failed to separate a reasonable interpretation of the court's actual analysis from your own. You would write up an analysis of the current status of the law that would not be an accurate description of what the case actually supported. You would then apply that law to your client's situation and reach a result, or potential results, that would not be an accurate prediction of the outcome before a future court. After reading your analysis in your memo, your supervising attorney might proceed to counsel the client about the next steps to take based on a flawed understanding of the relevant law.
>
> Of course, once you had developed a reasonable interpretation of the case's analysis based on the three requirements, and what it indicated for your client, you might then be asked by your supervisor to come up with any arguments, however creative and novel, that you could make on behalf of your client. At that stage, you might come up with the idea of arguing to the court to change its current approach based on three requirements and to adopt a new approach based on a totality test.

In this regard, analyzing a judicial opinion in your legal writing class, where you are working through the analysis as a lawyer in practice, will likely be quite different from analyzing an opinion for a doctrinal class focused on an individual subject area of the law. In a doctrinal class, you will not be analyzing the law of a particular jurisdiction to solve a specific client's legal problem and therefore will not be "stuck with" the constraint of the law as it actually exists. Instead, you will be much freer to pull apart a court's analysis, criticize it, and hypothesize better outcomes and ways to reason to those outcomes.

H. ANALYZE ANY CONCURRING OR DISSENTING OPINION

Having analyzed the majority opinion, you should then read any concurring or dissenting opinion. In a concurring opinion, a judge agrees with the result that the majority reached but does not agree with the majority's approach to the analysis. In a dissenting opinion, a judge disagrees with the majority's decision and likely also disagrees with the majority's analysis.

Concurring and dissenting opinions will not be the foundation for your analysis, including being sources that you may cite to in a memo as authority for the current status of the law since they are not the "law" of the jurisdiction. Despite the fact that these opinions generally are not the "law" itself, however, you may find them helpful, and you may cite them as additional support in a memo in certain instances. For example, in explaining their disagreement with the majority's analysis, concurring or dissenting judges may clarify aspects of the majority opinion. They might make clear an idea in the majority opinion that was ambiguous and therefore could be interpreted in more than one way. A concurring or dissenting judge may also explicitly articulate an idea in their opinion that was only implicit in the majority opinion.

I. USE THE COURT'S LANGUAGE TO DESCRIBE IMPORTANT IDEAS IN THE ANALYSIS

After you have analyzed a case using the ideas explored in this chapter, you'll be ready to summarize your understanding of that case in a tangible form for your notes, as explained in Section D4 above. As you summarize, you'll need to distinguish between ideas that you should paraphrase and ideas that you should use verbatim. On the one hand, you should paraphrase general aspects of the court's discussion. On the other hand, you should use the court's own language when the court has stated important ideas in a unique manner.

> **Example of using the court's phrasing**
>
> In explaining its analysis of a bystander's cause of action for negligent infliction of emotional distress, a court states that a bystander must "gain a sufficient sensory perception of the negligent act and the direct victim's injuries." You would probably not paraphrase the concept of "sensory perception of the negligent act and direct victim's injuries" because you would recognize that the court was expressing an important aspect of its analysis in unique language. You would therefore use the court's exact phrasing and would not paraphrase it. You would be especially confident in doing so if you had found that a series of courts had used this exact phrasing in analyzing this cause of action.

CHECKLIST

☐ Review how legislatures enact statutes and courts decide cases.

☐ Understand the difference between analyzing cases to determine the law of a jurisdiction and analyzing cases to learn the doctrine of a specific area of law.

☐ Read a case actively:
- Skim for an overall sense of the case's content;
- Distinguish between the court's text and the editorial features;
- Reread the court's text to actively engage with its content, including using some form of narrative writing, outlining, or visual representation of ideas, such as diagrams or pictures; and
- Summarize your understanding of the case in some tangible form.

☐ Analyze the majority opinion thoroughly:
- Determine the procedural history of the case; and
- Distinguish between issues that are relevant to your client's situation and those that are not.

☐ Analyze each relevant legal issue in the majority opinion:
- Determine the procedural and substantive decision(s) the court reached;
- Identify the facts that were relevant to the court's decision(s), distinguishing background facts from legally significant facts;
- Evaluate the court's interpretation of the law and the court's application of that law to the controversy before it;
- Distinguish between analysis that supports the court's decision and analysis that it considers but rejects;

CHAPTER 6 • Analysis of Individual Judicial Opinions

- Separate analysis that is relevant to your legal issue from analysis that is not; and
- Consider dicta.

☐ **Distinguish between the court's analysis and your own opinion.**

☐ **Analyze concurring or dissenting opinions.**

☐ **Summarize the court's analysis:**
- Paraphrase general ideas; and
- Use the court's exact language to describe important ideas.

CHAPTER 7

Synthesis of Judicial Opinions

A. INTRODUCTION

Many of the legal problems you'll work on as a lawyer will be based on court decisions, including problems where the courts are interpreting their own common law decisions, problems where the courts are interpreting a provision in a constitution, or problems where the courts are interpreting a term in a statute or regulation. In all of these situations, you will likely need to work with a group of cases to develop an analysis of the current status of the law in the jurisdiction relevant to your client's legal problem. To understand how to develop such an analysis, you first need an overview of the process of synthesizing opinions, which is explained in Section B. You also need to understand the different types of tests courts use, which is discussed in Section C.

With that understanding in mind, you'll need to learn how to work with a group of cases to develop the analysis, including identifying the courts' overall test, the tests' components, and the courts' reasoning for that test, as explained in Section D. When working through the cases, you'll use explicit ideas and potentially implicit ideas from the cases, which is discussed in Section E. Section F describes how to use diagrams and charts to keep track as you synthesize cases. You'll learn important considerations in describing the analysis that results from your synthesis in Section G. Illustrations of this entire process are included in Section H.

B. UNDERSTANDING THE PROCESS OF SYNTHESIZING CASES: AN OVERVIEW

While in some legal problems you'll find that a court in the jurisdiction will have fully articulated in a single case its analysis on a given legal issue, most often you will encounter situations where the courts have not clearly set out their entire analysis in any single case. In this situation, you'll need to recognize important ideas throughout a group of cases and combine these ideas, or in other words synthesize them, to develop a complete and accurate understanding of the courts' analysis. This understanding is the analytical foundation for your memo where you will explain the analysis to your readers.

To develop this analytical foundation, you'll begin by analyzing cases that are mandatory authority in your jurisdiction—as explained in Chapter 3—which include cases from the highest appeals court and any intermediate appeals court. You'll use persuasive cases—trial court cases from your own jurisdiction or cases from other jurisdictions—only after you've fully analyzed all mandatory cases in your own jurisdiction, which is discussed in more depth in Chapter 8.

Mandatory cases from your jurisdiction will be relevant to your analysis in all of the following situations. First, a court may discuss its analysis and reach a decision as to whether the facts before the court satisfy that legal issue. Second, a court may discuss the legal issue, developing its analysis, but avoiding reaching a decision on the facts before it. Finally, a court may have discussed helpful dicta, which was explained in Chapter 6.

In synthesizing cases from your jurisdiction that are relevant to your client's legal issue, you must begin with a presumption that these cases join together to create a consistent analysis where each case reiterates or adds relevant ideas. This presumption is reasonable because courts must use relevant precedent of their jurisdiction as they decide disputes that come before them, given the doctrine of *stare decisis* that you learned about in Chapter 3. (However, see Chapter 8 for some more complex situations that may be exceptions to this general rule.)

C. UNDERSTANDING DIFFERENT TYPES OF TESTS

As you develop analysis based on judicial opinions, you'll find that courts use a variety of tests at different points in their analyses of legal issues. The most common include: Bright-line tests, balancing tests, totality tests, checklists of requirements, and threshold tests. In simple analyses, the courts may choose just one of these tests. In complex analyses, the courts may use a combination.

Also be aware that you may encounter different ways to describe each of the tests discussed below. Courts in different jurisdictions, as well as law professors and lawyers, may use different terminology to describe the same kind of test.

1. Bright-line tests

You will often encounter "bright-line" tests that are definitional in nature. For instance, courts may develop categories that satisfy and categories that do not. Using this kind of test, courts generally have less leeway in reaching a decision in the case before them than when they use tests that allow more flexibility, such as where they balance factors or evaluate a combination of factors, as discussed in the sections below.

> **Example of bright-line test**
>
> "The courts in our jurisdiction have found that a bystander may recover for negligent infliction of emotional distress only if the bystander has an immediate or extended family relationship with the direct victim."
>
> In the bright-line test, a court has described two categories of relationships that satisfy this requirement: Immediate family or extended family. Either a bystander has such a relationship or not, which restricts a court's inquiry.
>
> To have a sufficient relationship, a bystander must be either an immediate family member or an extended family member of the direct victim.

Of course, bright-line tests are not actual "definitions" as we think about them in a dictionary since they may change and develop as the courts in any given jurisdiction work out their approach to a legal issue case by case over time. Such a test may also be more complex than the example given above and not necessarily indicate as certain an outcome in a client's situation.

For another example of a bright-line test, see Comment 22 to the Sample of a Formal Objective Memorandum in Appendix I.

2. Balancing tests

You also may encounter "balancing tests." Using this kind of test, courts weigh two or more factors against each other to see whether the overall result takes care of the courts' concerns.

> **Example of balancing test**
>
> In the language below, a court identifies that it is using a balancing test by explaining that a court "must weigh" one factor "with" another factor. Using this balancing test, a court would have much more flexibility in reaching a decision on the facts of a case before it than the court using a bright-line test in the example in Section 1 above.

> To decide whether the familial relationship between the bystander and direct victim is sufficient, courts must weigh the factor of degree of kinship with the factor of depth of prior emotional attachment between the parties.

In addition, courts may describe a "balancing test" as a "sliding scale" test. Here, the courts would evaluate how the relative weight of two factors achieves a result consistent with the courts' concerns. For instance, if one factor is exceptionally strong, then that strength might compensate for the relative weakness, or even absence, of a second.

> **Example of sliding scale test**
>
> In the language below, a court specifically describes its test as a "sliding scale" test.
>
> > To decide whether the familial relationship between the bystander and direct victim is sufficient, the courts use a sliding scale based on the degree of familial kinship and the actual nature of the emotional attachment between the two. When the degree of kinship is very close, less objective data must be introduced about the actual nature of the emotional attachment between the parties. In contrast, when the degree of familial kinship is much more distant, more objective data must be introduced about the attachment.

3. Totality tests

Using a totality test, the courts evaluate the overall combination of three or more factors to evaluate whether that combination achieves a result that is consistent with their concerns.

In some legal problems, you will be able to determine from the relevant cases that the courts use a combination of factors, but you will not be able to determine the exact nature of that combination.

> **Example of totality test**
>
> In the language below, a court explains that is using a totality test by stating that courts must "evaluate the overall combination of" several factors. The court goes on to identify those specfific factors.
>
> > To determine whether the grandparents should be granted visitation rights with the grandchild, courts **shall evaluate the overall combination of the following factors:** The nature of

> the grandparents' prior interaction with the child; the nature of the grandparents' prior interaction with each of the parents; and the benefits to the child of visitation.

In other legal problems, however, you will be able to determine more precisely how the courts actually manipulate the factors in the combination. The following are three possiblities of how courts might view a combination:

- The courts evaluate three or more separate factors but all factors do not necessarily have to be present as long as the overall combination of those present achieves the right result, given the courts' concerns.
- The courts require all factors to be present but present only to the degree that the overall combination achieves the right result, given the courts' concerns.
- The courts weigh one factor most heavily, given the nature of how it takes care of the courts' concerns, but adds the weight of other factors to the extent necessary for the overall combination to achieve the right result, given the courts' concerns.

For another example of a totality test, see Comment 12 to the Sample of a Formal Objective Memorandum in Appendix I.

4. Checklists—series of requirements

Courts often use a kind of "checklist" that sets out two or more requirements that must each be satisfied.

> **Example of checklist of requirements**
>
> In the language below, a court identifies that it is using a checklist of requirements by stating that a court "must find" and then listing several different ideas.
>
> > To decide whether a grandparent should have visitation rights with a grandchild, a court **must find** that the grandparents' prior interaction with the child was long-standing and beneficial; that the grandparents' prior interaction with each of the parents was amicable; **and** that visitation would be beneficial for the child.

For other examples of checklist tests, see Comments 8 and 21 to the Sample of a Formal Objective Memorandum in Appendix I.

5. Threshold tests

Courts may use a threshold test where they set out an initial requirement. If that threshold is not met, then the analysis ends. If that threshold is met, then further aspects to the test must be satisfied.

> **Example of a threshold test**
>
> In the language below, a court identifies that it is using a threshold test by stating that bystanders must "first" satisfy a certain requirement. The court goes on to explain that, if a bystander satisfies that first requirement, the bystander must meet another requirement.
>
> > Bystanders must first satisfy the requirement that they have some kind of an immediate or extended family relationship with the direct victim. If a bystander has one of these types of relationship, then the bystander must provide sufficient objective evidence of a deep emotional bond with the direct victim.

D. IDENTIFYING THE COURTS' OVERALL TEST AND ITS COMPONENTS

Although you will begin to read cases during your research process to locate cases in your jurisdiction relevant to your client's legal problem, once you have found some cases, you must read them more carefully, a step that makes use of the skills that you learned in Chapter 6. As you read the cases one by one, you should begin by determining the courts' overall test for the legal issue, which is discussed in Section 1 below. Section 2 describes the next step of determining the courts' analysis for each component of that test.

Each time you begin working with a new group of cases, keep in mind that no legal writing textbook can give you hard and fast rules to follow as you analyze the variations of legal problems that you will encounter as a student and as a lawyer. You should therefore not view the process outlined below as a rigid, linear way of working with a group of cases. Instead, use the process as a beginning. Be ready then to change course, depending upon what you encounter as you read any particular group of judicial opinions.

The bottom line is that, if you have a good sense of the important points to consider, and if you are thorough, you will end up with an accurate and sufficient analysis. This result will be true even if you later determine that a different process would have been more efficient.

1. Determine the courts' overall test and the courts' reasons for that test

In general, you should determine the courts' overall test and the courts' reasons for that test before delving into an analysis of each component, for several important reasons. First, in a series of decisions over time, courts may have added to or modified their overall test. If you begin with an in-depth analysis of one component of that test, you may waste time on something that is irrelevant to the *current* status of the jurisdiction's law. Second, by gaining a cohesive sense of the entire test, you'll be able to see how the components fit together. That knowledge may then give you insights into the courts' specific analysis of each component.

Finally, before you focus on individual components, you need to understand the courts' reasoning as to why they chose the overall test. Remember that courts tend to justify the approaches they use to their analysis on the basis that that analysis achieves results consistent with broad policy rationales whose goal is fairness among individuals or entities in society. These policy rationales, therefore, provide a necessary context for the courts' specific analysis for all components.

> **Example of determining the courts' overall test and the reasons why they chose that test**
>
> In working through a group of cases in your jurisdiction to determine if a defendant entered a "dwelling house," one of the elements under the jurisdiction's burglary statute, you find that the courts have chosen an overall test based on two components and have explained their reason for choosing that approach.
>
> > Overall test: To determine if a structure is a "dwelling house," the courts use a test with two components, both of which are requirements: The structure must be "used as part of" and "conveniently reachable from" the main residence.
> > Explaining the reasons for the test: The courts explain that they use this overall test because the purpose of the statute is to protect the "sanctity of the home."
>
> Once you've determined the overall test that the courts use and the courts' reasoning, you would move on to figuring out the courts' analysis for each of the two required components, including that the structure must be "used as part of" and must be "conveniently reachable from" the main residence. See Section 2 below.

a. Use a thorough process as you read the group of cases

So, how do you read a group of cases in a logical and thorough manner in order to determine the courts' overall test and the courts' reasons for choosing that test? At this point, you will be looking either at an electronic list of cases on your computer screen or at a pile of print copies on your desk. You must begin by choosing one case to read first, a decision that involves a range of competing considerations discussed in Section i below. Next, you must decide the order in which to read the rest of the cases in the group, a decision discussed in Section ii.

i. *Choose a first case to get started*

You know you must choose one case to read first, but there may not be one obvious choice as to the "best" case to help you develop the analysis. As a first consideration, you should evaluate the cases as to the level of the deciding court. If the highest appeals court in your jurisdiction decided all the cases, then all those cases would be equally authoritative. However, if the group includes decisions by both the highest and intermediate appeals courts in your jurisdiction, then you should consider beginning your analysis with the more authoritative decisions by the highest appeals court. You probably would not begin with trial court cases in most circumstances because the analysis in these decisions is only persuasive to the appellate courts, as you learned in Chapter 3.

To choose which of the highest appeals court cases to read first, try skimming through all the cases to locate ones that appear to be most helpful to understanding the courts' overall test. In fact, you will likely have already begun this step during your research process. Look for cases where the highest appeals court more fully develops its analysis, both in terms of the specific test it uses and its reasoning to justify that test, including its policy rationales. Then check whether later courts, both highest and intermediate, appear to rely on these cases by citing them and discussing them as especially important to the courts' analysis. If so, reading this kind of case early on may provide you with a good foundation of ideas as to the courts' analysis, and give you a sense of which case or cases to read next.

You might be wondering whether you should always begin with the most recent case of the highest appeals court in the jurisdiction. If you have a subgroup of several "central" cases by the highest appeals court, you might choose to read the most recent one first. This kind of case is likely to reflect the current analysis by the most authoritative court in the jurisdiction, including the specific test and policy rationales for that test, and would therefore likely be very helpful in developing your analysis.

However, choosing the most recent case to read first is not always the most useful way to begin. For instance, if the courts in your jurisdiction have explicitly established much of their approach in earlier cases, later cases may just be applying that established analysis to new sets of facts. In this situation, recent decisions might explain the courts' analysis in less detail because they would simply be relying on prior cases that developed the ideas in more depth. In fact, in some legal problems, the oldest case in a group might be the "best" place to begin. If the court in that case adopted a new test for the legal issue, the court will likely have justified that decision with an in-depth discussion of that choice—analysis that all later cases in the jurisdiction then build on.

You also might be wondering whether you should always begin by reading the case that, like the other cases, is discussing the relevant legal issue but that is the most factually similar to your client's situation. And the answer is "yes and no." Beginning with this kind of case might point you in the right direction, especially if the case includes a well-developed articulation of the current analysis of the highest appeals court. However, choosing to begin with a factually similar case that had little developed analysis might not be helpful at all. This kind of a case would not add much to your understanding of the courts' overall approach to the test, which would be necessary to predict the outcome in your client's situation.

Of course, if you locate a case that has identical facts to your client's situation, then you probably would begin there since that case would likely govern the outcome for your client. Don't forget, though, that, if you have a group of relevant cases, you would still have to verify that the court's analysis in that one case was consistent with the analysis of the other cases in the group.

ii. Proceed with the rest of the cases

After reading the first case, you should check your understanding of the court's overall test, and reasons for that test, with the analysis by the other opinions, especially other decisions by the highest appeals court. Again, you must keep in mind that, whatever case you begin with, you are only reading one case in a group of relevant cases. You must therefore not become convinced of the ideas from *that single case* until you have verified it *with the cases as a group*. Synthesizing the ideas from a group of cases often provides insights that one case may not, no matter how developed its analysis.

After reading the first case, therefore, you might go on to other cases that discuss the analysis in depth, since these cases might verify the ideas or add ideas to the analysis found in the first case. Or, if you had not done so already, you might choose to read the most recent case by the highest appeals court to determine if that court has further developed its overall test. Contrasting an older "central" case by the highest appeals court with the most recent case might help uncover developments in the courts' approach to that test, even if they are fairly subtle.

After reading a few cases in this manner, you should then consider working through all of the cases in the jurisdiction in either chronological or reverse chronological order, possibly by court level, to verify the courts' test and the reasons for that test that you determined from the first few cases you read. By doing so you might find that the first few cases provided you with a sufficient foundation that the rest of the cases support explicitly or implicitly. Or, instead, you might find that reading chronologically demonstrates a shift in the courts' approach that was not obvious from the first few cases.

b. Reevaluate the courts' overall test as you determine the courts' analysis of the components

Once you've developed a basic understanding of the courts' approach to their overall test and the courts' reasoning for that test, you should remain open to revising that understanding on the basis of your in-depth analysis of each component, which is discussed in Section 2 below. Moving to a more specific analysis of each part, you will reread the cases from a different point of view, which may help you reach a more sophisticated understanding of how these parts fit together into a coherent whole. Again, you should not view this process as linear. Instead, you should view the process as one that may require moving back and forth between determining the courts' overall test on the one hand and their analysis of each component on the other.

2. Develop an analysis of each component of the courts' overall test

Once you have an understanding of the courts' overall approach to their test — including any components to the test, their relationship, and why the courts chose that test — you are ready to focus on each component. At this point, you should then reread the group of cases again to develop an in-depth analysis for each component, using the same general process as described in Section 1 above.

In general, you will be looking for answers to the following types of questions, which are discussed in more depth in the sections below. How do the courts initially describe a component — the courts' "label"? What is the basic role of the component: Is it a consideration or a requirement? How do the courts develop their analysis of the component — their "explanation"? What "reasoning" do the courts use to justify their analysis of the component and its relationship to the courts' overall test for the legal issue?

a. Determine a "label" for the component

To begin, you must determine a "label" that indicates the substantive focus of the component.

> **Example of determining a label for the component**
>
> In determining whether a bystander may recover for negligent infliction of emotional distress in your jurisdiction, the courts use three requirements, one of which is that "a bystander's emotional distress must result in serious physical or mental symptoms."

> By using this phrase, the courts have communicated that this particular component focuses on the idea of the bystander's emotional distress resulting in specific symptoms and generally what those symptoms must be.

b. Determine the component's role in the courts' overall test

You must also determine the role that the component plays in the overall test. Is the component a requirement or, instead, a consideration that is evaluated in some manner but not required? You must understand the precise role of each component in the courts' overall test to develop your analysis accurately.

> **Example of determining a component's role in the overall test**
>
> In the previous example, by using the word "must," the courts made clear that the role of this component is a requirement in the courts' overall test.

c. Determine an explanation of the courts' analysis for the component

Once you've determined the courts' label and confirmed the role of the component in the overall test, you must figure out an explanation of the courts' analysis for that component. For instance, you may find that the courts are using a specific test for that component—see the discussion of tests in Section C above.

> **Example of determining an explanation of the courts' analysis for the component**
>
> In the negligent infliction of emotional distress example from above, once you identified that the courts' overall test was based on a checklist of three requirements, you would move on to figuring out an explanation of the courts' analysis for each of these three required components. For the requirement that a bystander's emotional distress must result in serious physical or mental symptoms, you decide that the courts use the following bright-line test:
>
> > _Explanation_: To satisfy this requirement, symptoms must be permanent and undermine to a great degree a bystander's ability to function in personal or professional endeavors.

In simpler problems, you may need to address only one layer of analysis that you can explain in a sentence or two. In more complex problems, however, you may need to work through several layers of analysis to identify the general concepts and then explain those general ideas in more specific terms. In this situation, you might need to develop paragraphs of analysis. Each legal problem will be different, and you'll need to develop the confidence and expertise to recognize the depth of analysis needed, depending on the ideas you encounter in the specific group of relevant cases in light of your own client's facts. In some situations, for instance, as you develop your explanation, you'll realize that the court uses a complex test to determine the component. In that situation, you may need to break that test down to its subparts and develop an analysis for each.

Instead of the word "explanation," lawyers may use other ways to describe this step of the analysis. For instance, they may use "standard" or "rule explanation." Whatever term is used, however, the focus of this step is the same: Determining an explanation for the courts' analysis.

d. Determine the courts' reasoning for the component

When working on the analysis of a component, you'll also need to determine the courts' reasoning. For most legal issues, you'll find that this step has two related aspects. You'll need to identify the specific reasons why the courts chose the particular component and then how those reasons help achieve the courts' broad policy rationales that underlie the overall test. Behind most analyses are important policy rationales about creating fairness among individuals and entities in society.

> **Example of determining the courts' reasoning for the component**
>
> <u>Courts' overall test and its components</u>: In developing their approach to when a bystander may recover for negligent infliction of emotional distress, the courts in your jurisdiction have chosen an overall test based on a checklist of three requirements. The courts explain that the goal of this test is to determine which bystanders should be allowed to recover because they have suffered genuine emotional distress.
>
> As one of the three components to the overall test, the courts require that a bystander's emotional distress result in serious physical or mental symptoms.
>
> <u>Reasoning that supports the choice of the physical or mental symptom requirement</u>: The courts require that a bystander's emotional distress result in serious physical or mental symptoms because such symptoms help objectively verify that the distress is genuine.

> Connecting the reasoning behind the specific requirement to the broader tort policy rationales behind the courts' overall test: The courts developed their overall test to ensure that they are treating plaintiffs and defendants fairly, an important policy goal in tort law. The courts use the "physical or mental symptom" requirement, for instance, to help distinguish between plaintiffs who are able to provide objective verification that their emotional injury is genuine, and therefore should be allowed to recover, from plaintiffs who should not be allowed to recover.

E. WORKING WITH EXPLICIT AND IMPLICIT IDEAS TO DEVELOP THE ANALYSIS

The difficulty of determining the courts' analysis from a group of cases may vary, depending upon the degree to which the courts in the jurisdiction have explicitly articulated their ideas and the degree to which those ideas are only implicit in the cases. In general, you should begin working with the explicit language the courts articulate as they reason to a result on the facts before them, which is discussed in Section 1 below. When those explicit ideas are not sufficient to develop a complete understanding of the courts' analysis, however, you must work with ideas that the courts have implicitly relied on but never articulated as the basis for their decisions, which is discussed in Section 2. In many analyses, you will need to use explicit and implicit ideas to fully develop your understanding of the courts' overall test and their reasons for choosing that test — as explained in Section D1 above — as well as the analysis for the different components, including their labels, roles, explanations, and reasoning, as discussed in Section D2 above. Finally, Section 3 discusses using your client's facts to determine the necessary level of detail for the explanation of the courts' analysis.

1. Begin with the courts' explicitly articulated ideas

To begin the process of synthesizing ideas from a group of cases in your jurisdiction to determine the overall test or a particular component, you should work with the courts' explicit statements about the test or component. If the courts say they are using certain principles to explain their analysis, you should begin with this foundation of ideas. Judges often — though not always — express many, or even all, important ideas unambiguously and explicitly as they reason to a decision for the parties before the court. These ideas join with the explicit ideas from the other relevant cases to articulate, at least to some degree, the courts' analysis, including the overall test, the components of that test, and the underlying reasoning, including policy rationales.

When examining the cases for explicit ideas, you will sometimes find an idea that is explicit in all relevant cases, as explained in Section a. However, in other situations, you may encounter groups of cases where an idea is explicit in only some of the cases, as discussed in Section b.

a. Ideas that are explicit in all relevant cases

In the easiest situation, the courts use the same language to express an aspect of the analysis explicitly and rely on this idea to reason to a result on the facts before them in all of the relevant cases. Synthesis in this situation simply requires recognizing the thematic use of the same idea expressed in the same way throughout the group of cases.

In other situations, the courts discuss an aspect of the analysis but use different words to express the idea. You may think that courts from the same jurisdiction, given the doctrine of *stare decisis*, should express the same idea in the same words. Once you recognize how case law develops over a period of time, you will understand why courts, even in the same jurisdiction, might choose different language to explain the same idea. Decisions by the same court over a period of time are actually decisions of entirely different groups of judges sitting on that court. In addition, those judges often struggle to articulate a difficult idea and therefore try different formulations in different cases over time until they decide on the best phrasing to communicate that concept.

When the courts appear to be using different language to express the same idea, you will need to identify these words and compare their meaning carefully. You must then test back that phrasing within the analytical framework of each individual case to be sure that each of the courts are, or reasonably seem to be, using the term in the same manner as they reason to a result. By working through this process, you'll be able to distinguish between the situation when the courts are expressing the same idea in different ways and the situation when the courts are describing different pieces of the analysis.

Assuming that you reach the conclusion that the different phrasing reasonably expresses the same idea, you must then decide which language best conveys the sense of the courts' analysis. In making that decision, you should begin by trying to determine whether the highest appeals court of your jurisdiction prefers one articulation to another. Has that court used one way of articulating the idea more often? Did the highest appeals court use one articulation in earlier cases but then change that language in more recent cases?

If it's not clear which language the highest appeals court prefers, then decide which articulation would best communicate that piece of analysis to another lawyer. Remember that ultimately you will have to convey this idea clearly in person or in writing to your supervisor or other members of your team.

b. Ideas that are explicit in some cases but only implicit in others

You will encounter situations where some of the relevant cases in the group articulate explicitly an aspect of the courts' analysis, but some do not. In this circumstance, you should begin by working with those cases that have explicitly stated the analysis. You would then take that analysis and test it back on the other cases to verify that these cases also support this idea.

This verification process has two steps. First, you must ensure that analysis that some courts have articulated could reasonably explain how the rest of the courts could have reached the result they did on the facts before them, even though they never explicitly discussed the idea. Second, you must ensure that the explicit ideas are consistent with any explicit reasoning that these other courts used to justify their decisions. If the explicit ideas from some of the cases test back on the rest of the cases in this manner, then you can be reasonably sure that these cases, too, support these ideas even though you reached that conclusion by inference.

This process makes sense when you think about how courts in our legal system decide cases over time. In some circumstances, courts simply rely on prior cases that fully express an aspect of the analysis and don't reiterate the analysis of the prior courts in the case they are currently deciding. Here, the courts might simply cite to the prior cases but not set out those cases' explicit analysis. In other circumstances, courts struggle to develop an aspect of the analysis and only do so after a series of cases. While the analysis may only be explicit in some of the later cases, the earlier cases are, in fact, consistent with the later cases; in fact, these early cases developed the foundation that helped later courts draw all ideas together and make them clear. For a further discussion of this concept, see Chapter 8, Section B.

2. Work with courts' implicit ideas, if necessary

In analyzing a legal problem, you may need to look beyond the courts' explicit ideas and consider ideas that the courts have not yet expressed at all. In some circumstances, ideas may not be explicit in any of the relevant cases and therefore completely implicit. In other circumstances, the courts may have explicitly articulated some of their analysis. However, these explicit ideas will not be sufficient by themselves, either because they are too general or because the courts leave important ideas unstated.

When these situations occur, you will need to look beyond the courts' explicit statements and analyze what the group of cases implies about the courts' analysis even when no court has actually articulated the ideas. You will find, especially in complex analyses, that you may need to uncover important aspects of the courts' analysis that the courts have not yet discussed but were arguably implicitly relying on in reaching their decisions.

When working with implicit analysis, you'll need to use your own words to explain the courts' ideas, but the cases themselves must reasonably support those words. While you may feel as if you are "making up law," remember that you are simply expressing ideas yourself that reasonably explain why a group of cases in your jurisdiction came to the results they did on the facts in each case. In other words, you are making explicit an inferential step in the courts' analysis.

To ensure that that you sufficiently ground your inferences on ideas in the cases, you must follow a careful methodology:

- Brainstorm descriptions that you think take into account the facts and results and relevant explicit ideas of all the cases in the group;
- Test those descriptions back on the cases' facts and results and any relevant explicit language;
- Revise or discard descriptions that are inconsistent with the cases; and
- Be ready to cycle through this process several times.

a. Begin by brainstorming descriptions of the implicit ideas

You might begin by working with the cases that reach a positive result on the overall test or component. Brainstorm and play around with different possible descriptions for why these courts reached the result they did on the facts before them. Do you see themes of similar facts that may have influenced the courts? How can you articulate in your own words why the courts found these facts sufficient? Does any explicit language in any of the cases help you figure out what the courts were concerned with?

Then move on to the cases that that did not reach a positive result on the overall test or component at hand and ask the same questions. Brainstorm and play around with different possible descriptions for why these courts reached the result they did on the facts before them. Do you see themes of similar facts that may have influenced the courts? How can you articulate in your own words why the courts did not find these facts sufficient? Does any explicit language in any of the cases help you figure out what the courts were concerned with?

Next, compare the ideas you've come up with in the two subgroups of cases. Try to express in your own words an overall description that reasonably makes sense of the courts' positive and negative decisions on the facts before each court. As part of this process, be sure to continue to evaluate any relevant explicit language in the cases.

Remember that you will rarely find a "bulls-eye" answer—one perfect description—since none of the courts articulated the idea themselves. Instead, the cases as a group will likely support a range of possible descriptions that are reasonable, and whether that range is wide or narrow will vary from problem to problem. For instance, in a large number of cases, the courts will likely have addressed many different factual situations, which might reduce the number of reasonable descriptions of the courts' analysis. In contrast, in a smaller group of cases, the courts will have addressed many fewer fact patterns, which may allow a greater number of descriptions that reasonably make sense of why the courts came to the decisions they did.

b. Test the descriptions back on the cases

Once you have come up with one or more potential descriptions of the analysis, you must then test each one back on all the relevant cases in the group. As you did with explicit ideas—see above—you should consider beginning with the cases where the court reached a positive decision on the facts before it and then proceeding to those cases where the courts reached one that was negative. In many situations, working with the cases in this manner may more quickly point out when a description is consistent with the whole group of cases and when it is not.

While a description does not need to have been articulated by any one court within the group, it should generally be consistent with all relevant cases in the jurisdiction and must be consistent with decisions by the highest appeals court. First, your description must reasonably explain how each court in the group reached the decision it did on the facts before it. Second, that description must also be consistent with any relevant explicit ideas in the cases, such as the courts' explicitly articulated doctrine and reasoning. (However, see Chapter 8 for some more complex situations that may be exceptions to this general rule.)

Important caveat: You must be careful when you are working with a case where the court does explicitly discuss the relevant analysis in the abstract but does not reach an actual decision as to whether the facts before the court satisfy that analysis. In this situation, you may use the court's explicit language to verify your description. In contrast, you may not use the facts of the case. Facts that are not tied to the court's decision provide no foundation whatsoever to verify whether your description of the courts' analysis is reasonable or not.

Example of testing descriptions back on the cases

Imagine that you are working with a group of cases where the courts use two requirements. As to the first requirement, the courts explicitly require a distance between two places that is short enough to allow a reasonable person to easily walk between the places. However, the courts have never developed explicitly when a distance is "short enough," and therefore you begin to work with the cases to come up with an articulation of what the courts implicitly meant by this phrase.

> In Case A, the court began by discussing the first requirement in the abstract, stating the "courts require a distance between two places that is short enough to allow a reasonable person to easily walk between the places." However, the court reached no decision as to whether the facts before the court—a distance of two miles—satisfied the requirement, given that the court found that the second requirement was not met.
>
> In coming up with a description that explains what the courts as a group implicitly meant by a "short enough distance," you could use Case A to verify that courts did, in fact, use that explicit phrasing as they described the requirement. However, you could not test any hypothesized explanation of what the courts implicitly meant by "short distance" back on the facts of two miles in Case A since the court reached no decision on the sufficiency of those facts. Without that decision, Case A cannot verify whether any particular description of "short distance" is a reasonable interpretation of the courts' analysis or is not.

c. Revise or discard descriptions that are inconsistent with the cases

Using this methodology, you will be able to distinguish between a description that is reasonably supported by the relevant cases in the jurisdiction, even though implicit, and a description that does not test back and is therefore outside a "reasonable zone" of ways to describe the analysis for this group of cases. When the cases do not reasonably support a description, given the methodology above, you must take one of the following two steps.

In some circumstances, you'll find that your description clarifies some aspects of the courts' reasoning process but is still inconsistent with other aspects. When this occurs, you must go back to the drawing board, brainstorm ideas, and then use the new ideas to revise any inconsistent aspects of the description so that it reasonably explains the whole group of cases. Then you must test this revised description back on the cases.

In other circumstances, you must discard a description because it is completely inconsistent with some aspect of the group of cases and therefore clearly wrong. Remember that the relevant group of cases is the foundation for your hypothesized description of analysis inferred from the cases; the cases are the check that you are not "making up" law that the cases do not support. Therefore, you must discard any description if it cannot explain how a relevant case reached a result, given the facts before that court, or if it is contradicted by any relevant reasoning explicitly articulated by any of the courts. (See Chapter 8, however, for some relatively rare exceptions to this important general rule.)

d. Be ready to cycle through this process several times

You should expect to cycle through this process several times as you work with a group of cases to figure out what the cases imply. Although you may brainstorm ideas that appear reasonable at first, you will often have to conclude that they do not test back sufficiently on the facts and results, and explicit language, of all the relevant cases. For this reason, you'll often have to refine your descriptions and go back through the process, or discard your description and move on to another. While you are more likely to have to refine or discard ideas when you are learning this process in law school, even experienced lawyers must go through trial and error when working with implicit ideas.

3. Use your client's facts to determine the necessary level of detail for the explanation of the courts' analysis

As you learned in Chapter 1, the purpose of an objective analysis is to develop a reasonable interpretation of the legal analysis relevant to your client's issue and then predict how a future court would likely use that analysis to reach a decision on your client's facts. Therefore, as you develop the analysis on a particular legal issue, you may find that the facts of the client's situation will affect the level of detail necessary in the explanation of the courts' analysis. For instance, in a legal problem based on judicial opinions, the courts' explicit language may specifically identify the client's facts as sufficient or insufficient. When the outcome based on the relevant law is so completely clear, you may not need to develop the explanation further than noting the relevant explicit language. In the corresponding application-prediction, a section that you will learn more about in Chapters 10 and 13, you would simply need to demonstrate how those explicit ideas dictate a clear result on the client's facts.

In other situations, however, your facts may guide you to provide a more in-depth explanation because the courts' explicit language does not provide a clear answer for your client. Only with an in-depth explanation will you be able to support a reasonable prediction on your client's facts in the corresponding application-prediction.

> **Example of using the client's facts to determine the necessary level of detail for the explanation**
>
> Imagine that your explanation of the courts' analysis, based on explicit language in the relevant cases, is that a "structure must be used for storing food." The relevant fact of your client is that she uses her structure only to store canned goods. In this situation,

> your analysis of the law clearly identifies "food" as dispositive. You therefore feel certain that a future court would view the client's use of the structure as sufficient since "canned goods" clearly falls in the "food" category.
>
> > Our client likely will successfully satisfy the requirement that a structure be used for storing food since she stored canned goods in her shed. See Case B; Case A.
>
> In contrast, imagine the same law but a different client who uses the structure to store only gardening equipment used to grow vegetables in the backyard. Whether "food" could be extended to cover gardening implements used to grow food would only be clear based on a more in-depth analysis to determine what the court was concerned about when it framed the analysis as to "food." In this situation, therefore, you would need to develop a more complete analysis of the law and then use that analysis to predict the outcome a future court would reach on your client's facts.

F. KEEPING TRACK OF IDEAS AS YOU SYNTHESIZE CASES

You should consider using diagrams and charts as you synthesize ideas from a group of cases. Diagrams often help as you develop the courts' overall test for a legal issue, as discussed in Section 1 below. Charts work well as you develop your analysis for each particular component of that test, as is discussed in Section 2. As you learned in Chapter 2, these techniques allow many writers to more easily "see" ideas and connections between ideas.

1. Consider using a diagram to refine the courts' overall test

You should consider working with visual representations of ideas in a diagram as you determine the courts' overall test. Begin to work on a diagram as you read through the cases the first time and continue to refine the content as you read the cases again. Be open to moving ideas around to explore new relationships among aspects of the analysis, or deleting ideas if they turn out to be irrelevant. In addition, change how the diagram represents the analytical structure of the courts' overall test if your subsequent analysis of a component indicates such a change is necessary.

2. Consider using a chart to synthesize cases as you develop the analysis of components

You should also consider working with a chart to help you with the process of synthesizing cases as you develop your analysis for each component. A chart draws together all the necessary information for each case in juxtaposition visually to the information for the other relevant cases. As you work with all the information in this manner, you may be able to more easily "see" themes of explicit or implicit ideas throughout some or all of the cases. You'll also end up with the important information in one convenient place and therefore be able to avoid repeatedly reading and rereading a series of cases.

a. Setting up the chart

i. Include basic information for each case

To begin with, set up the chart in the following manner. Group cases together by level of court in chronological order, or reverse chronological order. For each case, include the case name, court, citation, and date of decision. In this manner, you will include the important general information about the cases in one place.

ii. Include the facts of each case relevant to the particular component

Next, add the facts of each case that the court relied on, or appeared to rely on, to reach a decision on the particular component. Isolating these facts from facts relevant to other issues in the courts' analysis will help you as you work with the explicit and implicit ideas of the cases.

Remember that you may find these facts in more than one location in the case, as you learned in Chapter 6. Many of these facts will be located in that part of the case where the court addresses the specific component. However, you may also find relevant facts at the very beginning of the case. In a complex case that addresses many separate legal issues, for instance, the court may begin the case with a general overview of the situation before the court, and this overview may include facts that are, or arguably are, relevant to the courts' analysis of the specific component at issue.

iii. Include the decision that each court reached on the component

Also include on the chart each court's decision as to the component. For instance, if it's a requirement, was it satisfied? If it was a consideration—e.g., a factor—did the court use it and rely on it?

In many situations, however, you will not find it easy to figure out the court's decision relevant to a particular component. First, remember that, in any individual case, a court will likely reach a series of decisions as to each legal issue, as is discussed in Chapter 6. Before you can include the court's "decision" on your chart, you must determine which decision is relevant to the component you are analyzing.

Determining the court's decision may also not be easy because courts do not always clearly state or explain the result they reach on each component, even if they have clearly discussed that piece of the analysis. Nevertheless, you should try to determine what the result was, even if the result is not completely clear.

iv. Include any explicit language relevant to the component

Once you've included the relevant decision of each court, you should insert all the explicit language each court uses relevant to the component under consideration. Work through each case and isolate any relevant explicit language. Incorporate that language into the chart, using quotation marks, and include relevant page number references as a reminder that the language was explicit in the case. Remember that the range of what you may find in each case is very broad: You may find no explicit language at all or you may find whole paragraphs.

This part of the chart for each case may therefore contain a court's abstract discussion of an analysis of the law, including an explicit test; explicit explanations of how that test is satisfied; and explicit reasoning that indicates why that test is used, including broader policy rationales. This part of the chart may also include how the court applied those abstract principles to the facts of the case before the court and reached a decision for the parties.

v. Include any necessary implicit analysis relevant to the component

Finally, include places on the chart where you can insert ideas that you infer from the cases — those ideas, discussed in Section E2 above, that are not articulated by the courts but are implicit. When inserting these ideas, include a notation of "implicit" to remind yourself that these ideas have not been explicitly articulated by the courts.

b. Using the chart to synthesize ideas

Once you have filled in the chart with all of the necessary information, you are ready to work with this information to develop the analysis of the component under consideration. Having all the relevant explicit language from the cases in one place, you may more easily be able to "see" that some or all of the courts have used the same phrasing to articulate the same idea. You may also be able to compare and contrast phrasing more easily to reach a decision concerning whether a particular phrase expresses the same idea or ones that are different, as well as the role that phrasing plays in the analysis.

In addition, you might use the chart to figure out implicit ideas in the courts' analysis. Moving the cases around may allow you to see implicit "themes" of ideas that arise from the facts that the courts relied on to reach a decision, for instance. Having all the cases together also makes it easier to "test" a description of ideas back on all the relevant cases to ensure that it is adequately supported, even though never articulated by any court.

G. DESCRIBING THE RESULTS OF YOUR SYNTHESIS

As you develop a description of analysis synthesized from judicial opinions—analysis that is wholly explicit, wholly implicit, or a combination—you must learn to express your ideas accurately, completely, and with sufficient breadth to fully capture your synthesized ideas. To take this step, you need to state your analysis in general principles and consider when to use paraphrased or verbatim language.

1. Using general principles

When describing the analysis you developed from synthesizing cases, you should state your ideas in general principles—language that takes into account ideas from the relevant legal authority and is phrased with sufficient breadth to apply to a range of situations. You'll probably begin to use general principles due to the very process of synthesizing the ideas throughout a group of cases.

> **Example of expressing analysis with general principles**
>
> Imagine that a court in your jurisdiction has decided two cases relevant to your legal issue.
>
> Case One: The court found that the bystander satisfied the relationship requirement. In reaching this decision, the court reasoned that:
>
> > The bystander in the case before the court, Jon Snow, has satisfied the relationship requirement since he is a spouse of the direct victim of the negligence, Mary Snow.
>
> Case Two: The court found that the bystander satisfied the relationship requirement. In reaching this decision, the court reasoned that:
>
> > The bystander in the case before the court, Anthony Puorro, has satisfied the relationship requirement since he is the father of the minor child, Maria Puorro, who was the direct victim of the negligence.

> To express your analysis, you would need to state these ideas as general principles. To do so, you would synthesize the court's specific decisions as to Jon Snow and Anthony Puorro and state this idea in a broad enough manner to be useful in deciding future situations. Looking at the relationship in Case One—spouses—and the relationship in Case Two—parent to minor child—you would determine that the courts require an "immediate family" relationship between the bystander and the direct victim. **To state that analysis using general principles, you would write something like:**
>
>> *Bystanders* will satisfy the relationship requirement when they have **an immediate family relationship with the direct victim of the negligence.**

2. Using verbatim language or paraphrasing

You will consistently confront the following two important questions as you work on conveying your analysis from judicial opinions in general principles. First, should you use the exact words of the courts, paraphrase those words, or use your own words? Second, if you use the actual words of the courts, do you need to use quotation marks?

a. Choosing between using the courts' verbatim language or your own words

As you develop your general principles of analysis, you'll need to decide whether to use the courts' exact words, to paraphrase those words, or even to use your own words to describe ideas that the courts have only implied. With some groups of cases, you'll find that the courts consistently discuss the same important idea using the same phrasing. In this situation, you probably should use the exact words of the courts and not paraphrase. Changing any of the words could undermine an accurate analysis.

Often, however, when working with a group of cases—as explained above in Section E1a—you'll find that the courts have used inconsistent phrasing as they express a particular aspect of the analysis. After determining that the courts are expressing the same idea, you must decide which articulation communicates the idea most precisely and use that phrasing as the basis for your general principles.

Finally, when you are working with implicit ideas from a group of cases, you must use your own words to explain the ideas that you are inferring from the cases, a process that was discussed in Section E2 above.

b. Deciding when to use quotation marks around verbatim language

In any situation where you are using the exact words of the courts, you must decide whether to use quotation marks. Many lawyers believe there's no need to do so. Your readers will understand whether the language is verbatim based on the citation signal that introduces the citation to the legal authority, as is discussed in Chapter 14. In addition, there is no need to be concerned about plagiarizing from primary legal authority, as is also discussed in Chapter 14. However, other attorneys always use quotation marks to emphasize the places where you have used the courts' precise language.

If you choose to use quotation marks for analysis explained in general principles, however, you must be careful. Remember that your initial job is to synthesize the ideas in the group of cases. In the situation where the courts have expressed the same idea in various ways, you must go through the process, as described in Section E1a above, to decide which articulation best expresses the idea. Only when you've chosen the best language should you decide whether to add quotation marks.

If you follow this process, you'll avoid failing to synthesize the ideas and merely stringing together a series of "quotes" that all express the same idea. Analysis expressed in this manner is problematic. Encountering a series of quotes, your readers will have to spend their own precious time figuring out whether the quotes express the same idea or ones that are different—a job that's yours as author.

H. ILLUSTRATIONS OF SYNTHESIZING CASES

The following examples illustrate this process of synthesizing ideas from a group of cases. The lawyer would first determine the overall analytical structure of the courts' test and then move on to develop an analysis for each component of that test. In both steps, the lawyer would need to read through and analyze the relevant group of cases in the jurisdiction, as discussed in Section D above. During this process, the lawyer might have to work with explicit and with implicit ideas, as discussed in Section E.

> **Example of synthesizing a group of cases that interpret a statutory term**
>
> Imagine that one required element in a statute in your jurisdiction governs your client's situation. You discover that the legislature did not define this element and, without a definition, it is not clear whether your client's situation satisfies this statutory element. You do find, however, that the courts of your jurisdiction have interpreted this

element in several cases, and so you proceed to analyze what this group of cases indicates about the meaning of that statutory term.

As a first step, you would determine what the cases indicate about the overall test that the courts use to decide when this statutory element is satisfied. In synthesizing the ideas from the cases, you conclude that, to determine if this element is met, the courts use a test with three requirements. To reach this conclusion, however, you might have encountered either of the following situations. You might have found that the courts were explicit that they were using three requirements because throughout the cases the courts used phrasing such as "must" or "require" or "requirement." Alternatively, you might have encountered the situation where the courts only implied that they were using three requirements by how they reached their decisions based on the facts before each court, and you would have reached that conclusion by inference. For instance, if the courts allowed a plaintiff to recover when a component was satisfied but did not allow the plaintiff to recover when the component was not, you would reasonably be able to infer that the courts viewed that component as required.

Once you had figured out the courts' overall approach to interpreting this statutory element, you might then move on to develop an analysis for each component of the analysis—an analysis of each requirement. That analysis, depending upon the cases and your client's facts, might require you to develop one layer of analysis or might require several layers. How do the cases describe each requirement—the courts' "label"? What do the cases indicate about how each requirement is satisfied, including whether the courts use a further test for each of the requirements—an explanation of the courts' analysis? Why do the courts use each requirement—the courts' reasoning? And so forth. For each aspect of this part of the analysis, you might encounter a situation where the courts explained their analysis explicitly or you might encounter a situation where the explanation for what satisfied a particular requirement, or part of what explains that, would only be clear from synthesizing the cases together and implying that part of the courts' analysis.

Example of synthesizing a group of cases in a common law situation

Imagine a second situation where the courts in your jurisdiction have developed the following overall approach to analyzing a particular common law tort that you think could be the basis for a claim for your client. In synthesizing the ideas from the group of relevant cases, you conclude that, to recover for this tort, a plaintiff must satisfy a test based on two requirements, each of which furthers specific aspects of the courts' policy concerns.

Once you've figured out this overall analytical structure to the courts' approach—that they use a test with two requirements—you then would work with the cases and move on to determine the courts' analysis for the first requirement, one component of that test. Here, after synthesizing the cases, you determine that the courts use a totality analysis for that requirement where they evaluate a combination of four factors. To reach this conclusion about the totality analysis, however, you might have encountered a situation where the courts were explicit about all aspects of this totality idea or one where some aspects were explicit but others implicit.

You might have found that the courts explicitly described their analysis to determine whether the first requirement was satisfied: That they use a totality test; that, in applying this totality analysis, they use four factors; and that they require that each of these four factors be sufficiently present to result in an overall combination that achieves the courts' policy concerns as to this legal issue.

Instead, you would more likely encounter the situation where the courts only implied some of this analysis by how they reached their decisions based on the facts before each court, and you could only reach certain conclusions about the analysis by inference. For instance, you could have encountered the following situation. The courts did explicitly articulate that they evaluated three factors in an overall combination. However, the group of cases supported a logical inference that the courts were in fact also using a fourth factor, even though the courts never explicitly identified that factor as part of the test. If that fourth factor would make a difference in predicting a result in your client's situation, then as a sophisticated lawyer you would include that fourth factor as part of your analysis of the courts' overall test.

Once you had figured out the courts' analysis above, you would then move on to develop the next layer of analysis, which would include an analysis of each factor in the totality test. This step of the analysis might require you to develop one further layer of analysis or several more layers. How do the cases describe each factor—the courts' "label"? What do the cases indicate about when the courts find each factor sufficiently present—an explanation of the courts' analysis? Why do the courts use each factor to achieve certain policy objectives for this tort— the courts' reasoning? And so forth. For each aspect of this part of the analysis, you might encounter a situation where the courts explained their analysis explicitly. However, you might also encounter a situation

> where part or all of the courts' analysis of a particular factor would only be clear from synthesizing the cases together and implying the courts' analysis.

CHECKLIST

☐ Recognize that you often must synthesize a group of cases to determine the analysis of a legal issue.

☐ Understand that courts use different types of tests:
  - <u>Bright-line tests</u>, where the courts use a definitional-type analysis, which often includes categories that satisfy the analysis and ones that do not;
  - <u>Balancing tests</u>, where the courts balance two or more factors against each other to reach a result;
  - <u>Totality tests</u>, where the courts evaluate some kind of overall combination of three or more factors to reach a result;
  - <u>Checklists—series of requirements</u>, where the courts use two or more requirements; and
  - <u>Threshold tests</u>, where the courts use a requirement as a first step and then other steps only if that initial requirement is met.

☐ Identify the courts' analysis:
  - Use a process to develop the courts' overall test and the courts' reasons for that test:
    - Choose a first case to get started;
    - Proceed with the rest of the cases; and
    - Reevaluate the courts' overall test as you determine the courts' analysis of the components; and
  - Work with the group of cases to determine an analysis of each component of the courts' overall test:
    - State a label for the component;
    - Explain the component's role in the overall test;
    - Develop an explanation of the courts' analysis for the component; and
    - Identify the courts' reasoning for the component.

☐ Work with explicit and implicit ideas from the cases to develop the analysis:
  - Begin with the courts' explicitly articulated ideas:
    - Ideas that are explicit in all relevant cases; and
    - Ideas that are explicit in some cases but only implicit in others; and

- Work with courts' implicit ideas, if necessary:
  - Brainstorm descriptions of the implicit ideas;
  - Test the descriptions back on the cases;
  - Revise or discard descriptions that are inconsistent with the cases; and
  - Repeat this process several times.
- Determine the necessary level of detail for the explanation of the courts' analysis.

☐ **Keep track of ideas as you synthesize cases:**
- Consider using diagrams to refine the courts' overall test; and
- Experiment with charts to synthesize cases as you develop the analysis of components.

☐ **Describe the results of your synthesis:**
- Use general principles;
- Decide when to use verbatim language, to paraphrase, or to use your own words; and
- Determine whether to use quotation marks around verbatim language.

CHAPTER 8

Synthesis of Judicial Opinions in Complex Analyses

A. INTRODUCTION

As you know, many legal problems are based wholly or in part on court decisions, including problems where the courts are interpreting their own common law, where the courts are interpreting a provision in a constitution, or where the courts are interpreting a term in a statute or regulation. In Chapter 7, you learned that you'll often need to develop a description of the courts' analysis yourself by synthesizing the explicit and implicit ideas throughout a group of cases because courts do not necessarily fully articulate their analysis when reaching a decision for parties before them.

To accurately reflect the courts' analysis, as you learned in Chapter 7, your description must test back on the facts, results, and explicit ideas of all the cases together. When a description does not test back, you must go through the process again. You must either amend the description, or discard it and formulate a new one. At that point, you would test the revised or new description back on all the cases. In most situations, that process will convince you that you have articulated an accurate description of the courts' analysis since the courts of the jurisdiction used a consistent approach to answer the question.

However, you need to be prepared to handle more challenging situations when synthesizing groups of cases. You will likely encounter situations, as discussed in Section B below, where you will not be easily able to identify the courts' consistent approach because the law is insufficiently developed. You also might face a situation where the courts have developed contradictory approaches instead of a consistent approach, as discussed in Section C.

In other situations, as discussed in Section D, your proposed description of the courts' analysis may not test back on a case from your jurisdiction because you determine that the particular case is irrelevant to the courts' analysis. Finally, in any of these situations, you might decide to add persuasive cases — such as opinions from other jurisdictions — to strengthen your analysis based on the mandatory cases from your own jurisdiction. This possibility is discussed in Section E.

B. SYNTHESIZING CASES THAT INDICATE A CONSISTENT BUT UNDEVELOPED APPROACH

You will often encounter situations where you'll struggle to identify the courts' consistent approach to a legal issue because the courts have not yet sufficiently developed the law. For instance, you might find that recent decisions reflect a more complete analysis than earlier decisions in the jurisdiction, which would raise a question concerning whether the courts were developing one consistent approach or ones that were contradictory. Upon further analysis, however, you could conclude that the courts were developing a consistent approach over time on the basis that their current analysis was relying on the analytical foundation of earlier cases. You could reach this conclusion by testing back the current analysis on the earlier cases and finding that it was consistent with the facts, results, and explicit ideas of those cases, even though the courts' earlier descriptions of their analysis were incomplete.

You might also encounter the situation where the courts in the more recent decisions do not pull all aspects of their analysis together, in contrast to earlier cases where that analysis was more complete. Given that courts often develop their analysis piecemeal as they decide individual cases over a period of time, you might need to combine important ideas that are scattered throughout a group of cases. You could then test back your description of how these ideas cohesively fit together on the facts, result, and explicit language of all cases in the group in order to be confident that the courts were developing one consistent approach.

To verify your conclusion that the courts were developing a consistent approach in both of the above situations, you would also evaluate the way in which later courts discussed and cited to earlier cases. In groups of cases that combine to create a consistent approach to a legal issue, each court is likely to indicate that its analysis is part of a cohesive whole by positively citing to and discussing previous cases.

As you synthesize cases in situations where the courts have not sufficiently developed the law, you may find that your initial description does not test back on the facts, result, and explicit analysis of all the relevant cases. You would therefore need to either amend that description, or discard it and formulate a new one, to come up with a reasonable interpretation of the courts' consistent approach.

C. SYNTHESIZING CASES THAT INDICATE CONTRADICTORY APPROACHES

In addition to dealing with situations where the courts' analysis of the law is insufficiently developed yet suggests a consistent approach—as discussed in Section B—you will likely encounter rarer situations where the courts have used contradictory approaches and have not resolved that conflict. In some circumstances, the courts will have explicitly discussed that they have not sufficiently resolved their approach to a legal issue and that consequently different approaches have emerged. In the alternative, the possibility of contradictory approaches may be implicit in a group of cases that has not developed the law sufficiently and that therefore does not indicate clearly where future courts could take the analysis.

To determine a reasonable analysis under these circumstances, you should recognize that, when you find a group of cases that suggests a conflict, the level of court of the opinions—highest appeals or intermediate appeals—might affect your synthesis process. In some situations, as discussed in Section 1 below, the highest appeals court will be using competing approaches to the issue and will not have adopted one approach over the other. In other situations, discussed in Section 2, the intermediate appeals courts will be using competing approaches and the highest appeals court will not have resolved that conflict.

1. Contradictory approaches in highest appeals court cases

You might conclude that the highest appeals court has used contradictory approaches when dealing with a particular legal issue and has not adopted one approach over the other. You might think the likelihood that a highest appeals court would use approaches that contradict each other is rare since the highest appeals court is the final arbiter of a jurisdiction's law. However, this possibility makes sense when you think about the way in which courts decide cases over time.

In each individual case, the court's primary responsibility is to decide the dispute between the parties before it. In doing so, a court will address the relevant issue in so far as it needs to decide the dispute, but often may not necessarily pull together all aspects of relevant prior decisions into one cohesive statement of the courts' overall approach. Given this process over time, especially when the courts are developing an area of law and having difficulty, the courts themselves may not even be aware that the way in which they've written their opinions results in competing ways to view the emerging law.

When this occurs, you must be able to synthesize the cases together to identify the contradictory approaches, as discussed in Section a below. You must then attempt to predict which approach the highest appeals court would choose when confronted with a case that directly raised that question, as discussed in Section b.

a. Determine the contradictory approaches

To determine whether the highest appeals court has used contradictory approaches, you would use the following process as you analyzed the group of cases. First, you would locate and evaluate the different themes of explicit and implicit ideas that indicated different approaches to the analysis. You would then determine whether those approaches were contradictory, and therefore did not logically combine into one consistent approach to the legal issue.

As part of this process, you would evaluate whether throughout the group of cases the court appeared to be justifying its decisions based on different policy rationales. When a court is struggling to develop an area of law over time, it may, even without realizing it, develop different approaches to its analysis in order to achieve objectives that change as society's values change.

You might find additional evidence of a conflict in the way in which later courts discuss and cite to earlier cases. In some instances, courts will rely on different lines of cases as they develop contradictory approaches. In other instances, later courts may rely on the same case or cases to support the particular approach being applied, resulting in the situation where the same case is described by two different courts in a contradictory manner.

Example of determining contradictory approaches of highest appeals court

Imagine that you are working in a jurisdiction where the highest appeals court has adopted a bystander's cause of action for negligent infliction of emotional distress. In its original decision, the court used two requirements. The first requirement focused on the bystander's physical distance from the scene of the negligent act injuring the direct victim. The second requirement focused on the bystander's experience of the negligent act as it occurred, or of the direct victim immediately afterwards. As the court developed its analysis over time in the cases that followed, two different themes of ideas emerged as to whether the court viewed these two requirements as completely separate or whether it viewed them as necessarily interacting together.

On the one hand, in some cases the court discussed the bystander's experience separately from the physical distance. In these cases, the court analyzed the physical distance by focusing on the actual distance between the bystander's location and the location of the seriously injured direct victim. To justify this analysis, the court explicitly explained that, although using the distance per se was somewhat arbitrary, viewing distance in this manner was fair since doing so served to limit the scope of the defendant's liability to a small pool of bystanders.

On the other hand, in some cases the court analyzed the two requirements together by evaluating how the distance affected the degree to which the bystander gained an experience of the direct victim's injuries. To justify this analysis, the court explicitly explained that analyzing distance in relation to experience avoided arbitrary line-drawing and therefore achieved a better balance between the scope of a defendant's liability and the ability of a seriously injured bystander to recover.

As you read the cases, you also noted that all the cases cited each other, regardless of which approach to the analysis an individual court used. However, you also determined that the way the court discussed prior cases in the opinions disagreed to some degree, depending upon the approach the court was using in a particular opinion.

Given your analysis of all the cases, therefore, you could conclude that the highest appeals court appeared to have developed two competing, contradictory approaches to these two requirements. While the court in the different opinions used the same general policy rationales, it used these rationales differently, depending upon the approach it was applying in a particular opinion. In addition, the court in each individual opinion described the analysis to support the approach it was applying in that opinion, which resulted in opinions with contradictory descriptions of the court's analysis.

b. Predict how the highest appeals court would likely resolve the conflict

Once you had identified that the highest appeals court was using contradictory approaches, you would attempt to predict which approach the court would most likely adopt in the future. You would therefore evaluate the cases again to look for clues as to the court's thinking.

You might begin by assessing whether the highest appeals court had applied one approach more than the others, especially in recent cases. If it had, you could conclude that the court was coming to prefer that approach to the other. You might even find that the court had implicitly discarded an older approach for a more current one. In addition, you would evaluate whether the court appeared to favor policy rationales that were more likely satisfied by one approach or the other because that, too, might indicate something about the court's preference.

Depending upon what you found in the decisions by the highest appeals court, you might develop a sense that the court actually appeared to favor one approach. In the alternative, you might not be able to determine which of the two approaches the court might ultimately choose.

2. Contradictory approaches in intermediate appeals court cases

You might also encounter a situation where the intermediate appeals courts in your jurisdiction had used contradictory approaches to an issue. If the highest appeals court had decided that one approach was preferable to the other, then that approach would be the law of the jurisdiction, since the highest appeals court is the final arbiter of the jurisdiction's law.

However, in the situation where the highest appeals court had not yet addressed the conflict and either had reconciled or chosen between the approaches, you would need to develop your analysis, using the same steps as discussed in Section 1 above. You would begin by determining that the intermediate appeals courts were using two competing, contradictory approaches. Once you had completed that step, you would attempt to predict which approach the highest appeals court would most likely adopt in the future.

To make this decision, you would look to see whether the highest appeals court had addressed this issue at all, even in dicta, in order to find some clue as to how that court would rule in the future if given the chance. You would also look to see whether, in addressing related aspects of the law, the highest appeals court had emphasized any policy rationales that might provide insight as to how it would view the competing approaches.

Depending upon what you found, you might develop a sense that the court would likely choose one of the approaches. In the alternative, you might only be able to conclude that the highest appeals court might choose either.

> **Example of contradictory approaches of intermediate appeals court**
>
> Imagine that you are working in a jurisdiction with more than one intermediate court of appeals, which you learned about in Chapter 3. You want to file a claim for intentional infliction of emotional distress for your client. In particular, you are analyzing how the courts in your jurisdiction have approached the issue of a debt-collector's "extreme and outrageous conduct."
>
> You find that the highest appeals court requires that a debt-collector's conduct be "extreme and outrageous" for a plaintiff to recover. In support of that analysis, the highest appeals court had addressed general policy rationales as to why they chose to evaluate "extreme and outrageous conduct" in a debt-collector situation. All subsequent developments of how a court should find a debt collector's conduct as "extreme and outrageous," however, came from decisions by the intermediate appeals courts.

> In some decisions, the intermediate appeals courts analyzed "extreme and outrageous" conduct by using a totality test based on five factors. In other decisions, the intermediate appeals courts used a totality test based on four factors and explicitly excluded the fifth factor of the other courts as "irrelevant" and not based on good policy.
>
> In analyzing the jurisdiction's approach to this requirement of "extreme and outrageous conduct," you would first have to figure out the two conflicting approaches developed by the intermediate appeals courts and then move on to predicting which one would be adopted in the future by the highest appeals court. On the one hand, you might be able to predict that the highest appeals court would likely adopt one approach, given its explicit discussion of the policy rationales it most favored. On the other hand, you might only be able to predict that the highest appeals court might choose either of the two approaches.

D. EXCLUDING UNIQUE OR WRONGLY DECIDED CASES

In some rare situations, as you synthesize a group of cases, you'll determine that a particular case is irrelevant to the courts' analysis. You will likely reach this conclusion because your proposed description based on your synthesis will not test back on one of the cases yet that description still appears accurate based on the rest of the cases in the group. In this situation, you could decide that the particular case is irrelevant to the courts' analysis for either of the following reasons. First, the court might have relied on unique facts that require a different analysis from the rest of the cases, which is discussed in Section 1 below. Second, the court might have incorrectly decided the case, which is discussed in Section 2. When a case falls into either of these categories, you must exclude that case on the basis that it is irrelevant to the courts' mainstream analysis. Once you have excluded the case, you can then test your description back on the rest of the cases.

1. Cases based on unique facts

Sometimes you will encounter a group of cases where it appears that one court is using an approach that contradicts the analysis of the rest of the relevant cases. Upon a more careful evaluation, however, you determine that the court did not develop a contradictory approach but, instead, chose a different analysis to take into account the unique facts presented by the situation before it. Having reached this conclusion, you would exclude this case as irrelevant to your analysis and only then continue to test back your description on the rest of the cases.

While you might encounter a situation where the courts explicitly limit certain types of analysis to certain unique factual situations, in many instances you would need to infer this result. To do so, you would begin by evaluating what about the specific facts seemed to cause the court to use a different analysis from the rest of the cases. You might find that the fact that the courts used one analysis with one set of facts but a different analysis with another set made sense, especially if the courts' policy rationales varied depending upon the factual situation. A difference in the courts' policy rationales might indicate that the courts viewed certain factual situations as raising issues that other situations did not.

In addition to evaluating what it was about the specific facts that may have caused the court to use a different analysis, you would evaluate the manner in which the greater number of courts had discussed and cited to the case with unique facts. On the one hand, the courts in those decisions might not have cited to and discussed that case at all, which would be strong evidence that they did not view the case as relevant to their mainstream analysis. On the other hand, these courts might have discussed the case, but in a manner that indicated that they viewed that case as limited to its unique facts.

Finally, in the same manner, you would evaluate how the court in the case with unique facts discussed and cited to any prior cases in the rest of the decisions. On the one hand, the court might not have cited to or discussed any of these cases at all, which would indicate that it viewed the situation before it as limited to its unique facts and therefore not part of the mainstream analysis. On the other hand, the court might have discussed prior mainstream cases in a manner that demonstrated that those cases' analysis was not helpful in deciding the unique facts before the court.

> **Example of case based on unique facts**
>
> Imagine that you are analyzing the issue of negligent infliction of emotional distress in your jurisdiction. As you research, you find that most of the cases addressing this question involve some kind of accident caused by the defendant's negligence and that that accident injures the plaintiff physically and emotionally.
>
> However, you also locate one case that addressed this issue in a sexual abuse situation. As you work with this group of potentially relevant cases, you find that the analysis of all the cases based on negligent accidents form a consistent approach to the analysis. However, you also conclude that, in the case based on sexual abuse, the court used very different analysis. Given the unique facts of sexual abuse, you

> wonder whether your description of the courts' current analysis of the issue must take into account the analysis of the sexual abuse case or whether it does not.
>
> In evaluating all the cases, you find that the court articulated policy concerns in the negligent accident cases that are consistent yet seem very different from the policy rationales that the court articulated in the abuse case. In addition, you find that the highest appeals court has never cited to or discussed the sexual abuse case as it reached a decision in all the subsequent negligent accident cases. Correspondingly, you find that the abuse case did not rely on prior cases based on negligent accidents. Given these indications, you would probably conclude that the courts implicitly do not view cases based on sexual abuse as relevant to their analysis based on negligent accidents.

2. Incorrectly decided cases

a. Intermediate appeals court's decisions that contradict the analysis of the highest appeals court

Intermediate appeals courts generally develop their analysis consistently with that of the highest appeals court, since the highest appeals court is the final arbiter of the jurisdiction's law, as you learned in Chapter 3. Despite this general rule, on rare occasions you might encounter an intermediate appeals court's decision based on analysis that is inconsistent with that of the highest appeals court and therefore incorrectly decided. In that situation, you would have to exclude the case as irrelevant to your analysis. Once you have done so, you could proceed to test back your description of the courts' analysis on the rest of the relevant cases in the jurisdiction.

b. Highest appeals court's decisions that apply incorrect analysis

Sometimes you'll encounter the situation where the highest appeals court decided one case using an approach that contradicts the analysis that the court used in the majority of its other cases. Upon a more careful evaluation of the case in light of the rest of the cases, however, you make the subtle distinction, using the considerations below, that you've encountered the rare occurrence when the court simply applied an incorrect analysis.

To begin with, you would consider the weight of authority. A case is more likely applying an incorrect analysis when it does not reflect the viewpoint of a large number of other cases. Furthermore, the weight of authority is even better evidence when the court's policy rationales underlying the approach of most of the cases are different from the policy rationale the court used in the case that is potentially incorrect. The highest appeals court develops an approach to an area of law to achieve certain policy objectives for the citizens of the jurisdiction. When the court has consistently justified its approach on the basis that the approach achieves certain objectives, a case that disagrees with or ignores these policies is more likely aberrational and therefore incorrectly decided.

You would also evaluate whether the courts in the majority group cite to and discuss the potentially incorrect case. You might find that in subsequent cases the highest appeals court had never cited that case at all or at some point had stopped citing to and discussing that case in support of its current analysis. When it did so, the court might have been indicating that it viewed that case as incorrectly decided, even though the court never explicitly overruled the case. In the alternative, you might find that the court discussed the case in the opinions in the majority group but in a manner that provided additional evidence that the court viewed the case as irrelevant to its mainstream analysis.

> **Example of case with incorrect analysis**
>
> Imagine that you are working in a jurisdiction where the highest appeals court had set out several requirements for a bystander's cause of action for negligent infliction of emotional distress. In developing its analysis, the court stated that the first requirement was aimed at analyzing the degree to which the physical distance between the bystander and injured direct victim affected the intensity of the bystander's experience of the direct victim's recent injuries from the negligent act. To justify this analysis, the court explicitly reasoned that defendants should not be liable to bystanders when physical distance prevents them from sufficiently experiencing the effect of the negligent act on the direct victim.
>
> After this initial case, the majority of decisions by the highest appeals court applied this analysis to a variety of factual situations and focused on when the physical distance allowed a bystander to gain a sufficient experience and when it did not. In all of these cases, the courts explicitly discussed that this analysis was necessary to fairly balance the rights of seriously injured bystanders with defendants whose potential liability should be reasonable.
>
> As you analyzed this group of consistent cases, however, you found that in one lone case the court applied the idea of physical distance as a completely separate requirement from how it affected the bystander's experience. The court reasoned explicitly that using such an arbitrary cut off, without regard to the bystander's experience, was necessary to weight most heavily the court's concern that a defendant's scope of liability be sufficiently limited. While that lone court did cite to prior cases by the highest appeals court that used the original analysis, all

> subsequent cases by the highest appeals court never cited to or discussed that case.
>
> In this situation, you could conclude that the highest appeals court had not developed two competing, contradictory approaches. Instead, you could infer that the lone case applying physical distance separately used incorrect analysis. You would find support for this inference based on the weight of authority against that one case; the fact that that one case justified its different analysis on weighting the defendant's scope of liability more heavily than did the majority of decisions; and the fact that later decisions never cited this case in support of the mainstream analysis.

E. USING CASES FROM OTHER JURISDICTIONS TO GUIDE YOUR SYNTHESIS

In an objective analysis of the current status of the law, you might sometimes benefit from using cases from other jurisdictions as persuasive authority to help guide your synthesis of the cases in your own jurisdiction. Doing so might assist you when you are dealing with the situations discussed in Sections B through D above. For instance, you might add support for your own courts' implicit analysis by incorporating explicit articulations of that same analysis by courts from other jurisdictions. Combining the cases in this manner would provide more weight behind your implicit ideas, even though the analysis of other jurisdictions' courts would only be persuasive.

You might also turn to persuasive cases when the courts in your own jurisdiction had not yet developed certain aspects of their approach to an area of law that would be helpful in predicting an outcome on a factual situation like your client's. In particular, persuasive cases that had actually addressed factual circumstances like your client's might be very helpful. By using the cases in this manner, you would be able to flesh out your analysis of the law and consequently be better able to predict the future court's reaction to your client's factual situation.

In adding ideas from persuasive cases, however, you should separate analyzing the approach of your own courts from analyzing the approach of courts whose decisions would be only persuasive. You would begin by analyzing the cases decided by your own courts since they provide the analytical foundation to the jurisdiction's law. Based on this analysis, you would then move on to analyze the approach taken by courts from another jurisdiction. Separating these two steps, you would be more likely to develop a complete and accurate analysis of both approaches and consequently be able to more accurately predict whether your own courts would view ideas from another jurisdiction as relevant and helpful.

In deciding whether the future court would accept analysis from persuasive cases, you would need to decide whether the analysis of the courts from another jurisdiction was sufficiently consistent with the approach of your own courts. First, the two sets of courts would need to use approaches that were consistent in content, even if that content were described in different words.

Second, even if the approaches were consistent, you should evaluate whether the two sets of courts base their analysis on relatively the same policy rationales. Courts in your jurisdiction will be much more likely to incorporate ideas from persuasive cases into their own analysis if the two approaches are based on similar policies.

If you conclude based on the above considerations that a future court in your jurisdiction might view the persuasive cases as helpful, then you would take these ideas and use them to help guide and support your analysis. Again, you would use the analysis of your own courts as the foundation for your description of the current status of the law in your jurisdiction. Then, at appropriate points, you would transition into the analysis based on persuasive cases, making clear in the text and in the citation that you were discussing ideas from another jurisdiction as additional support.

CHECKLIST

☐ Understand how to synthesize a group of cases when the jurisdiction's courts use a consistent approach that is difficult to identify.

☐ Understand how to synthesize a group of cases when the jurisdiction's courts use contradictory approaches:
  - The highest appeals court has used contradictory approaches that it has not resolved; or
  - The intermediate appeals courts have used contradictory approaches and the highest appeals court has not resolved that conflict.

☐ Recognize that you may need to exclude a case from your synthesis when you determine that:
  - The case is based on unique facts that require a different analysis from the rest of the cases; or
  - The case is incorrectly decided because:
    - The case is an intermediate appeals court's decision that contradicts the analysis of the highest appeals court; or
    - The case is a highest appeals court's decision that applies incorrect analysis.

☐ Consider when you need to use cases from other jurisdictions to inform your synthesis of cases from your jurisdiction.

CHAPTER 9

Questions of First Impression

A. INTRODUCTION

This chapter provides a general introduction to analyzing questions of "first impression" in a jurisdiction, which may arise in two different ways. First, as is discussed in Section B, you may face a legal problem governed by a constitutional or statutory provision that the courts or authorized agencies have not interpreted. Second, you may encounter a situation where the courts must consider adopting a new approach to their common law, as is discussed in Section C.

B. LEGAL ISSUES GOVERNED BY UNINTERPRETED CONSTITUTIONAL OR STATUTORY PROVISIONS

In some legal problems, the courts or authorized agencies in the jurisdiction won't have interpreted the governing constitutional or statutory provision. When you encounter this kind of situation, you must anticipate how a future court would determine the reasonable meaning of the provision.

To predict a future court's process, you would first need to determine the specific methods—also known as "canons of construction"—used by the courts in the jurisdiction to analyze constitutional or statutory provisions. In particular, you would need to know the canons that your jurisdiction's courts tended to use and the weight that the courts give them. You would also need to understand whether the courts used these methods differently depending upon whether they were interpreting a constitutional provision or one that was statutory.

Although the specifics vary among jurisdictions, courts in most jurisdictions follow common canons of construction when interpreting constitutional or statutory language for the first time to determine the drafters' intent in promulgating the provision. Those canons generally guide courts to begin by examining the text, as discussed in Section 1, and the context of that text, as explained in Section 2. From there, those canons direct courts to consider sources extrinsic to the provision, examples of which are explained in Section 3.

1. Textual evaluation

The canons of construction generally direct courts to begin the determination of what the drafters intended by evaluating the language that the drafters chose to convey their ideas. For example, a court would go through the same process of analysis that you learned about in Chapters 4 and 5 and would ask the following question: Evaluated from a common sense perspective, what do the words chosen by the drafters indicate about what they intended to accomplish? This canon of construction is known as the "plain meaning doctrine."

> **Example of the plain meaning doctrine**
>
> Here is how one Massachusetts court articulated this doctrine as it evaluated the language of a statute to determine the legislature's intent: "The general rule of construction is that where the language of the statute is plain, it must be interpreted in accordance with the usual and natural meaning of the words." *Commissioner v. AMIWoodbroke, Inc.*, 634 N.E.2d 114, 115 (Mass. 1994) (interpreting statute addressing corporate tax issue).

In addition to using the plain meaning doctrine, a court might use canons of construction that evaluate how the drafters constructed the text of the provision.

> **Example of a canon of construction**
>
> In the following example where a court was interpreting the legislative intent behind a criminal statute, the court discussed the canon that, if the drafters included one idea explicitly in the provision, they then intended to exclude any contradictory idea that they did not explicitly include.
>
> > [T]he canon of construction *expressio unius est exclusio alterius*, holds that "to express or include one thing implies the exclusion of the other, or of the alternative." *Black's Law Dictionary* 661

> (9th ed. 2009) . . . This canon applies "only where in the natural association of ideas the contrast between a specific subject matter which is expressed and one which is not mentioned leads to an inference that the latter was not intended to be included within the statute." *Int'l Sav. and Loan Ass'n v. Wiig*, 82 Hawai'i 197, 201, 921 P.2d 117, 121 (1996).[1]

Courts use a variety of similar canons as guidance when interpreting constitutional and statutory language. However, the relevance of these methods varies by jurisdiction, as does the order in which the courts apply them when evaluating specific language. For instance, the following quote summarizes some of the specific canons of construction used by the United States Supreme Court when interpreting federal statutes:[2]

- *Noscitur a sociis*: interpret a general term to be similar to more specific terms in a series.
- *Ejusdem generis*: interpret a general term to reflect the class of objects reflected in more specific terms accompanying it.
- Follow ordinary usage of terms, unless Congress gives them a specified or technical meaning.
- Follow dictionary definitions of terms, unless Congress has provided a specific definition. Consider dictionaries of the era in which the statute was enacted. Do not consider "idiosyncratic" dictionary definitions.
- "May" is usually precatory, while "shall" is usually mandatory.
- "Or" means in the alternative. . . .
- Punctuation rule: Congress is presumed to follow accepted punctuation standards, so that placements of commas and other punctuation are assumed to be meaningful.

2. Textual context

Canons of construction may also direct courts to consider sources beyond the text — either in the provision itself or in surrounding provisions — that indicate the drafters' intent. For example, a court could look to a statute's heading in

---

1. *Fagaragan v. State*, 320 P.3d 889, 907 (Haw. 2014) (italics added).
2. The Rehnquist Court's Canons of Statutory Construction, National Council of State Legislatures, http://www.ncsl.org/documents/lsss/2013PDS/Rehnquist_Court_Canons_citations.pdf (outline was derived from the Appendix to "Foreword: Law As Equilibrium," William N. Eskridge, Jr., Philip P. Frickey, 108 Harv. L. Rev. 26, November, 1994. Format modified by Judge Russell E. Carparelli, Colorado Court of Appeals, Sep. 2005) (footnotes omitted).

which the legislature summarized the content of the section. That heading might clarify ideas in the text of the statute that followed.

Similarly, as you learned in Chapter 4, a court could assess any definitions section where the legislature defined terms in the statute. The court could also evaluate any policy section that explained the legislature's concerns in that area of law.

A court might also look to other related provisions. For example, a court could look for similar language in the same subject area of the jurisdiction's statutory code. In statutes that address related substance, the legislature might have provided indications of the result it was intending to achieve in the statute under consideration or why it viewed that result as important. The court might also find evidence of intent reflected in the overall organizational framework for that subject area of the code.

In some instances, a court might look to prior versions of the provision under consideration. Changes from one version of a provision to the next, as to what the drafters deleted or added or rephrased, might indicate ideas relevant to understanding the current version.

When evaluating a statute that has legislative history, a court might look to how the original bill worked its way through the legislative process and ultimately how the legislature enacted it into law. Here, the court might rely on sources that were sufficiently reliable as evidence of the legislature's intent. For instance, the court might be swayed by a written committee report that supported a bill the committee sent to the legislature. Such a report summarizes the point of view of the legislators who studied the subject in depth and came up with specific recommendations for the legislature. The court could therefore view this analysis as reliable evidence of the legislature's intent in enacting the bill into law. In contrast, a court would be less likely to rely on statements of individual legislators during oral debates on the passage of the bill. Unlike a written committee report, such statements might be the point of view only of individual legislators and not necessarily the view of the legislature itself as it enacted the statute.

3. External Sources

Beyond the text itself, a court might use the canons of construction to consider external sources for guidance to interpret the provision. For example, these sources might include similar provisions and cases interpreting those provisions from other jurisdictions; common law in the jurisdiction that addressed the same subject and that predated the provision; authoritative secondary authority; and the historical context surrounding the enactment of a statutory or constitutional provision.

a. Sources of law from other jurisdictions

A court might look to constitutional or statutory provisions from other jurisdictions as persuasive authority, especially when a provision was similar and courts of that jurisdiction had interpreted that provision in a way that was helpful. Especially relevant would be judicial interpretations of similar language and discussions of the underlying policy rationales.

b. A jurisdiction's common law related to the same subject matter

In some situations, a court might look to a jurisdiction's common law that predated the enactment of a constitutional or statutory provision and addressed the same subject matter. For example, common law was the original source of some areas of law before the legislature codified that common law into statutes. While the statute then supersedes the prior case law, a court might look to discussion in the prior cases, such as the courts' policy rationales, as evidence of the legislature's intent.

c. Secondary authority

A court interpreting a constitutional or statutory provision might look to secondary authority that addressed the particular provision under consideration. Authors of law review articles or treatises often provide in-depth, thoughtful discussions of such provisions and make recommendations about how the courts should interpret them. Such thorough discussions sometimes influence courts, especially when they are authored by a renowned expert in that area of law.

d. Historical context of the provision

In some circumstances, a court might find relevant the historical context surrounding the passage of a provision. That context might help explain why the issue came before the drafters and why they chose to address that issue with the particular provision. For example, when interpreting a statute, a court might use the historical context of the provision if authoritative legislative history leading to the enactment of the statute supported it. A committee report, for instance, might have discussed the specific social problems that created the need for legislative action.

C. SITUATIONS WHERE THE COURT MUST CONSIDER A NEW APPROACH TO THE JURISDICTION'S COMMON LAW

A court might encounter a controversy where a party argues that the court should adopt a completely new approach to the jurisdiction's common law, such as a new tort action. In this type of situation, the court could not rely on prior cases in the jurisdiction that addressed the approach. Instead, to justify its decision, the court would need to look to other sources, such as analogous law, both statutes and cases, in its own jurisdiction; cases by courts in other jurisdictions; and authoritative secondary sources.[3]

1. Analogous law in its own jurisdiction

A court would likely look to analogous law in its own jurisdiction to determine whether to take a novel next step in the jurisdiction's common law. First, the court might look to analogous common law, evaluating whether the policies and doctrine underlying the courts' approach in similar subject areas would be helpful in deciding whether to adopt a new approach in the case before the court. In addition, the court might evaluate whether the legislature had enacted, refused to enact, or repealed any statutes and, by doing so, had indicated policy concerns that should affect the court's decision.

2. Cases from other jurisdictions

A court might also look to cases from other jurisdictions that address the same or similar approaches to the one the court is considering. In particular, the court might be influenced by the analysis of persuasive cases, including how other courts developed their approach and supporting policy rationales. The court might also be swayed by the number of courts from other jurisdictions that have already adopted — or refused to adopt — the approach it is considering.

3. Secondary sources

Finally, a court might look to authoritative kinds of secondary authority that might help identify the ramifications of adopting a new approach. These types of sources, such as law review articles or treatises, might provide in-depth, thoughtful discussions of the law and policy rationales relevant to the court's

---

3. For an example of a court developing a new tort cause of action, see *Tarasoff vs. Regents of University of California*, 551 P.2d 334 (Cal. 1976), where the highest appeals court in California, the Supreme Court of California, adopted a cause of action for a therapist to have a duty to warn a third party or others of the danger from a voluntary outpatient. Before this landmark case in 1976, no state court recognized a therapist's duty to warn third parties or others of danger when that danger arose only from a voluntary outpatient. In reaching its decision, the Supreme Court evaluated and relied on a wide range of sources of law and secondary authority. See also *Dziokonski v. Babineau*, 380 N.E.2d 1295 (Mass. 1978), where the Supreme Judicial Court of Massachusetts added a new common law cause of action, a bystander's cause of action for negligent infliction of emotional distress.

analysis. The court might rely on an author's recommendations, especially if the author was a renowned scholar in the area of law and especially if other courts had relied on that author's ideas to reach a similar decision.

CHECKLIST

☐ **Analyze questions of first impression regarding a constitutional or statutory provision by following the jurisdiction's approach for using canons of construction in such situations:**
- Textual evaluation;
- Textual context;
- External sources to the provision itself, including:
  - Law from other jurisdictions;
  - The jurisdiction's common law;
  - Authoritative secondary authority; and
  - Historical context surrounding the enactment of the provision.

☐ **Analyze questions of first impression regarding a new approach to the jurisdiction's common law by following the jurisdiction's approach in such situations:**
- Analogous law of the jurisdiction;
- Persuasive cases from other jurisdictions; and
- Authoritative secondary sources.

CHAPTER 10

Analytical Foundation of Predictions

A. INTRODUCTION

As you have already learned, your work supervisor and other members of your team will count on you to achieve two important goals in a Discussion Section of an objective memorandum. First, your supervisor will want an objective analysis of the current status of the law for all relevant issues. To achieve this goal, you'll need to develop a reasonable interpretation of the legal authority relevant to your client's issue — an analysis that is neutral and isn't slanted for the client. To develop this analysis of the law, you'll use the skills you learned in Chapters 2 through 9. You will then need to present this analysis in a memo, ideas that are explored in Chapters 11 and 12.

In addition to an objective analysis of the law, your supervisor will expect a prediction of what that law indicates neutrally on the facts of your client's situation. Throughout this textbook this step of analysis is described as an "application-prediction," because you will be applying the law and predicting how a future court will use that law to reach an outcome on your client's facts for all the relevant issues.

You will learn how to present application-predictions in an objective memo in Chapter 13. But first you need to understand their analytical foundation. To begin, you need to understand the purpose of application-predictions in a formal objective memo, which is discussed in Section B. As discussed in Section C, based on your analysis of the law, you need to learn when to include a single prediction or when to include a prediction and counter-predictions. Section D addresses when case comparisons are necessary in an application-prediction and when they are not. Finally, you should be prepared for assignments that go beyond a formal objective memo and require you to consider potential arguments, which is addressed in Section E.

B. UNDERSTANDING THE PURPOSE OF APPLICATION-PREDICTIONS IN AN OBJECTIVE MEMO

Given that the overall purpose of this kind of memorandum is objective analysis, in application-predictions you must apply a reasonable analysis of the current status of the law neutrally to your client's facts. You must then predict the outcome a future court could reasonably reach, regardless of whether that outcome is favorable or unfavorable for the client or simply not clear. Sometimes you'll find that the law clearly indicates a definitive answer for your client—again, one that might be favorable or unfavorable. At other times, the law will only indicate possibilities, and you'll need to identify each possible conclusion that a court could reasonably reach.

Based on the foundation of this objective analysis, your supervising attorney will be able to take the next steps in representing the client. For instance, your supervisor might counsel the client about whether to file an action in court; begin drafting some kind of agreement, such as a contract or lease; or proceed to negotiate with the other side's attorney.

> **Example of the purpose of application-predictions**
>
> Imagine that your law firm is representing a client who has been harassed by a debt collector in Massachusetts. The issue is whether the client could successfully recover against the debt collector for violations of consumer protection laws. To advise the client about the chances of prevailing, your supervisor would need to understand the Massachusetts legal authority that governs this claim; a reasonable interpretation of what that legal authority requires; and a neutral assessment of whether the client's situation would be sufficient given that legal authority.
>
> If the client's situation definitely does not satisfy some aspect of the claim, then your supervisor must inform the client that a lawsuit on this basis cannot go forward. If the client's situation seems unclear as to whether all aspects of the claim can be satisfied, then informing the client of the likelihood of success will be very important, given the high cost of litigation. Your analysis could also provide a basis for negotiating with the debt collector's attorney and reaching a settlement without the costs associated with extended litigation.

In an objective memo, an analysis of the current status of law explains a reasonable interpretation of the relevant law and therefore prepares readers for the analysis in the corresponding application-prediction. Analytically, therefore, all important ideas relevant to that "law" in both parts of the memo must be entirely consistent in content to provide readers with a cohesive analysis that is easy to understand quickly. Chapter 13 will discuss the presentation of application-predictions.

C. DECIDING WHEN TO INCLUDE SINGLE OR ALTERNATIVE POSSIBLE PREDICTIONS

In an objective memo, readers expect that you will apply your analysis of the law to your client's situation and use your best judgment to predict the outcome or the potential outcomes before a future court. For some legal problems, you'll be able to predict with a fair degree of certainty that a future court would reach a particular outcome on a client's facts. In other legal problems, however, you may not be able to predict with any certainty that the court would reach only one result, and therefore you will need to develop one or more alternative predictions of the outcomes that a court could reasonably reach. This situation may occur for a variety of reasons: The client's facts themselves may make determining the result uncertain given the current status of the law; the current status of the law may be unclear; or a combination of both these possibilities may be present.

You'll often struggle to decide whether to provide a single prediction or a prediction and alternative counter-predictions. In particular, as a first-year student developing an application-prediction in your first objective memo, you may struggle to make such a judgment. To gain confidence, remind yourself what your law practice readers need from an objective memo. In addition, you might try imagining that you are the judge who is deciding the question.

Begin by reminding yourself what your busy law practice readers need from your objective memo. These readers need the memo to predict the decision, or potential decisions, that a future court could reasonably reach by applying the current status of the law to the client's situation. In contrast, these readers do not need a memo based on decisions that a future court could not reasonably reach. For instance, imagine that you turned in to your supervisor a memo that evaluated several different questions relevant to a legal issue and provided alternative predictions for each of those questions, even though a future court would most likely reach a certain result in all but one. Your supervisor would be frustrated by having to spend her own time making the judgments that she expected you to have made since you were assigned this project. Remember that the purpose of an objective memo depends upon your ability to analyze the law and make good judgments about what that law reasonably indicates for the client.

You should also keep in mind that your readers are lawyers who do not expect that you are guaranteeing your prediction of what a future court will decide. Instead, your readers expect you to use your best judgment, given that the law rarely — if ever — provides complete certainty. When you predict that a future court will likely reach a certain result, you'll still use language such as "probably" or "likely" to indicate the slight chance that your prediction isn't accurate. When you predict that a future court could reach alternative results, you'll use language to indicate that uncertainty: A future court would *probably* reach one outcome but *could* reach another outcome, or outcomes.

In addition to keeping in mind what readers need, you may feel more confident in making these judgments if you imagine that you are the judge deciding the case. Judges base their decisions on the same information that you have as the lawyer: Judges analyze the current status of the law — as you have learned to do in Chapters 3 through 9 — and decide what that law reasonably indicates on the facts of the situation before them. If you think that the answer on any given issue would be clear for you as the judge, you should predict that result without discussing alternative possibilities. If, in contrast, you think that as a reasonable judge you would struggle to reach a decision on the client's facts — that your decision would be a "close call" — you should include a prediction of the more likely result as well as a counter-prediction or predictions for that issue.

Sections 1 and 2 below discuss the situations when you would likely use a prediction and counter-predictions, given that the likely result would not be certain but a close call. These situations include ones where the client's facts create uncertainty, or the law creates uncertainty, or both.

1. Counter-predictions when the law is clear but the result is uncertain given the client's facts

In many situations, you'll find that you will not be able to predict with reasonable certainty what a future court would decide on your client's facts, even when the law is reasonably clear. In some circumstances, the nature of the client's facts may allow the court leeway to reach different outcomes as it applies the law. In other circumstances, some of the client's facts may be contested and thus the result could vary depending on which version the court accepts.

In an application-prediction in these circumstances, therefore, you would need to predict whether the future court would find that the client's facts were sufficient or insufficient under the courts' approach, or whether the outcome was unclear. For any reasonable possibility, you would need to predict the result the future court would reach and then explain how the court would justify that result.

> **Example of an uncertain result because the facts allow the court leeway**
>
> Imagine that your explanation for the courts' requirement is that "a structure must be *predominately* used for storing food." The relevant fact of your client is that she uses about two thirds of her structure to store canned goods and one third to store gardening equipment. Given the courts' analysis, whether a future court would decide that the structure was used "predominately" to store food might be a close call. If so, you would include a prediction and counter-prediction in the application-prediction: A future court could decide that the structure was "used predominantly" for food storage, given that food storage was two thirds of the structure's use, but the court could also decide that two thirds was not enough.

> **Example of an uncertain result because the facts are in dispute**
>
> Using the same legal question from the previous example, imagine that the facts are in dispute as to how your client used the shed. Your client claims that at the time of the incident she used the shed exclusively to store canned goods. Other witnesses, however, claim that your client only used one third of the shed to store canned food at that time. Given the courts' analysis, the outcome would depend upon which version of the facts a future court accepted. Thus, in the application-prediction, you would probably need to make a prediction based on one version of the facts and a counter-prediction based on the other version.

2. Counter-predictions because the law is unclear

In some legal problems, the relevant area of law may be unclear, as you learned in Chapter 8, because the courts seem to have developed contradictory approaches to the legal issue—either explicitly or implicitly—and have not resolved that conflict. This lack of clarity—which you would explain in the analysis of the law portions of your memo—might require you to develop a prediction and also counter-predictions for that issue. This situation could occur because the highest appeals court has developed competing approaches to the law and has not adopted one approach over the other or the intermediate appeals courts have developed competing approaches and the highest appeals court has not resolved that conflict.

In both circumstances, when developing your description of the courts' analysis of the law, you would need to explain these different approaches and explain why the future court might be persuaded to adopt a particular approach, based on the policy justifications of prior courts. In the application-prediction, you would include a prediction for the result you think is most likely and then develop counter-predictions regarding the outcome for the client under the other possibilities.

> **Example of an uncertain result because the law is unclear**
>
> Using the example from Section 1 above, imagine that your explanation for the courts' analysis is that "a structure must be used for storing food." The relevant fact of your client's situation is that she uses the structure to store gardening equipment that she uses to grow vegetables in the backyard. To determine whether "storing food" could be extended to cover storing gardening implements used to grow food, you would need to analyze this issue in depth to determine what the courts in prior cases were concerned about when they framed the law as to "storing food."
>
> The language of some of the opinions suggests that something beyond strictly storing food, such as items related to food production, might satisfy the requirement. However, the language of other cases states that a future court would be unlikely to expand the requirement beyond storing food items.
>
> In this situation, you would need to explain these two possibilities in your description of the courts' analysis of law for this issue. In the corresponding application-prediction, you might need to include a prediction using the narrow analysis of storing only food items and a counter-prediction based on the potentially expanded analysis that storing items related to food production could satisfy the requirement.

D. DETERMINING WHEN CASE COMPARISONS ARE NECESSARY

1. Comparing to precedent because the legal analysis is dependent upon facts

The analysis of some legal issues depends upon an in-depth examination of the facts. When you develop an application-prediction based on this type of analysis, you must support all predictions of the possible outcome on your clients' facts by comparing those facts to the facts of similar and dissimilar cases, both in circumstances where you predict a reasonably certain result and where you predict alternative results. Since a future court would apply its understanding of the law to the facts of the situation before it to reach its decision, the court would need to support that decision by relying on prior cases that reached a similar outcome and distinguishing cases that reached a dissimilar outcome. Your case comparisons track that decision-making process and confirm your determination of whether the analysis supports a single prediction or a prediction and counter-predictions.

> **Example of an application-prediction that requires factual comparisons to cases**
>
> Imagine that you have developed the following analysis of the law:
>
>> The courts require that a plaintiff's emotional distress result in serious physical or mental symptoms. To satisfy that requirement, a plaintiff's symptoms must be permanent and substantially undermine the plaintiff's ability to function in personal or professional endeavors.
>
> Based on this analysis, using your best judgment, you predict that a future court would decide that your client's symptoms satisfy this requirement. In justifying that prediction, you would need to compare your client's facts as similar to cases that reached the same outcome as your prediction—that the plaintiff satisfied the requirement—and as dissimilar to cases that reached the opposite outcome:
>
>> A future court likely would conclude that our client satisfied the requirement that his emotional distress result in serious physical or mental symptoms since our client's symptoms are permanent and have substantially undermined his ability to function in personal or professional endeavors. To reach that decision, the court would view our client's symptoms of periodic migraine headaches that are permanent, and that prevent him from working full-time, as similar to the plaintiff in Case X whose bouts with vertigo were permanent and prevented her from taking care of her minor children. In contrast, the court would view our client's symptoms as different from the symptoms of the plaintiff in Case Y that did not satisfy the requirement. In that case, the plaintiff's injuries were not permanent because they healed completely. In addition, these injuries did not undermine his ability to function in personal and professional endeavors since he missed only one week of work and merely could not drive for a month.

2. Not comparing to precedent because specific facts are not relevant to the analysis

You will not need to be able to support predictions and counter-predictions by comparing the facts of your client to the facts of precedent in certain situations. Some legal problems involve a question of law where more than one approach to that law is possible, but the result based on that approach is not dependent on the particular facts. Dealing with this kind of a question, a future court will use the general situation before it to identify the possible approaches that are relevant. However, it will choose to adopt any particular approach purely based on the policy rationales it finds most convincing, no matter what the specific facts might be. In this situation, the court will not need to be able to justify its decision by comparing the specific facts before it to the specific facts of relevant precedent. In developing your application-prediction for this type of issue, therefore, you would not be able to use case comparisons to support your predictions or counter-predictions.

> **Example of an application-prediction that does not require factual comparisons to cases**
>
> Imagine that the highest appeals court in your state had never addressed whether parents were immune from suits brought by their minor children because of negligence in automobile accidents. Further imagine that two intermediate appeals courts in this jurisdiction had developed contradictory approaches to this issue. One intermediate appeals court refused to apply parent-child immunity in negligent car accident situations on the basis that that immunity did not achieve good policy results for the jurisdiction. The other intermediate appeals court applied immunity based on other policy considerations.
>
> Further imagine that your client is a minor child who was seriously injured due to alleged parental negligence in a car accident, and the child's representative wants to bring a suit against the parent to recover damages. The legal question before a future court, then, would be whether the highest appeals court would apply immunity, or not, in your client's situation.
>
> In your analysis of law, you discuss each approach to immunity and why the highest appeals court might follow the approach it found most convincing based on policy rationales. Applying your analysis to your client's situation, you predict that a future court would be more likely to refuse to apply parent-child immunity in negligent car accidents, reasoning that immunity would not achieve good policy results for the jurisdiction and the parties before the court. Under this outcome,

therefore, your client would be able to bring the negligence claim to court. However, you also provide a counter-prediction that a future court might apply parent-child immunity in this situation based on other policy considerations. Under this outcome, your client would be precluded from going forward with the lawsuit.

In this situation, you would be predicting whether the future court would be more convinced to apply, or refuse to apply, parent-child immunity in negligent automobile accident situations based on policy rationales. The court would use the specific case of the client—a child suing a parent for injuries arising out of a negligent automobile accident—as the basis to choose which possible approach to immunity was relevant to the case before it. However, the court would reach its decision based on policy that was most convincing and would not need to consider the specific facts of the automobile accident. If parental immunity applied, the parents would be immune from suit regardless of the specific facts of the automobile accident.

In developing your application-prediction for the immunity question, you would mirror the future court's decision-making process as you predicted which approach it would adopt, and why, and which approach it was less likely to adopt, and why. For the same reason as a future court, you would not be able to develop comparisons of your client's facts to the facts of precedent because the only relevant facts would be identical: A child suing a parent on the basis of injuries arising out of a negligent automobile accident. The specific facts regarding the parent's action in the automobile accident would be irrelevant.

However, the facts of the automobile accident could be relevant in the next step of the case. If the court rejected parental immunity, the plaintiff—the child's representative—would have to show that the parents were negligent. At that stage of the litigation, the specific facts of the accident would be relevant to determine if the parents were negligent. If you analyzed the negligence issue in your memo, you would at that point include case comparisons in the application-prediction for that part of your analysis.

E. MOVING FROM MAKING PREDICTIONS TO DEVELOPING ARGUMENTS

As discussed in Sections B and C above, a formal objective memo includes reasonable interpretations of the current status of the law and a prediction and possible counter-predictions of what that current law reasonably indicates for the client in the corresponding application-prediction. You need to be prepared, however, for the situation where a supervising attorney requests that you move beyond making predictions based on the current status of the law to developing potential arguments using your understanding of that law. In this situation, you would be asked to develop creative, novel arguments about extending or changing the law in order to give your client a chance to prevail.

When drafting this type of assignment, you should consider taking two separate analytical steps. As a first step, you should develop an objective description of the analysis of the law just as you would in a formal objective memo. You then should use that foundation to determine a reasonable prediction and relevant counter-predictions just as you would in any formal objective memo.

Only at that point would you proceed with the next step of coming up with arguments about extending or changing the law to help your client. You might base such arguments on novel and creative ways of interpreting or applying the law. While the court would be less likely to adopt arguments that went beyond a reasonable interpretation of the current law and how it should be applied, you might be able to convince a judge of your viewpoint.

CHECKLIST

☐ Consider the purpose of application-predictions in formal objective memos.

☐ Decide to include a single prediction or alternative possible predictions by recognizing when counter-predictions may be necessary:
- The current status of the law is clear but the result is uncertain given the client's facts; and
- The status of the law is unclear.

☐ Determine if case comparisons are necessary to demonstrate how the future court would justify its result:
- The analysis is dependent upon the facts and therefore a court will compare the situation before it to similar and dissimilar precedent to justify its result; and
- The analysis is not dependent upon the facts and therefore a court will not need to compare the facts of the situation before it to the facts of precedent.

☐ Understand the difference between making predictions and developing arguments.

PART III

THE DISCUSSION SECTION OF AN OBJECTIVE MEMO

CHAPTER 11

Effective Overall Organization

A. INTRODUCTION

As you learned in Chapter 1, you must accomplish two main goals in the Discussion Section of an objective memo. First, using the skills you learned in Chapters 3 through 9, you must provide an objective analysis of the current status of the law, which is based on a reasonable interpretation of the legal authority relevant to your client's legal question. This analysis will be abstract and without reference to your client's facts. Second, as you learned in Chapter 10, you must explain what that law indicates objectively on the facts of your client's situation. Here, you must apply the law neutrally to your client's facts to predict the outcome, or potential outcomes, before a future court, even if unfavorable for your client.

Once you've developed this analytical foundation for your memo, you are ready to begin drafting the Discussion Section. As a first step, which is discussed in this chapter, you must think about—and ultimately choose—an overall organization for the Discussion Section that will most effectively communicate your analysis to busy law practice readers. Section B discusses a situation where your memo addresses more than one legal issue. Section C explains how to organize the discussion for each legal issue that does not involve a question of first impression because the courts of the jurisdiction have addressed all parts of the analysis, whether based on constitutional or statutory provisions or the common law. Section D addresses how to organize the discussion of a legal issue that involves a question of first impression.

B. OVERALL ORGANIZATION FOR DISCUSSION SECTIONS WITH MORE THAN ONE LEGAL ISSUE

When a Discussion Section addresses more than one legal issue, you need to provide your readers with an overview of those issues—usually in an introductory paragraph or two—and then organize the Discussion Section around each legal issue separately. This organization is logical because each legal issue will be based on its own unique analysis that will need to be developed in the abstract and then applied separately to the client's facts. You should organize the discussion for each separate legal issue, using the guidelines explained in Section C.

> **Example of organizing around independent legal issues**
>
> Imagine that you have been asked to analyze whether your client may be charged under two unrelated statutory crimes. You would organize around separate analyses of each crime because the crimes are independent legal issues. The analysis of the statutory provisions for each crime, and any cases interpreting them, would be unique and would therefore need to be applied separately to the client's facts.

Even when your memo involves independent legal issues, you must evaluate whether the relationship among those issues requires you to order the analyses in a certain manner.

> **Example of legal issues that require a certain order**
>
> Imagine that your memo addresses the following two legal issues as to whether a statute governs your client's situation: Is the statute constitutional and, if it is, has your client satisfied all statutory elements? In this situation, you would logically need to address the constitutionality of the statute first, since the statute would govern your client's situation only if it were constitutional. You would then address whether your client's situation satisfied the statutory elements second.

> **Example of legal issues that do not require a certain order**
>
> Imagine that you have been asked to analyze whether your client will be able to recover damages for an intentional tort and the tort of negligence. In this situation, you would organize around separate analyses

> of each tort. You could begin with the analysis of either, because they are independent legal issues where the analysis of one does not relate to the analysis of the other.

Even when the legal issues do not require a certain order, however, you might choose a specific order to help busy readers.

> **Example of helpful organization**
>
> In the second example above, imagine that you are convinced that the client would recover for the intentional tort, and therefore that you could convey that analysis very concisely. However, you are much less certain about the negligence claim, with the result that you would need to develop the analysis in greater depth. In this situation, you might choose to help your readers by beginning with the simpler analysis of the first legal issue — the intentional tort — before moving to the lengthier discussion of the second legal issue — the negligence claim.

C. ORGANIZATION OF LEGAL ISSUES THAT DO NOT INVOLVE A QUESTION OF FIRST IMPRESSION

Many legal issues do not involve questions of first impression because the courts of the jurisdiction have addressed all parts of the analysis. In these situations, you must use the statutory or constitutional scheme, when relevant, and the courts' analysis to present your ideas in a manner that allows your readers to grasp the overall analysis of the legal issue quickly and easily.

To begin, you'll need to include introductory paragraphs for each independent legal issue. These paragraphs, discussed in Section 1 below, need to provide an overview of the analysis that prepares readers for the in-depth discussion that follows. For that in-depth discussion, you must choose an effective organization, as explained in Section 2. Section 3 discusses the order in which you should consider drafting the introductory paragraphs and the rest of the discussion.

1. Introductory paragraphs

In the discussion for each independent legal issue, you must use introductions to guide your readers. Therefore, you should begin such a discussion with an overall introductory paragraph or paragraphs that provide readers with an overview of the entire analysis. You must first introduce the relevant legal authority, which is discussed in Section a. As explained in Section b, you must then decide whether to introduce the courts' analysis at that point or only later on in the discussion that follows the introductory paragraphs.

a. Introduce the legal authority

You should begin a discussion of a legal issue by introducing the overall analysis based on the legal authority. As you draft these introductory paragraphs, you'll need to decide on the necessary amount of detail about the controlling authority, which will depend on the nature of that authority and how it breaks down.

i. Begin by introducing relevant statutory or constitutional provisions

If a legal issue is controlled by statutory or constitutional provisions, you should begin the introduction by identifying the relevant provision or provisions. When the statutory or constitutional provisions include only one relevant piece, you would identify that piece as the focus of the analysis and then provide an introduction to the courts' interpretation of that idea, as discussed in Section b below.

> **Example of introducing a statutory provision and courts' interpretation**
>
> Imagine that you're addressing the legal issue of what type of label your client must include on packing for a particular consumer good. The issue is controlled by a statutory provision that provides that such labels must be "conspicuous," but no statutory provision explains that term. In working through the group of cases in the jurisdiction that interpret the term, you find that the courts have developed an analysis with a four-part test. In your overall introduction, you would introduce the statutory provision and identify the focus of the discussion on the "conspicuous" term. You would then proceed to introduce the courts' analysis of the four-part test, using the ideas explained in Section b.

If the relevant statutory or constitutional provisions have different pieces, your overall introduction should identify those pieces and how they relate. However, if the pieces of the provisions break down into further parts, you probably would not introduce that more specific analysis in the overall introduction. Instead, you would include another introductory passage for each of those additional parts at relevant portions of your discussion, using the guidelines discussed in Section 2a below. Similarly, you would probably not include the courts' analysis in the overall introduction since the courts' analysis would be more relevant later on as you discussed each piece of a statutory or constitutional provision and its parts in more depth, as is explained in Sections b and 2b below.

> **Example of introducing a statutory provision with several parts**
>
> Imagine that you're analyzing one of the jurisdiction's burglary statutes, which states that an individual commits burglary in the second degree when "the individual breaks and enters a dwelling house with intent to commit a crime therein." The statutory provision does not explain "breaks and enters" or "intent to commit a crime therein," but does define "dwelling house" as any structure that meets two criteria.
>
> In the introductory paragraph, you would identify the language of the statutory provision by explaining that the discussion following the introduction would analyze each of the following pieces of the provision: "Breaks and enters," "dwelling house," and "intent to commit a crime therein." You would probably not introduce the provision's two criteria for "dwelling house" because that part of the analysis would be more relevant in the analysis for that question later in your discussion. Similarly, you would not include the courts' analysis for any of the three pieces in the overall introduction since those analyses would be more relevant to each of the subsequent in-depth discussions of "breaks and enters" and "dwelling house" and "intent to commit a crime therein."

When introducing statutory or constitutional provisions—or pieces of those provisions—you might be able to quote the relevant language from the statute or constitution because quoting would be sufficiently concise. However, in other situations, you might decide that you should paraphrase some language and quote only the most relevant part. See Chapter 4, Section G.

ii. Begin by introducing common law if it controls the legal issue

If common law controls the legal issue, you should probably begin the overall introduction by stating that the jurisdiction has not enacted a relevant statute addressing the issue, and therefore that you based the analysis on common law. You would then identify the particular common law question and proceed to introduce the courts' analysis of that question, as discussed in Section b below.

> **Example of introducing a legal issue controlled by common law**
>
> Imagine that you're addressing the legal issue of whether your client can be found liable for negligent infliction of emotional distress. In the jurisdiction, common law controls the issue because the legislature has not enacted any relevant statutory provisions. In working through the group of cases dealing with the question, you find that the courts have developed an analysis with a three-part test. In your overall introduction, you would explain that common law controls the issue because the legislature has not enacted an applicable statute. You would then proceed to introduce the courts' analysis of the three-part test, using the ideas explained in Section b.

b. Introduce the courts' analysis when relevant

Once you have identified the underlying authority and, if necessary, the pieces of that authority, you would then go on to introduce the courts' analysis for all relevant pieces. As explained in Section a, you might introduce the courts' analysis in the overall introductory paragraphs or in introductions at later points in the discussion, depending on the analytical structure of the underlying authority.

When you introduce the courts' analysis, you would include the courts' overall test, the test's components and their relationship, and the courts' reasons for the test. That type of summary prepares busy readers for the in-depth discussion that follows, which will focus on the courts' analysis.

> **Example of introducing a statutory provision and the courts' interpretation**
>
> Imagine that you're addressing the legal issue of whether your client entered a structure that is a "dwelling house," one of the elements under the jurisdiction's burglary statute. In working through the group of cases in the jurisdiction that interpret this element, you find that the courts have developed the following analysis. The courts have used an overall test, explained their reasons for that test, and identified the test's two required components. The courts have also developed an analysis of when each of the two components is satisfied.
>
> In the introductory paragraphs for this element, you would need to provide your readers with an overview of the analysis that is developed in more depth in the discussion that follows. For this legal issue, you would first need to make clear that the memo is analyzing "dwelling house" in the burglary statute. You then would go on to describe how

> the courts determine when a particular structure is a "dwelling house," including the courts' overall test and the courts' reasons for that test. Finally, you would identify the components of the test and make clear that these components are requirements.

For an example of an introduction to the Discussion Section in a memo with one legal issue based on a common law question, see Comment 6 to the Sample of a Formal Objective Memorandum in Appendix I.

c. Organize the introduction to help your reader

For introductions to all types of legal issues, you should focus only on the current status of the law that will govern the client's problem and therefore should omit detailed historical background. Busy law practice readers are primarily interested in current law and in general don't want to be distracted by the process by which legislatures or courts reached their current approach to the analysis.

Furthermore, you should describe the concepts using general principles that are abstract and not tied to the facts of the client, a concept that you've already encountered in Chapter 7, Section G1. In fact, generally these introductions should not include a summary of what the law indicates for a client's facts at all because most supervisors don't find such a summary necessary. They reason that this type of statement is repetitious with the Brief Answer and Conclusion sections, which you'll learn about in Chapter 15. However, an introduction could begin or end with a quick summary of what the law indicates for the client.

Finally, you need to remember that you are providing an overview of the analysis that is developed in more depth in the discussion that follows. Therefore, you should provide just enough detail in an introduction to give readers a sufficient context to understand the more in-depth analysis that follows.

2. The discussion after the introduction

For the discussion of a legal issue that follows introductory paragraphs, you must choose an organization that is based on the logic of the relevant legal authority. This logic will likely reveal itself as you analyze that authority, using the process discussed in Chapters 2 through 8. In fact, you'll probably consider, preliminarily reject, and reconsider a variety of potential organizations as you work on your analysis.

As you begin to shift your focus from developing the ideas to expressing them to your readers, you'll continue to think about which organizations are consistent with the logic of the analysis for the legal issue. At this point, you'll also begin to consider which of the possible organizations would be most helpful for busy law practice readers.

In determining the best organization, or possible organizations, you'll find the following guidelines helpful. As discussed in Section a, for a legal issue controlled by statutory or constitutional provisions, consider first organizing around those provisions and then any relevant pieces of those provisions. As discussed in Section b, at the relevant point, organize around the courts' analysis. Finally, Section c explains that, at points in the analysis helpful for your readers, you should develop, and organize around, separate discussions of an analysis of the law and an application-prediction.

a. Organize around relevant statutory or constitutional provisions

When you are faced with a legal issue that is controlled by either statutory or constitutional provisions, you should organize the discussion after the introduction around those provisions, and any pieces of a provision, following the process described in Chapters 4 and 5. Such an organization reflects the analytical structure of the constitution or statute. At any point necessary for your readers, you should provide an introduction to a part of the analysis. You would also incorporate the courts' analysis at the relevant points in the discussion and organize that analysis by using the guidelines discussed in Section b below.

> **Example of organizing the discussion around related statutory provisions**
>
> Imagine that you're analyzing one of the jurisdiction's burglary statutes, which states that an individual commits burglary in the second degree when "the individual breaks and enters a dwelling house with intent to commit a crime therein." The statutory provision does not explain "breaks and enters" or "intent to commit a crime therein," but defines "dwelling house" as any structure that meets two criteria. In the introductory paragraph, you would identify the relevant language of the statute. You would make clear that the discussion that followed the introductory paragraphs would analyze each of the following: "breaks and enters," "dwelling house," and "intent to commit a crime therein."
>
> After the introductory paragraph, you would organize around separate discussions of "breaks and enters," "dwelling house," and "intent to commit a crime therein." For the discussions of "breaks and enters" and "intent to commit a crime therein," you would begin with an introduction that identified the relevant language of the statute for each of those ideas. You would then introduce the courts' analysis, focusing on the courts' overall test that determines whether that language is satisfied or not. You would organize the discussion of the courts' test, using

> the guidelines described in Section b below. For the discussion of "dwelling house," you would begin by identifying that term and then introduce the provision's two-criterion definition. You would then organize the discussion of the courts' test for each criterion, using the guidelines described in Section b below.

b. Include an introduction to the courts' analysis

As you develop your discussion of a legal issue, you should organize around the courts' analysis at the point helpful for your readers. First, as is explained in Section a above, once you have broken down the discussion of a legal issue around the applicable statutory or constitutional provisions, or relevant pieces of such provisions, you will need at some point to introduce and organize around the courts' analysis of the constitutional or statutory language. Second, you should use the courts' analysis to organize the discussion of a legal issue that is controlled by the jurisdiction's common law.

In organizing around the courts' analysis, you would focus on the courts' overall test and the components of that test. First, you should organize around the components, as discussed in Section i. Then, as discussed in Section ii, you should decide whether to break down the analysis of each component further and organize around more specific pieces of the courts' analysis.

i. Consider organizing around the components of the courts' overall test

When the courts' overall test is based on more than one component, you should consider organizing around a separate analysis of each. Organizing in this manner follows the logic of the courts' analysis and will therefore help your readers.

> **Example of organizing around components of the courts' overall test**
>
> Imagine that you are working with a courts' checklist test of two requirements, a test you learned about in Chapter 7. Given the nature of this test, you would organize the discussion around separate analyses for each requirement.

When an analysis is based on separate, and therefore equal, requirements, you may discuss the requirements in any order, unless you decide that a particular order would be most helpful for readers. In contrast, some analyses are based on ideas that must be discussed in a certain order.

> **Example of organizing around a test that requires a certain order**
>
> Imagine that you are working with the courts' threshold test, which is a test that you learned about in Chapter 7. This kind of test requires that something must be met before other aspects of the test come into play. In this situation, your memo would need to analyze that threshold before it proceeded to analyze subsequent aspects of the test, since those would become relevant only if the threshold were satisfied.

For an example of a memo where the discussion is organized around the components of the courts' test, see Comment 9 to the Sample of a Formal Objective Memorandum in Appendix I.

ii. Decide whether to break down the analysis of each component

Depending upon the analysis, you may decide to break down the analysis of each component again, one or more times, and organize your analysis around each subpart. Again, no formula will help you make this decision in every analysis. Instead, you must understand the courts' test well enough to figure out the ideas, and the relationship among ideas, that will be the basis for these choices. You must also keep your readers in mind and choose a structure that helps them grasp your analysis quickly and easily.

> **Example of breaking down the analysis of a component**
>
> Imagine that you are working with the courts' checklist test based on two requirements. As you work with the first required component, you realize that, to satisfy that requirement, a plaintiff must satisfy two further sub-requirements. As you organize the first requirement, therefore, you would organize around an analysis of the first sub-requirement and then an analysis of the second.

c. Separate analyses of the law from application-predictions

You'll need to address two separate aspects of the analysis for the different components of the courts' test. You will first need to develop, and organize effectively, an analysis of the law, which is discussed in more depth in Chapter 12. Here, you will use general principles that are abstract and not tied to the facts of your client. When you have completed this step, you'll then move on to the corresponding application-prediction where you'll apply that law to the client's facts and predict what a future court would conclude in your client's situation. You will learn more about organizing this section in Chapter 13.

A discussion that separates these two steps is much easier for readers to understand quickly. As you already know, these readers are relying on your memo to provide them with a thorough grounding in both the law and what that law indicates for the client. By encountering an analysis of the law that is abstract and without reference to the client, your readers will more easily gain an understanding of what the legal authority reasonably means. With that understanding, your readers will be much better able to grasp why that law supports the predicted outcome, or potential outcomes, on the client's facts in a separate application-prediction. In contrast, readers who encounter a discussion that merges these two steps are more likely to be confused, since they must attempt to understand at the same time what the law means and how it should be applied to the client's facts.

> **Example of separating the analysis of the law from the application-prediction**
>
> Imagine that the analysis for your legal issue is based on a courts' test that has three components, each of which is a requirement. After the overview in your introduction, you would organize the rest of the discussion around analyses for each of the three requirements. As you analyzed each requirement, you would first develop an analysis of the law using general principles that were abstract and not tied to the facts of the client. When you finished that step, you would move on to developing an application-prediction where you would apply that law to the client's facts and predict what a future court would conclude in the client's situation.

This separation of law and application to the client's situation will also help you as the author of the memo. In developing an abstract analysis of the law, you'll more easily determine where you need to further develop ideas and where you were insufficiently precise. In proceeding to apply that law to the client's situation separately, you will be better able to determine whether you sufficiently developed the preceding law to predict a reliable outcome in the client's situation. You'll also be able to compare the two steps of the analysis and check the consistency of ideas throughout both. Doing so, you may figure out areas where you are still unclear about certain aspects of the analysis and need to revise your memo before submitting it to your supervising attorney.

For an example of the analysis of law for a component explained separately from the corresponding application-prediction, see Comment 25 to the Sample of a Formal Objective Memorandum in Appendix I.

3. Order of drafting the discussion

You should consider the order in which you might draft the different parts of the discussion of a legal issue. What order you may choose in any given instance, however, will likely depend upon your own individual working style and the particular analysis of a legal problem.

a. Introductory paragraphs and the discussion that follows

As you begin to draft the discussion of a legal issue, you need to decide the order in which to draft the introductory paragraphs and the in-depth discussion of the analysis that follows. On the one hand, you might choose to draft first the introductory paragraphs that set out the analytical framework for the analysis. You would be able to use this framework as an important reference point as you developed the in-depth analysis for each piece of that framework in the rest of the discussion.

On the other hand, you might decide to write the overview only after you had drafted the rest of the discussion. With the analysis of each piece already developed in depth, you might more easily describe the overall analytical framework, including the pieces of that framework and their relationship.

However, as long as you are thorough as you develop your analysis, you'll end up in the same place whether you begin with the overview or the in-depth discussion of the analysis. You'll need to begin with one, move on to the other, and then check that they are consistent in content and in phrasing.

b. Abstract analysis of the law and application to the client's situation

As you learned in Section C2c above, to accurately determine and effectively communicate the analysis for any given piece of a legal issue, you'll ultimately need to explain your abstract analysis of the law and only then proceed to the application of that law to your client's situation. In your early drafts during the preliminary drafting stage when you are writing to yourself to explore ideas, however, you do not need to follow this same order. In fact, you should figure out the order that best helps you develop the ideas.

You might be someone who should begin with the analysis of the law because you'll benefit from working first to understand the abstract ideas. With this understanding, you'll feel more comfortable taking those abstractions and applying them to the concrete situation of your client's specific facts.

In contrast, you might be someone who will need to take an early understanding of the law from the brainstorming stage and more quickly begin to explore what those ideas mean as applied to the client's situation. Working with the concrete nature of your client's specific facts, you'll more easily begin to develop an understanding of the law.

Just as with the order of drafting the introductory paragraphs and the rest of the discussion, explained in Section a above, you'll end up in the same place whether you begin with a preliminary application-prediction or analysis of the law, as long as you are thorough. You'll begin with one, move on to the other, and then check that they are consistent in content and in phrasing, as discussed in Chapter 16.

D. ORGANIZATION OF LEGAL ISSUES THAT ARE A QUESTION OF FIRST IMPRESSION

As you learned in Chapter 9, you might encounter a legal issue that involves a question of first impression because the courts of the jurisdiction have not addressed all aspects of the analysis. These situations can include legal issues involving a constitutional, statutory, or common law question. When developing the discussion of such an analysis, you would need to anticipate how the future courts would analyze the question, using the techniques you learned in Chapter 9, and then use the same organizational principles discussed in Section C to present that analysis in your memo.

CHECKLIST

- [ ] For a memo with more than one legal issue, structure the overall organization of the Discussion Section around each legal issue.

- [ ] Develop the overall organization for each discussion of a legal issue that is not a question of first impression:
  - Begin with an overview of the analysis in introductory paragraphs:
    - Introduce the relevant authority and overview of analysis based on that authority, including controlling statutory or constitutional provisions or common law;
    - Introduce the courts' analysis for pieces of the analysis when relevant;
    - Describe all ideas using general principles that are abstract and not tied to the facts of the client;
    - Provide an overview of the analysis without repeating the more in-depth analysis of the discussion and without including historical background;
    - Consider adding an overview with a quick summary of what the law indicates for the client, depending upon the instructions of the supervisor; and
  - Choose an effective organization for the discussion that follows the introductory paragraphs:

- Organize initially around controlling statutory or constitutional provisions and relevant pieces of the provisions, if applicable;
- Organize around the courts' test and components of that test at relevant points; and
- Separate analyses of the law from application-predictions.

☐ Experiment with the order in which to draft the discussion of the analysis:
- Consider whether to begin with the introductory paragraphs and then move to the rest of the discussion or the reverse; and
- Consider whether to first fully develop the abstract analysis of the law and apply those developed ideas to the client's specific facts or to first use a preliminary understanding of the abstract ideas to explore what those ideas mean as applied to the client's situation to further develop the analysis of law.

☐ Organize the discussion of questions of first impression around the anticipated analysis of the future courts.

CHAPTER 12

Analyses of the Law: Effective Structure

A. INTRODUCTION

You learned in Chapters 6 through 8 how to develop analysis based on judicial interpretations, and you learned in Chapter 9 how to analyze questions of first impression. Chapter 11 then discussed the first step of presenting your analysis in the Discussion Section of an objective memo. For each separate legal issue, you learned to begin with an introduction that identified the underlying law. For an issue based on judicial interpretations, whether of a constitution, statute, or the courts' own common law, you then learned that the introduction should proceed to identify the courts' overall test, including its components.

You are now ready to consider effective techniques to present the courts' analysis for each component of a test, which includes two steps. In this chapter, you'll learn the first step: How to organize those parts of a Discussion Section that present an analysis of the current status of law based on judicial interpretations—law that is abstract and not stated in terms of the client's situation. You'll learn the second step in Chapter 13, which explains how to organize application-predictions that apply that abstract law to the client's situation and predict the outcome, or potential outcomes, before a future court.

B. BASIC STRUCTURE OF AN ANALYSIS OF THE LAW BASED ON JUDICIAL INTERPRETATIONS

To convey the analysis of law for a component, you first need to express your ideas in general principles, as is discussed in Section 1 below. Using these general principles, you should identify the component's "label" and the component's role in the overall test, which is explained in Section 2. As discussed in Section 3, you should provide a complete and accurate explanation of the courts' analysis and support that explanation with the courts' reasoning, which is explained in Section 4. Once you've taken these steps, you would likely need to provide examples from court decisions to illustrate your ideas, a concept explained in Section 5. Finally, Section 6 reminds you that you must support all ideas with citation to legal authority.

1. Use general principles to express your analysis

In an analysis of the law based on judicial opinions, as you learned in Chapter 7, Section G1, you must explain your analysis in general principles. To do so, you must use language that takes into account the important ideas from the relevant cases and you must phrase that language with sufficient breadth to apply to a range of situations. When you present the analysis to your readers in the memo, you must use these general principles and not simply describe a series of cases as to what each individual court decided based on the specific facts before it.

To demonstrate why articulating ideas in general principles is so important, imagine that you are working on a legal problem based on cases decided by the courts of your jurisdiction. Your supervisor asks you to quickly give her a verbal update about what these cases as a group indicate about the current status of the law. In discussing your analysis of these cases in person, you would instinctively know not to describe individual cases, one after the other. Instead, you would explain the important ideas in general terms to give your supervising attorney a cohesive overview of the courts' analysis.

You would use that same generalized language to convey the analysis in your memo. When a lawyer only describes cases one by one, without using general principles to explain the relevant ideas, the memo insufficiently conveys the analysis. Such a memo is equivalent to handing the supervisor copies of all the cases and saying, "OK, on the basis of these cases, *you* do the work of synthesizing these cases together and figuring out what they indicate about the courts' analysis." This type of final product fails to accomplish its major goal—to present a complete analysis to the readers.

Of course, in many legal problems, illustrations of individual cases provide readers with a better sense of the analysis in general principles. You will learn in Section 5 below, therefore, how to craft these illustrations effectively.

2. Begin with the component's "label" and the component's role in the overall test

As you introduce an analysis of the law for a particular component, you must begin with a topic-transition sentence—see Section D2 below. In this first sentence, you should identify the label for the component. By doing so, you introduce your readers to the first step of the courts' analysis—how the courts indicate the component's substantive focus. You should also clarify the role the component plays in the courts' overall test. Is the component a requirement or, instead, a consideration that is evaluated in some manner but not required? Finally, you must use a precise transition to remind readers how this component and its particular role relates to the other components within the framework of the courts' overall test.

> **Example of drafting an effective topic-transition sentence**
>
> Imagine that you are drafting a memo based on a courts' overall test that is a checklist of requirements, which you first learned about in Chapter 7, and that you are drafting a discussion of the second requirement in your memo. Your first sentence would need to identify the courts' label and make clear that this component is a requirement. It would also need a transition from your prior discussion of the first requirement to remind readers that the courts based their overall test on a checklist of requirements. To provide all of this information effectively, your sentence would be something like:
>
>> In addition to the first requirement [*reminding the readers that this component is one of the requirements in the courts' overall checklist test*], the courts require that [*indicating that the component under consideration plays the role of a requirement*] bystanders gain a sensory perception of the negligent act and the resulting injuries of the direct victim [*identifying the courts' label*]. Ortiz; Spellman.

You'll often find that you'll need to work through several attempts to construct an effective topic-transition sentence. As explained in Chapter 7, sometimes the courts will provide you with all these ideas fairly explicitly. In other situations, you will have to imply the necessary ideas. In either case, you can be more confident that you've reached a complete and accurate understanding of the courts' ideas if you are able to craft a sentence that achieves all of the necessary goals. If you are unable to do so, you may still be struggling to understand the courts' analysis.

3. Develop an explanation of the courts' analysis

After you've identified the component's label and the component's role in the overall test, you'll need to provide an explanation of the analysis for that component. For many analyses, your explanation will include a specific test that determines whether the component is satisfied or sufficiently present.

Using the process described in Chapter 7, you'll sometimes find that the courts explicitly state the ideas in their analysis in one or more cases. In this circumstance, you'll find it relatively easy to use that language to develop a complete and accurate explanation of the courts' analysis. At other times, you'll find that the courts don't explicitly articulate important ideas. In that circumstance, you may need to take an inferential step and explain part or all of the courts' analysis in your own words.

As a novice legal writer, you'll probably struggle at times to determine when you've fully explained your understanding of the courts' analysis. In some legal problems, your explanation will be fairly short—maybe just a sentence or two. However, in more complex analyses, you may need several paragraphs or even pages to explain the important nuances of the courts' ideas. Just remember that you must express the important ideas in a complete and accurate manner.

> **Example of a short explanation**
>
> Using the issue from the example in Section 2 above, the paragraph below adds in bold an explanation of the courts' analysis for the requirement. The citation signal "see" is used when ideas were implicit in the group of cases—see Chapter 7 for a discussion of implicit analysis and Chapter 14 for a discussion of this signal.
>
>> In addition to the first requirement, the courts require that bystanders gain a sensory perception of the negligent act and the resulting injuries of the direct victim. *Ortiz*; *Spellman*. **Bystanders satisfy this requirement when they arrive at the scene immediately after the negligent act and encounter the severely injured direct victim.** *Ortiz*; *Spellman*. **In this situation, bystanders encounter the vivid injuries of the direct victim within an emergency atmosphere that captures the intensity of the event.** *See Ortiz*; *Spellman*. [*describing in general principles an explanation for this component that you developed from synthesizing the ideas in the cases*]

4. Describe the courts' reasoning

You should go on to support your explanation with the reasoning for the component, which you first learned about in Chapter 7. Your readers will better understand the analysis if they have a sense of why the courts chose that component. Again, sometimes you'll find that the courts explicitly state their reasoning in one or more cases. At other times, you'll need to take an inferential step and articulate that idea in your own words. Furthermore, much like the explanation, in some situations, you'll be able to explain the reasoning in a sentence or two. In other analyses, you may need to describe the reasoning in much more detail—and space—to demonstrate how the specific component relates to the courts' broad policy rationale.

> **Example of the courts' reasoning in one sentence**
>
> The following example adds in bold the courts' reasoning for the requirement to the example from Sections 2 and 3 above:
>
> > In addition to the first requirement, the courts require that bystanders gain a sensory perception of the negligent act and the resulting injuries of the direct victim. *Ortiz*; *Spellman*. Bystanders will satisfy this requirement when they arrive at the scene immediately after the negligent act and encounter the severely injured direct victim. *Ortiz*; *Spellman*. **In this situation, bystanders encounter the vivid injuries of the direct victim within an emergency atmosphere that captures the intensity of the event.** *See Ortiz*; *Spellman*. **This type of experience objectively verifies that a bystander is directly reacting to the negligent injuries of the direct victim with resulting severe and genuine emotional distress.** *Ortiz*; *Spellman*. [courts' reasoning as to why they use this component in their overall checklist test]

5. Use cases to illustrate the courts' analysis when helpful

a. Situations when the analysis depends on facts of cases

Once you've presented the label, explanation, and reasoning in general principles, you may need to illustrate those ideas by including examples of individual cases. In a case illustration, you describe how an individual court used the preceding analysis to reach a result on the specific facts before it. In issues that are dependent upon the facts of a specific situation, these illustrations help readers gain further insight into the analysis.

When using an illustration that is in the text of a paragraph, you'll describe the case in several sentences or more, depending upon the complexity of the court's analysis. You'll include the court's decision relevant to the specific explanation of the courts' analysis set out immediately beforehand in general principles; how the court reached that decision on the basis of that explanation; and the specific facts the court used to reach its decision. Depending upon the particular analysis, you might include the court's reasoning. As you describe these points, you will use past tense since the case was already decided.

> **Example of analysis stated in general principles followed by a case illustration in the text**
>
> By reading the following bolded case illustration, readers would understand how the court reached its decision by applying the explanation stated in general principles to the specific facts of the case.
>
> > In addition to the first requirement, the courts require that bystanders gain a sensory perception of the negligent act and the resulting injuries of the direct victim. *Ortiz*; *Spellman*. Bystanders will satisfy this requirement when they arrive at the scene immediately after the negligent act and encounter the severely injured direct victim. *Ortiz*; *Spellman*. In this situation, bystanders encounter the vivid injuries of the direct victim within an emergency atmosphere that captures the intensity of the event. *See Ortiz*; *Spellman*. This type of experience objectively verifies that a bystander is directly reacting to the negligent injuries of the direct victim with resulting severe and genuine emotional distress. *Ortiz*; *Spellman*. [*general principles setting out the court's analysis, including the label, explanation, and reasoning*]
> >
> > **For example, in *Ortiz*, the court found that the bystander, a minor child, gained a sensory perception because he arrived at the scene and encountered the direct victim, his mother, immediately after a vicious attack that had occurred due to the negligence of the property owner. *Ortiz*. When the child entered the scene, his mother's bedroom, he encountered her vivid injuries within an emergency context. *See Ortiz*. He found her hog-tied, with knife-cuts all over her body, and struggling to breathe. *Ortiz*. Until emergency services arrived, the child waited with his mother as she continued to choke. *Ortiz*.** [*several sentence case illustration in the text*]

For additional considerations in developing effective case illustrations, see Section C below.

b. Situations when the analysis does not depend on facts of cases

As you learned in Chapter 10, some legal questions are not dependent on the particular facts of a situation. Dealing with this kind of a question, a future court will use the general situation before it to identify the possible approaches to their analysis that are relevant. However, the court will choose to adopt a particular approach purely based on the policy rationales it finds most convincing, no matter what the specific facts of any precedent case might be. In this situation, the court will not need to justify its decision by comparing the specific facts before it to the specific facts of relevant precedent. In developing your analysis of the law for this type of issue, therefore, you would not need to use illustrations of specific facts from cases to support your analysis.

> **Example of analysis that does not require case illustrations**
>
> Imagine that your client is a minor child who was injured due to alleged parental negligence in a car accident, and the child's representative wants to bring a suit against the parent to recover damages. Further imagine that the highest appeals court in your state had never addressed whether parents were immune from suits brought by their minor child because of negligence in automobile accidents. Furthermore, two intermediate appeals courts in the jurisdiction had developed contradictory approaches to this issue. One intermediate appeals court refused to apply parent-child immunity in negligent car accident situations on the basis that that immunity did not achieve good policy results for the jurisdiction. The other intermediate appeals court applied immunity based on other policy considerations. The legal question would be whether a court would apply immunity, or not, in your client's situation.
>
> In your analysis of law, you would discuss each approach to immunity and why the highest appeals court might follow the approach it found most convincing based on policy rationales. In this situation, you would be analyzing whether the future court would be more convinced based on policy rationales to apply, or refuse to apply, parent-child immunity in negligent automobile accident situations. The court would use the specific case of the client—a child suing a parent for injuries arising out of a negligent automobile accident—as the basis to choose which possible approaches to immunity were relevant to the case before it. However, the court would reach its decision based on policy that was most convincing and would not need to consider the specific facts of automobile accidents in precedent cases. The only question would be whether parental immunity applied. If so,

> the parents would be immune from suit regardless of the specific facts of the automobile accident.
>
> In developing your analysis of the law, you would not include case illustrations detailing the facts of the automobile accidents. The only facts that would be relevant would be that a child was suing a parent because of injuries arising out of a negligent automobile accident. The specific facts regarding the parent's action in the automobile accident would be irrelevant.

6. Support your analysis with citation to legal authority

You must support your analyses of the law with citation to the relevant authority. Therefore, you should use accurate and complete citations to support all of your ideas in these parts of the Discussion Section. For an explanation of using citation to legal authority to support your discussion, see Chapter 14.

7. Sample of memo with an analysis of the law based on judicial interpretations

For an example of a memo with an analysis of the law conveyed with the techniques described in this section, see Comments 11 and 13 to the Sample of a Formal Objective Memorandum in Appendix I.

C. EFFECTIVE CASE ILLUSTRATIONS

In using case illustrations of the analysis that you explain with general principles, you must first decide which cases to describe, a step that is discussed in Section 1. Once you've made that decision, you can choose between three different forms: A longer form that describes a case in several sentences in the text, which you first learned about in Section B5 above and that is discussed in more depth in Section 2 below; a shorter parenthetical form that describes a case in a word, a phrase, or a sentence, and is placed in the citation sentence, which is discussed in Section 3; or, as explained in Section 4, a combination of a case illustration in several sentences in the text and additional case illustrations in parentheticals. You should always use one form or the other for any individual case at any particular point in your analysis, which is addressed in Section 5. Finally, as discussed in Section 6, you should try to organize your illustrations by the result the court reached in the cases.

1. Choosing which cases to describe

You must begin by choosing the case or cases that best illustrate your description of the law at that point in your analysis. In some legal problems, you will have only a few relevant cases and will therefore choose to describe them all to provide a sufficient number of helpful illustrations throughout the analysis.

In other problems, however, you will have a large number of cases, many of which will illustrate your analysis in an essentially redundant manner. To be concise in this situation, you would choose to describe only the case or cases that would provide your readers with the "best" illustration of that aspect of the analysis.

To make this decision—keeping in mind that reasonable lawyers might reach different conclusions about the "best" case—you should evaluate the level of the court that decided each case. A decision by the highest appeals court of the jurisdiction has greater authority than one by an intermediate appeals court and by a trial court. However, you should also consider the depth and specificity of the courts' analysis relevant to the issue. A better-developed decision by the intermediate appeals court would likely be a more helpful illustration than one by the highest appeals court where the discussion was only superficial.

In conjunction with the level of court and depth of analysis, you would give weight to whether the court provided detailed facts to support its decision and therefore the case would provide a more vivid illustration of your analysis. And, finally, the date a case was decided could be relevant, especially if nuances in the analysis or facts in a recent case indicated something additional or different about the courts' emerging approach to the issue.

2. Using case illustrations in the text

As you first learned in Section B5 above, you may choose to describe a case in several sentences in the text. In constructing this type of case illustration, you should consider the following guidelines, each of which is discussed below:

- Place case illustrations in the text effectively;
- Tailor the content of case illustrations in the text to your description of the analysis;
- Describe actions by the court consistently with legal conventions;
- Identify whether ideas are explicit or implicit; and
- Make clear the parties' relationship to the analysis.

a. Place case illustrations in the text carefully

In general, you should place descriptions of individual cases in the text soon after the analysis that they illustrate. Readers then will encounter the ideas that you explain with general principles, gain further insight into that analysis through an example or examples of those ideas, and then continue on to the next part of the analysis stated in general principles.

To put this general rule into effect, you must realize that you won't be able to use a formula that tells you exactly where to place case illustrations most effectively in all analyses. Instead, you must use the logic of the analysis itself. As you break down the analysis into its logical parts and develop each, you must evaluate where your readers would benefit from illustrations of how specific courts used your analysis—the explanation and underlying reasoning—to reach a result on the facts before them. Try to determine if readers would benefit from an illustration right where you are placing it. In some circumstances, you'll find there's only one "best" place to illustrate a piece of analysis. In other circumstances, you'll find you have legitimate choices, each of which has strengths and weaknesses.

b. Tailor the content of case illustrations in the text to the analysis

You must develop a case illustration in the text in a manner that allows your readers, who likely have not read and analyzed the case, to easily understand why the case illustrates the immediately preceding description of that part of the analysis.

i. Describe necessary aspects of a case

As you begin to craft a case illustration, think about where you are in your analysis by reviewing the immediately preceding ideas you stated in general principles. Then include any or all of the following aspects of a case that are necessary to illustrate those ideas: The court's decision; the facts the court relied on to reach that decision; an explanation of the court's analysis; and the court's reasoning for that explanation. In general, when you describe a case in several sentences in the text, you'll include all these aspects of a case, although for some analyses you won't need the reasoning.

> **Example of an illustration that includes the necessary aspects of the case**
>
> Imagine that you chose to describe the *Ortiz* case in several sentences in the text. Therefore, you would have included the court's decision and how the court reached that decision—based on the explanation of the courts' analysis you developed beforehand in general principles as applied to all the specific facts before the court. In particular, note all

> the specific facts in bold that make this description an effective illustration.
>
> > In addition to the first requirement, the courts require that bystanders gain a sensory perception of the negligent act and the resulting injuries of the direct victim. *Ortiz*; *Spellman*. Bystanders will satisfy this requirement when they arrive at the scene immediately after the negligent act and encounter the severely injured direct victim. *Ortiz*; *Spellman*. In this situation, bystanders encounter the vivid injuries of the direct victim within an emergency atmosphere that captures the intensity of the event. *See Ortiz*; *Spellman*. This type of experience objectively verifies that a bystander is directly reacting to the negligent injuries of the direct victim with resulting severe and genuine emotional distress. *Ortiz*; *Spellman*. [*general principles setting out the court's analysis—the label, explanation, and reasoning*]
> >
> > For example, in *Ortiz*, the court found the bystander, a minor child, gained a sensory perception because he arrived at the scene and encountered the direct victim, his mother, immediately after a vicious attack that had occurred due to the negligence of the property owner. *Ortiz*. **When the child entered the scene, his mother's bedroom,** he encountered her vivid injuries within an emergency context. *See Ortiz*. He found her **hog-tied, with knife-cuts all over her body, and struggling to breathe**. *Ortiz*. **Until emergency services arrived, the child waited with his mother as she continued to choke**. *Ortiz*. [*case illustration*]

ii. Begin by stating how the case relates to the preceding description of analysis

You must begin a case illustration in the text by making clear how it relates to the preceding description of that part of the analysis stated in general principles.

> **Example of an effective case illustration compared with a less effective one**
>
> In the "helpful case illustration" below, readers would understand from the first sentence—see the bolded ideas—how that case specifically illustrates the immediately preceding analysis in the first paragraph of general principles. In contrast, in the "less helpful illustration," readers would not understand that connection until the very end of the illustration—see the bolded ideas—which

would hinder their understanding of the connection between the analysis and why the case illustrated that analysis.

In addition to the first requirement, the courts require that bystanders gain a sensory perception of the negligent act and the resulting injuries of the direct victim. *Ortiz*; *Spellman*. Bystanders will satisfy this requirement when they arrive at the scene immediately after the negligent act and encounter the severely injured direct victim. *Ortiz*; *Spellman*. In this situation, bystanders encounter the vivid injuries of the direct victim within an emergency atmosphere that captures the intensity of the event. See *Ortiz*; *Spellman*. This type of experience objectively verifies that a bystander is reacting to the negligent injuries of the direct victim with severe and genuine emotional distress. *Ortiz*; *Spellman*. [general principles of analysis]

Example of a helpful case illustration:

For example, in *Ortiz*, the court found the bystander, a minor child, gained a sensory perception because he arrived at the scene and encountered the direct victim, his mother, immediately after a vicious attack that had occurred due to the negligence of the property owner. *Ortiz*. When the child entered the scene, his mother's bedroom, he encountered her vivid injuries within an emergency context. See *Ortiz*. He found her hog-tied, with knife-cuts all over her body, and struggling to breathe. *Ortiz*. Until emergency services arrived, the child waited with his mother as she continued to choke. *Ortiz*.

Example of a less helpful case illustration:

For example, in *Ortiz*, the bystander, a minor child, found the direct victim, his mother, hog-tied, with knife-cuts all over her body, and struggling to breathe. *Ortiz*. Until emergency services arrived, the child waited with his mother as she continued to choke. *Ortiz*. On the basis that the bystander-child arrived immediately on the scene and viewed the severe injuries of the direct victim, the court found that the child gained a sensory perception. *Ortiz*.

iii. Use consistent content and phrasing

To be effective, case illustrations must be consistent with the preceding description of the analysis, in both content and the phrasing of that content. When case illustrations are crafted in this manner, readers are able to skim through the description of the analysis in general principles and then easily learn more about that analysis when they encounter illustrations of how individual courts have used that analysis to reach a decision for the parties before the court.

> **Example of consistent content**
>
> Imagine that your memo is analyzing two separate common law causes of action and that some cases analyze and reach a decision on each. In this situation, you might describe these cases twice: Once in the part of your analysis that analyzes the first cause of action and once as you analyze the second. Using the case illustrations in this manner, you would provide your readers with a cohesive analysis of each cause of action.
>
> In contrast, as you discussed one cause of action, you would not describe that court's analysis on both causes of action since that would result in a case illustration that was inconsistent in content with the immediately preceding analysis.

> **Example of consistent phrasing**
>
> Imagine that your memo is analyzing a factor that is based on whether the plaintiff and defendant have a "close relationship." To be consistent, you would use the phrase of "close relationship" in both the explanation of the courts' analysis in general principles and in any corresponding case illustrations.
>
> In contrast, imagine that, as you developed your explanation, you described this factor using the phrase of "close relationship." In developing the corresponding case illustration, however, you described this idea using the phrase of "intimate emotional relationship."
>
> This inconsistency in phrasing would raise an important analytical question for your readers, thereby undermining their ability to grasp the analysis at this point in your memo: Are these two phrases describing the same idea in the analysis or different ideas? On the one hand, the word "close" and the phrase "intimate emotional" both appear to be getting at the same idea. On the other hand, the phrase "intimate

> emotional" might be further explaining what the court meant by "close," therefore indicating that these ideas play different roles in the analysis. Your readers would not be able to answer this important analytical question without going back to the actual cases, which would be frustrating in the busy environment of law practice.

Remember that, as you generated your description of the analysis in general principles, you could have synthesized ideas that have the same content but were expressed differently by different courts throughout a group of cases. At some point in this process, you would have chosen the "best" way to express that idea, as was discussed in Chapter 7. Having used that language in your description of the analysis, you would need to use the same language for that same idea in the case illustration that followed. If you were concerned that readers might be confused if they went back to the actual case and found the court's different phrasing, you could use that phrasing in the illustration but make clear how that phrasing related to the wording of the preceding analysis.

c. Describe cases consistently with legal convention

Be sure to describe all aspects of a case consistently with legal convention. For instance, courts "hold," "find," "reason," "explain," "state," and even "imply." Courts, however, do not "argue" or "believe." This distinction makes sense when you think about the role of the court. A court must come to a decision on the facts before it. Therefore, the court will "hold," "decide," or "find" because it based its analysis on certain ideas, given the facts before the court. However, given its role as decision-maker, the court doesn't "believe" and certainly doesn't need to "argue," which is something that the parties before the court must do.

d. Identify explicit or implicit analysis

When you illustrate individual cases, you must differentiate between ideas that courts express explicitly and ideas that are implicit, an important distinction that you learned about in Chapter 7. If the idea is explicit in a particular case, you may simply use such phrasing as the court "found," "held," "decided," "reasoned," "explained," or "stated." Encountering these words, readers will assume that the ideas are explicit. In contrast, if the idea is implicit, you must make that clear with phrasing like "the court reasoned implicitly," "the court implied," or "implicit in the case." You must also use the citation signal "see," which is discussed in Chapter 14.

e. Clarify the parties' relationship to the analysis

When you describe the parties to a case, you must make clear the role each plays in the analysis. Except in rare circumstances, therefore, do not describe a party by name, since a name generally indicates nothing about an individual's relationship to the analysis. In addition, in general don't use "plaintiff" and "defendant," except in criminal cases where "defendant" would identify the role of one party in the case.

> **Example of vague illustration due to use of party names**
>
> In the example below, the author used the actual names of the parties—see bolded names—and therefore obscured the parties' precise relationship to the analysis.
>
> > In *Ortiz*, the court found that **Samuel Ortiz** gained a sensory perception because he arrived at the scene and encountered **Carmen Ortiz** immediately after a vicious attack that had occurred due to the negligence of the **Cambridge Housing Authority**. *Ortiz*. When **Samuel Ortiz** entered the scene, **Carmen Ortiz's** bedroom, he found her hog-tied, with knife-cuts all over her body, and struggling to breathe. *Ortiz*. Until emergency services arrived, **Samuel Ortiz** waited with **Carmen Ortiz** as she continued to choke. *Ortiz*.
>
> > Readers would have to stop and figure out that Samuel Ortiz is a bystander; Carmen Ortiz is a direct victim; and the Cambridge Housing Authority is a property owner who was negligent. Taking that time would frustrate their ability to read fast and grasp your analysis easily.

f. Sample of memo with case illustrations in the text

For examples of case illustrations in the text of a memo, see Comment 13 to the Sample of a Formal Objective Memorandum in Appendix I.

3. Using parenthetical illustrations

Instead of choosing the longer form included in the text, you may use parenthetical illustrations to describe cases. This type of illustration is not included in the text but, instead, included within parentheses directly after the citation of a case in a citation sentence. Parenthetical illustrations are very flexible since they can illustrate analysis in a variety of ways, including describing a case using a word, a phrase, or a full sentence. While lawyers use the longer illustrations in the text in some circumstances, they often use shorter parenthetical illustrations to make their analysis concise.

During your first few months of law school, when you are just learning about legal analysis and how to convey it, you will likely find using the longer type of case illustration in the text to be helpful. By spelling out in depth what a court decided on the facts before it, and why, you may figure out ideas that you were unclear about as you initially generated your analysis in general principles. When this occurs, you will then be able to take the new ideas and revise your analysis so that it better informs your readers. However, as you become more proficient with conveying legal analysis, you will often find that using parenthetical illustrations is an effective tool to provide your reader with necessary information in a more concise manner.

To construct an effective parenthetical illustration, you should follow the same rules that you learned above for the longer form of case illustrations in the text, tailoring those rules to the shorter form as follows:

- Place parenthetical illustrations effectively;
- Tailor the content of parenthetical illustrations to your description of the analysis;
- Make parenthetical illustrations easy to read;
- Make parenthetical illustrations concise; and
- Construct a series of parenthetical illustrations consistently.

a. Place parenthetical illustrations carefully

Just as you learned with the form of case illustrations in the text in Section 2a above, you should place parenthetical illustrations soon after the ideas that they illustrate. Include them in the citation sentence that follows immediately after the sentence or sentences in which you explain your analysis with general principles. Readers then will be able to grasp the import of the discussion of analysis, move seamlessly into an example of those ideas, and then continue on to the next part of the analysis in general principles.

In fact, you'll find that you'll have more choices as to where to include parenthetical illustrations than with the longer form in the text. Parenthetical illustrations are shorter and therefore easier to insert at any point or points within your description of your analysis where they will help your readers understand the ideas more easily. For examples of placing parenthetical illustrations effectively, see Section b below.

b. Tailor the content of parenthetical illustrations to the analysis

Just as you would do with the longer form of a case illustration, you must develop the content of a parenthetical illustration so that your readers will be able to easily understand why the case illustrates the immediately preceding description of that part of the analysis. Remember that your readers have likely not read and analyzed these cases.

When you use parenthetical illustrations, however, you'll have more choices as to how to frame the content of your description. For instance, a parenthetical's content may just identify the relevant facts of the case; may describe the relevant decision of the court and how the court reached that decision on the facts; or may include any other information that would help readers further understand how an individual case illustrated the immediately preceding description of analysis. Parenthetical illustrations may be a word, a phrase, or a full sentence.

Examples of parenthetical illustrations that include the court's decision and the facts that it relied on to reach its decision

In the following example, the author chose to include in the parenthetical illustrations—highlighted in bold—the court's decision and the facts it relied on to reach that decision.

> In addition to the first requirement, the courts require that bystanders gain a sensory perception of the negligent act and the resulting injuries of the direct victim. *Ortiz*; *Spellman*. Bystanders will satisfy this requirement when they arrive at the scene immediately after the negligent act and encounter the severely injured direct victim. *Ortiz*; *Spellman*. In this situation, bystanders encounter the vivid injuries of the direct victim within an emergency atmosphere that captures the intensity of the event. *See Ortiz* **(gaining sensory perception by entering bedroom immediately after attack injured direct victim, seeing victim hog-tied with knife-cuts all over body, and waiting for emergency services as direct victim continued to choke)**; *Spellman* **(gaining sensory perception by arriving at accident scene immediately after car negligently injured direct victim, encountering victim lying on ground, and riding in ambulance)**. This type of experience objectively verifies that a bystander is directly reacting to the negligent injuries of the direct victim with resulting severe and genuine emotional distress. *Ortiz*; *Spellman*.

Example of parenthetical illustrations omitting information that is clear from the context of the paragraph

Here, the author chose to use parenthetical illustrations—highlighted in bold—that omitted the court's decision of "gaining sensory perception" because that was essentially clear from the context of the prior analysis stated in general principles.

> In addition to the first requirement, the courts require that bystanders gain a sensory perception of the negligent act and the resulting injuries of the direct victim. *Ortiz*; *Spellman*. Bystanders will satisfy this requirement when they arrive at the scene immediately after the negligent act and encounter the severely injured direct victim. *Ortiz*; *Spellman*. In this situation, bystanders encounter the vivid injuries of the direct victim within an emergency atmosphere that captures the intensity of the event. *See Ortiz* **(entering bedroom immediately after attack injured direct victim, seeing victim hog-tied with knife-cuts all over body, waiting for emergency services as direct victim continued to choke)**; *Spellman* **(arriving at accident scene immediately after car negligently injured direct victim, encountering victim lying on ground, riding in ambulance)**. This type of experience objectively verifies that a bystander is directly reacting to the negligent injuries of the direct victim with resulting severe and genuine emotional distress. *Ortiz*; *Spellman*.

Example of parenthetical illustrations that only include the specific facts of the cases

In the following example, the parenthetical illustrations—highlighted in bold—include only a general category of facts because that is all that is needed to illustrate the explanation.

> . . . Immediate family members satisfy the requirement. *Ortiz* **(parent/minor child)**; *Spellman* **(parent/minor child)**; *Lockleer* **(spouses)**. The courts reason that. . . . [*analysis in general principles continues*]

> **Example of parentheticals that include only a general category of information**
>
> In these parenthetical illustrations—highlighted in bold—the author identifies only general categories of information because that is all that is necessary to illustrate the explanation.
>
> > Wisconsin has abrogated many forms of tort immunity in personal negligence actions. *E.g., Zelinger* **(interspousal immunity);** *Goller* **(parental immunity).**

In addition, just as with the longer illustrations in the text, parenthetical illustrations must be consistent with the preceding description of the analysis, in both content and the phrasing of that content. When parenthetical illustrations are crafted in this manner, readers are able to skim through the descriptions of the analysis explained with general principles and then easily learn more about that analysis when they encounter illustrations of cases. For examples of consistency of content and phrasing, see Section 2biii above.

c. Construct concise parenthetical illustrations

Given their purpose to make analysis more concise, parenthetical illustrations must convey the important ideas in as few words as possible to help busy law practice readers.

To begin with, parenthetical illustrations are never more than one sentence. That sentence, then, should almost never be longer than two—or maybe three—lines. If a parenthetical illustration is too long, then either you need to use the longer form in the text instead or you need to reduce the length of the parenthetical.

To shorten a parenthetical illustration, begin by looking for words or phrases that are unnecessary to convey the content. Go on to edit out articles like "a" and "an" and "the," unless they are necessary for readers to understand the information. Finally, check that the sentence structure doesn't unnecessarily require that ideas be repeated or result in an awkward sentence.

> **Example of editing a parenthetical illustration that is too long**
>
> > ***Too long:*** *Ortiz* gaining ~~a~~ sufficient sensory perception when ~~the bystander~~ entered ~~his mother's~~ bedroom immediately after ~~the~~

> attack injured ~~the~~ direct victim, ~~his mother, and the bystander~~ saw ~~the~~ victim hog-tied ~~and~~ with knife-cuts all over ~~her~~ body, ~~and the bystander~~ waited ~~with his mother, the direct victim, during the time it took~~ for emergency services to arrive as ~~direct~~ victim continued to choke).
>
> *Concise: Ortiz* (gaining sensory perception by entering bedroom immediately after attack injured direct victim, seeing victim hog-tied with knife-cuts all over body, waiting for emergency services to arrive as victim continued to choke).

d. Make parenthetical illustrations easy to read

You must make parenthetical illustrations easy to read quickly. Remember that your readers are moving from the descriptions of the analysis that you explain with general principles to the case illustrations in parentheticals and then back to the next idea in the analysis. To help readers make these transitions, you should construct parenthetical illustrations using the following rules.

First, in general, begin a parenthetical illustration with a present participle (the "ing" verb form). Using this verb form helps readers move from the analysis to the illustration in the parenthetical.

> **Example of using a present participle in a parenthetical illustration**
>
> *Spellman* (gaining sensory perception by arriving at accident scene immediately after car negligently injured direct victim, encountering victim lying on ground, riding in ambulance).

Of course, you may need to vary from this rule based on the content of a particular parenthetical illustration. See examples in Section b above.

Second, you should always consider ordering ideas in a parenthetical from general ideas to more specific ideas. For instance, in a full sentence parenthetical, you would begin with the court's decision, the more general idea, and then follow with the facts that decision was based on, which are more specific ideas.

> **Example of ordering ideas from general to specific in a parenthetical illustration**
>
> *Spellman* (gaining sensory perception [*court's decision*] by arriving at accident scene immediately after car negligently injured direct victim, encountering victim lying on ground, riding in ambulance [*the facts court based decision on*]).

Finally, remember that parenthetical illustrations do not belong in the text of a sentence, since you should not ask your readers to attempt to understand both the ideas in general principles and a case description at the same time. Instead, you should include parenthetical illustrations in the citation sentence that follows the description of the analysis.

e. Present a series of parenthetical illustrations consistently

At some points as you convey an analysis of law, you may want to illustrate a series of cases that will provide your readers with a range of vivid examples of the ideas. Although a series can be very helpful, several cases together with parenthetical illustrations can disconnect the description of the analysis that comes before and after. To help readers transition from the analysis conveyed in general principles to a series of cases illustrating those ideas in parentheticals, craft the parenthetical information consistently in content, structure, and phrasing.

> **Example where parenthetical illustrations are consistent**
>
> The parenthetical illustrations below have consistent content, structure, and phrasing.
>
> *Ortiz* (gaining sensory perception by entering bedroom immediately after attack injured direct victim, seeing victim hog-tied with knife-cuts all over body, waiting for emergency services as victim continued to choke); *Spellman* (gaining sensory perception by arriving at accident scene immediately after car negligently injured direct victim, encountering victim lying on ground, riding in ambulance).

> **Example where parenthetical illustrations are inconsistent**
>
> The parenthetical illustrations below have inconsistent content, structure, and phrasing—highlighted in bold—and therefore hinder readers' comprehension.
>
> > *Ortiz* (**gaining sensory perception** by entering bedroom immediately after attack injured direct victim, seeing victim hog-tied with knife-cuts all over body, waiting for emergency services as victim continued to choke); *Spellman* (arriving at accident scene immediately after car negligently injured direct victim, encountering victim lying on ground, riding in ambulance; therefore, **gaining a sufficient experience**).

f. Sample of memo with parenthetical case illustrations

For examples of parenthetical case illustrations in a memo, see Comment 23 to the Sample of a Formal Objective Memorandum in Appendix I.

4. Using illustrations in the text and parenthetical illustrations together

In addition to choosing either the longer textual or the shorter parenthetical form of case illustration, you can use the two forms together to describe two or more cases at a specific point in the analysis. You would begin by describing one case in the longer textual form and then go on to describe additional cases in the shorter parenthetical form. This type of combination allows you to accomplish the following two important objectives. First, you can describe one case in depth to help a reader more clearly understand some particular point in the description of the analysis, if you feel that's desirable. Second, you can provide readers with additional illustrations in a very concise manner.

> **Example of using an illustration in the text and a parenthetical illustration**
>
> In the following example, the author chose to use the longer textual form for the *Ortiz* case since, given its vivid facts, it was a better illustration of the explanation than the *Spellman* case. The author then added the *Spellman* case in parenthetical form, and could also have

> included additional cases using the parenthetical form. Again, note that the illustration in several sentences comes first, followed by the citation signal of "see also" and then the supporting parenthetical illustration — all highlighted in bold.
>
> > **In addition to the first requirement, the courts require bystanders to gain a sensory perception of the negligent act and the resulting injuries of the direct victim.** *Ortiz*; *Spellman*. **Bystanders will satisfy this requirement when they arrive at the scene immediately after the negligent act and encounter the severely injured direct victim.** *Ortiz*; *Spellman*. **In this situation, bystanders encounter the vivid injuries of the direct victim within an emergency atmosphere that captures the intensity of the event.** See *Ortiz*; *Spellman*. **This type of experience objectively verifies that a bystander is directly reacting to the negligent injuries of the direct victim with resulting severe and genuine emotional distress.** *Ortiz*; *Spellman*. [*general principles*]
> >
> > **For example, in** *Ortiz*, **the court found the bystander, a minor child, gained a sensory perception because he arrived at the scene and encountered the direct victim, his mother, immediately after a vicious attack that had occurred due to the negligence of the property owner.** *Ortiz*. **When the child entered the scene, his mother's bedroom, he encountered her vivid injuries within an emergency context.** See *Ortiz*. **He found her hog-tied, with knife-cuts all over her body, and struggling to breathe.** *Ortiz*. **Until emergency services arrived, the child waited with his mother as she continued to choke.** *Ortiz; see also Spellman* **(arriving at accident scene immediately after car negligently injured direct victim; encountering victim lying on ground; riding in ambulance with victim).**

5. Choosing one form of illustration for an individual case

To describe any individual case at any particular point to illustrate the analysis, you must choose *either* the longer form in the text *or* the shorter parenthetical form. If you use both forms for the same case to illustrate a particular part of the analysis, your illustration of the case will be too disjointed because the relevant information will be in different places. Of course, you may choose different forms to describe the same case at different points in your description of the analysis.

Example of using different forms of case illustrations to illustrate the same case at different points in the memo

Using the *Ortiz* case from above, the author could choose the parenthetical form in the analysis of the relationship requirement and then the longer, several sentence form in the analysis of the "sensory perception" requirement in a different part of the memo.

Example of using a parenthetical illustration for Ortiz in one part of the analysis:

Immediate family members satisfy the requirement. *Ortiz* (parent/minor child); *Spellman* (parent/minor child); *Lockleer* (spouses). The courts reason that this type of relationship is based on a deep emotional bond. *Spellman*; see *Ortiz*.

Example of using a longer illustration in the text for Ortiz in a different part of the analysis:

In addition to the first requirement, the courts require bystanders to gain a sensory perception of the negligent act and the resulting injuries of the direct victim. *Ortiz*; *Spellman*. Bystanders will satisfy this requirement when they arrive at the scene immediately after the negligent act and encounter the severely injured direct victim. *Ortiz*; *Spellman*. In this situation, bystanders encounter the vivid injuries of the direct victim within an emergency atmosphere that captures the intensity of the event. *See Ortiz*; *Spellman*. This type of experience objectively verifies that a bystander is directly reacting to the negligent injuries of the direct victim with resulting severe and genuine emotional distress. *Ortiz*; *Spellman*.

For example, in *Ortiz*, the court found the bystander, a minor child, gained a sensory perception because he arrived at the scene and encountered the direct victim, his mother, immediately after a vicious attack that had occurred due to the negligence of the property owner. *Ortiz*. When the child entered the scene, his mother's bedroom, he encountered her vivid injuries within an emergency context. *See Ortiz*. In particular, he found her hog-tied, with knife-cuts all over her body, and struggling to breathe. *Ortiz*. Until emergency services arrived, the child waited with his mother as she continued to choke. *Ortiz*.

6. Organizing illustrations by the court's result

To help readers grasp the significance of case illustrations quickly, you should generally organize illustrations by the result the court reached rather than switching back and forth between cases with different results. Thus, you should group together the illustrations in which the court came to the same result—both longer illustrations and shorter parenthetical illustrations. Generally, you should begin with the positive examples—cases where the court found that the facts either satisfied the relevant analysis or had a positive influence on the court's decision. Then, you should provide the illustrations of cases that either did not satisfy the analysis or had a negative influence on the court's decision.

> **Example of organizing illustrations by result**
>
> In the example below, the author includes together the two cases that illustrate when a bystander encounters the vivid injuries of the direct victim in the first paragraph and then provides a case that illustrates the opposite result afterwards in the next paragraph. All of these illustrations are highlighted in bold.
>
> ... In this situation, bystanders encounter the vivid injuries of the direct victim within an emergency atmosphere that captures the intensity of the event. *See* ***Ortiz*** **(gaining sensory perception by entering bedroom immediately after attack injured direct victim, seeing victim hog-tied with knife-cuts all over body, waiting for emergency services as direct victim continued to choke);** ***Spellman*** **(gaining sensory perception by arriving at accident scene immediately after car negligently injured direct victim, encountering victim lying on ground, riding in ambulance).** This type of experience objectively verifies that a bystander is directly reacting to the negligent injuries of the direct victim with resulting severe and genuine emotional distress. *Ortiz*; *Spellman*.
>
> In contrast, bystanders do not gain a sensory perception when, after a lengthy period of time, they arrive at a location where the direct victim's injuries are no longer vivid and the overall atmosphere does not retain the intensity of the negligent event. *See* ***Freehold***; ***Cohen*****. In *Freehold*, the court found that the bystander did not gain a sensory perception of the negligent act and the direct victim's injuries.** *Freehold*. **There, the bystander encountered the corpse of the direct victim at a funeral home two days after a negligent accident.** *Freehold*. **The court implied that, since the direct victim's corpse had been prepared for the funeral,**

> it no longer exhibited the type of injuries that vividly reflected the negligent event. *See Freehold*. In addition, the calm, serene atmosphere of the funeral home was completely different from the emergency nature of an accident scene immediately after the event. *See Freehold*.

For examples of case illustrations organized by court's result, see Comment 14 to the Sample of a Formal Objective Memorandum in Appendix I.

D. ADDITIONAL ORGANIZATIONAL TECHNIQUES

Once you have learned the basic techniques to draft discussions of an analysis of law, as explained in Sections B and C above, you are ready to take on additional organizational techniques to handle even the most complex analyses: Transitions between ideas, topic-transition sentences, paragraph development, introductory and summary sentences or paragraphs, and headings.

1. Evaluate transitions

The effective use of transitional words or phrases will help you convey your ideas to readers more effectively and concisely. Evaluate whether you have used precise transitional words or phrases that connect ideas accurately at every level of the analysis:

- Between components of the courts' overall test;
- Between smaller pieces of those components;
- Between paragraphs;
- Between sentences; and
- Between ideas within a sentence.

a. Choosing accurate transitions

To craft precise transitions that connect ideas accurately, you must fully understand the underlying analysis, and how that analysis itself connects ideas. Many authors fail to provide sufficient transitions between ideas because they simply turn to a "list" of transitional words or phrases without realizing that it is the analysis itself that dictates the necessary connection.

> **Example of transitional words**
>
> Imagine that the courts have based an analysis on the following two ideas:
>
> - <u>A requirement</u>: Two places must have a sufficient physical relationship.
> - <u>Explanation of the courts' analysis of this requirement</u>: To determine whether this requirement is satisfied, the courts evaluate a combination of three factors.
>
> To convey the courts' analysis well, you would need to use a precise transition between these two ideas that accurately expresses their relationship—that of an overall requirement and the test that explains how to determine whether that requirement is satisfied. The examples below illustrate a precise transition that accurately conveys this relationship and an imprecise transition that does not.
>
> ***Precise transition that conveys an accurate connection between ideas:***
>
> > The courts require a sufficient physical relationship between two places. **To determine whether that relationship is sufficient,** the courts evaluate a combination of three factors.
>
> ***Imprecise transition that conveys an inaccurate connection between ideas:***
>
> > **Not only** do the courts require a sufficient physical relationship between two places, they **also** evaluate a combination of three factors.
>
> Using the transition of "not only/also," the author has made the two pieces of analysis appear equivalent—equally important—and this is contrary to the courts' actual analysis. In fact, from this transition, readers might reach the inaccurate conclusion that the court used two requirements—a physical relationship between two places and some combination of factors.

As you refine the drafts of your writing, especially the final edit of your memo, evaluate each and every transition. When you find one that does not precisely convey the relationship between two ideas, stop. Consider whether the transition accurately conveys your own understanding of the relationship between two ideas in the analysis. Sometimes you'll find that you understood the relationship but simply did not express it as well on the page for your readers. Other times, however, you'll find that you are still struggling to understand the relationship between two ideas in the analysis. An imprecise transition may be identifying a place in the analysis that needs further work.

b. Verifying that transitions connect ideas precisely

In particular, challenge yourself every time you use the transitions discussed below because these particular transitions may fool you into thinking that you have communicated a precise connection when you have not. While sometimes these transitions do express an accurate relationship between ideas, more often than not they convey a relationship that is too general or even inaccurate.

One such transition is "and" or any of its variations, such as "in addition," "as well as," and "also." When using this transition between two ideas, you must be sure you mean to indicate that the second idea is, in fact, equivalent to and on equal footing with the first.

> **Example of the precise and imprecise use of "and" as a transition**
>
> Think about the following statement, where the transitions are in bold: Apples **and** pears are **kinds of** fruit. In this statement, the transitions are correct. First, apples and pears are both kinds of fruit and therefore "and" between these items is precise because this transition accurately conveys the idea that these two items are equivalent. Second, the transitional phrase "kinds of" is precise, since "apples and pears" are specific examples of the generic class of "fruit." In contrast, therefore, it would be imprecise to say "apples and pears **and** fruit."

In addition, you should always evaluate transitions that list ideas in order, such as "first," "second," third," and so forth. You'll find that in many situations these transitions will not accurately reflect the most precise connection between ideas. On the one hand, you'll find these transitions useful when you want to indicate that two or more equivalent ideas should be examined in a certain order. On the other hand, like variations of "and," these transitions often obscure a more precise relationship between ideas and will therefore need to be replaced.

> **Example of using transitions, such as "first" and "second," which list ideas in order**
>
> As you did in the example in Section 1a above, imagine that the courts have based an analysis on the following two ideas:
>
> > <u>A requirement</u>: Two places must have a sufficient physical relationship.
> > <u>Explanation of the courts' analysis of this requirement</u>: The courts evaluate a combination of three factors.
>
> The two examples below illustrate a precise transition that accurately conveys this relationship and an imprecise transition that does not. In the second example, the author obscured the precise relationship between the two pieces of analysis by using the transitions of "first" and "second." In both examples, the transitions are in bold.
>
> ***Precise transition that conveys an accurate relationship between ideas:***
>
> > The courts require a sufficient physical relationship between two places. **To determine whether that relationship is sufficient,** the courts evaluate a combination of three factors.
>
> ***Imprecise transition that conveys an inaccurate relationship between ideas:***
>
> > **First,** the courts require a sufficient physical relationship between two places. **Second,** they evaluate a combination of three factors.

2. Construct topic-transition sentences carefully

As explained in Section B2 above, you should begin each analysis of law, and each paragraph within that analysis, with a topic-transition sentence. This kind of sentence provides readers with a "topic" that identifies the specific substantive focus at that point of the discussion. It also includes a "transition" that connects that topic back to the specific focus of the prior piece of analysis.

When you use these sentences well, you connect the important pieces of your analysis precisely so that readers understand exactly how ideas relate at every step. Without sufficient topic-transition sentences, in contrast, readers fall into "analytical holes" between ideas and those gaps prevent them from gaining a cohesive understanding of what you are trying to convey.

Use the following process to ensure that you have used topic-transition sentences well. Run a quick draft that includes only the first sentence of each paragraph. Read down these sentences, and check whether you have included the important ideas, ordered them logically, connected them precisely, and conveyed them clearly. If you have not, either you are still struggling with the analysis or you have not kept your busy readers in mind as you organized your paragraphs.

As you first craft these topic-transition sentences, you may have a tendency to spell out ideas in more depth and with more words than are necessary to be sure that you are complete and accurate. Therefore, work through each topic-transition sentence again and edit carefully for concision. First, evaluate whether the transition repeats ideas verbatim. If so, edit it carefully so that it still connects ideas precisely but in a more concise form, as is discussed in Chapter 16. Second, evaluate whether the part of the sentence that summarizes the topic of the paragraph could be more concise. You might be able to summarize some ideas even further and edit out words that are unnecessary to express the focus of the paragraph precisely.

For an example of topic-transition sentences, see Comments 20 and 24 to the Sample of a Formal Objective Memorandum in Appendix I.

3. Evaluate paragraph development

To convey analysis well at the paragraph level, you must be sure to identify the focus of the paragraph in the topic-transition sentence and then ensure that the rest of the paragraph develops ideas that are consistent with that focus. Put another way, all succeeding ideas in the paragraph must be relevant to the ideas in the first sentence. If they are not, then you need to revise either the first sentence or the rest of the paragraph, depending on which has gone astray.

Again, sometimes inconsistency between ideas in the topic sentence and the focus of the rest of the paragraph arises from a failure to organize well for busy readers. At other times, this kind of inconsistency will be a clue that, as author, you are still struggling with the analysis yourself.

4. Consider summary sentences or paragraphs

Especially in very complex analyses, you may need summary sentences or paragraphs at the beginning or at the end as you describe particular pieces of the analysis. Such a summary may be necessary to provide readers with a clear roadmap for the next part of the analysis, just as the introductory paragraphs do at the very beginning of the Discussion Section for the whole section—see Chapter 11. At the end of a complex analysis, a summary sentence or paragraph may also be helpful to tie all ideas together. Whether these beginning or ending summaries are helpful or necessary, however, depends upon the delicate balance of helping readers better understand the analysis yet not wasting their time with repetitious ideas. For instance, you'll need to judge whether a strong topic-transition sentence at the beginning of the next paragraph obviates the need for a summary sentence at the end of the prior paragraph.

5. Use headings

When a Discussion Section is long, lawyers often use headings to begin each major piece of the analysis. Each heading summarizes accurately in a phrase or full sentence the analysis that follows.

Readers use headings to read quickly and grasp analysis easily. They are able to skim the headings and gain a summary sense of the analysis when they don't have time to read the entire Discussion Section. Headings also allow readers to quickly locate a particular section and not waste time searching for relevant analysis.

To make them useful, however, you must craft headings carefully. First, headings should not take the place of a topic-transition sentence or summary at the beginning of the analysis that follows. If readers skip a heading, they need the text that follows to be complete on its own. Second, headings should identify the major aspects of the analysis that follows but should be a reasonable length. Very long headings impede readers' ability to read fast and grasp ideas easily. Third, headings should not divide down the analysis into so many individual parts that readers are not easily and quickly able to grasp the ideas and how they connect into a cohesive whole.

To help develop headings, you should consider writing a draft of the Discussion Section without them, verifying that you have included the important ideas and connected them with strong topic-transition sentences. Using that initial draft, proceed to insert headings. Begin by evaluating whether the placement of each heading helps or hinders your readers. Go on to check that the content of each heading summarizes accurately the ideas in the textual analysis that follows. End by making sure each heading is concise and readable.

For an example of a heading, see Comment 10 to the Sample of a Formal Objective Memorandum in Appendix I.

CHECKLIST

☐ Construct an effective analysis of the law based on judicial interpretations:
- Express analysis in general principles;
- Begin by stating the component's "label" and the component's role in the overall test;

- Provide an explanation of the courts' analysis;
- Describe the courts' reasoning;
- Use cases to illustrate the courts' analysis when helpful; and
- Support the analysis with citation to legal authority.

☐ **Develop effective case illustrations:**
- Carefully choose which cases to describe in case illustrations;
- Construct useful case illustrations of several sentences in the text:
  - Place illustrations in the text carefully;
  - Describe necessary aspects of a case;
  - Explain how each illustration relates to the preceding description of analysis;
  - Use consistent content and phrasing;
  - Describe actions by the court consistently with legal conventions;
  - Identify whether ideas are explicit or implicit; and
  - Make clear parties' relationship to the analysis;
- Construct useful parenthetical case illustrations:
  - Place parenthetical illustrations carefully;
  - Tailor the content of parenthetical illustrations to your description of the analysis;
  - Make parenthetical illustrations easy to read and concise; and
  - Construct a series of parenthetical illustrations consistently;
- Understand how to combine longer illustrations in the text with shorter parenthetical illustrations;
- Consider the use of one illustration form or the other at any particular point for any individual case; and
- Organize illustrations by the court's result.

☐ **Consider additional organizational techniques to help guide your readers through the analysis:**
- Evaluate transitions between ideas:
  - Ensure that transitions connect ideas precisely; and
  - Verify that common transitions connect the specific ideas accurately;
- Carefully construct and edit topic-transition sentences;
- Evaluate paragraph development;
- Determine the need for summary sentences or paragraphs; and
- Consider use of headings.

CHAPTER 13

Application-Predictions: Effective Structure

A. INTRODUCTION

As you have already learned, the Discussion Section of an objective memorandum has two goals. First, it must provide an objective analysis of the law for all issues relevant to the client's legal problem. You learned how to develop this type of analysis in Chapters 4 through 9 and how to present it to your readers in Chapters 11 and 12.

In addition, the Discussion Section must explain what that analysis of the law indicates in the client's situation. For each analysis of the law, therefore, you must provide a corresponding application-prediction where you apply the law neutrally to your client's facts and predict how a future court would likely use that law to reach a decision.

To present application-predictions effectively, you first need to understand their analytical foundation in a formal objective memo, which was explained in Chapter 10. Using that understanding, you need to learn a basic approach to placing application-predictions in the overall organization of the Discussion Section, as explained in Section B, and to structuring each individual prediction effectively, which is discussed in Section C. Section D then explains in more depth how to develop effective case comparisons and Section E discusses predictions and counter-predictions. Finally, you should consider a variety of techniques to refine your presentation, as explained in Section F, and be ready to confront more complex organizational issues as addressed in Section G.

B. PLACEMENT OF APPLICATION-PREDICTIONS

As you develop the Discussion Section, you must decide at what point or points to include an application-prediction. In many situations, the logic of how you've already organized the overall Discussion Section will dictate the most effective placement for the application-predictions. As you learned in Chapter 11, once you are beyond the beginning overview paragraph, you should organize your analysis around independent legal issues and then, if necessary, break down those issues into their components and perhaps even into logical pieces of components.

For each legal problem, at some point or points, therefore, you'll have the sense that you should develop an abstract analysis of the current status of the law for that piece and then go on immediately to an application-prediction. There, you'll apply that law to the client's situation and predict the outcome before a future court. By adding the application-prediction immediately after the analysis of the law, you'll provide your readers with a cohesive analysis: As soon as your readers understand your analysis of the law, they will find out what that law indicates on the client's facts.

> **Example of placing application-predictions**
>
> Imagine that you are working with the analysis of a legal issue that is based on three required components. Based on this analysis, in the Discussion Section beyond the overview paragraph, you have organized around the requirements. For each, you included an analysis of the current status of the law and then immediately presented an application-prediction where you applied that law to the client's facts. This organization provides your readers with a cohesive discussion of each requirement: For each requirement, as soon as your readers understand the analysis of the law, they encounter a prediction of whether the client's facts satisfied that requirement or not, or whether it was unclear.
>
> - Introductory paragraph(s)
>
> - Analysis of the law as to first requirement
> - Application-prediction as to first requirement
>
> - Analysis of the law as to second requirement
> - Application-prediction as to second requirement

Section G1 below discusses some additional considerations in placing application-prediction sections in more complex analyses.

C. STRUCTURE OF AN APPLICATION-PREDICTION WITH A SINGLE PREDICTION

As you learned in Chapter 10, when your analysis of the law indicates a reasonably certain outcome in your client's situation, in the corresponding application-prediction, you will need to develop only one prediction that addresses why the future court would likely reach that conclusion. For that prediction, you must include several parts. You must begin by stating your predicted outcome of what the future court would probably conclude on your client's facts, as discussed in Section 1. You must support that predicted outcome with the explanation you provided in the analysis of the law for that issue, as explained in Section 2. As discussed in Section 3, in general you should include comparisons to cases to support your predicted outcome. Section 4 addresses whether to incorporate the courts' reasoning at the end of the prediction. Finally, you should consider supporting your analysis with citation to legal authority, as explained in Section 5.

1. Begin with the predicted outcome

As you begin a single prediction, you should state in the first sentence what a future court would likely conclude on your client's facts. While in other kinds of writing before law school, you may have organized ideas by working up to a final conclusion, the rapid pace and busy nature of law practice requires ordering ideas differently. First, your readers will want to learn the bottom-line for the client immediately, since this idea is so important. Second, this bottom-line outcome for the client sets the stage for your readers to understand more easily the rest of your analysis that explains why the future court would likely reach this outcome.

When stating the predicted outcome, even when you are fairly certain of the result, you should use language that reflects the uncertain nature of legal analysis. All lawyers understand that predicting what a future court will do is not an exact science and that sometimes judges make decisions that appear inexplicable based on a reasonable interpretation of the current law. Most lawyers will therefore expect you to use language that incorporates that uncertainty, such as "probably" or "likely," even when predicting relatively certain outcomes. If you are unsure about the outcome, as discussed in Chapter 10, you must communicate that lack of certainty by providing counter-predictions, which is discussed in Section E below.

> **Example of stating a predicted outcome**
>
> In our client's case, the court will most likely find that our client, the bystander, gained a sensory perception of the negligent act and the resulting injuries of the direct victim. *See Ortiz; Spellman.*

2. Apply your explanation from the analysis of the law to support the predicted outcome

After stating in the first sentence your predicted outcome of what the future court would decide, you must go on to show why the future court would probably reach that result on your client's facts. To do so, you should use that part of your prior discussion of the abstract law that describes your explanation of the courts' analysis and apply that explanation to your client's facts. Your supervising attorney needs this step to check whether your predicted outcome is reasonable. Remember that you are predicting that the future court will use that same explanation to reach its conclusion on your client's facts.

Analytically, therefore, you must be consistent in how you use the explanation in both the analysis of the law and in the application-prediction. Most importantly, you must not change the content as you apply it to your client's facts; otherwise, your readers will have to stop reading and determine which content is accurate. Furthermore, you must not change the phrasing of this idea. If you do, you risk that your readers will waste time figuring out if the change in language reflects a change in substance.

3. Include case comparisons

As you know, when a court makes decisions based on an understanding of the current status of the law from prior cases, it must use these cases to support its decision on the facts of the situation before it. Therefore, in developing an application-prediction, in general you need to compare your client's facts to the facts of those cases to support the outcome that you predict the court will reach. To demonstrate why the future court would view those facts as similar or dissimilar, you would use your explanation from the analysis of the law.

> **Example of case comparisons**
>
> In the example below, the case comparisons—all highlighted in bold—include the facts of the client, the facts of precedent, and the explanation

that demonstrates why the two situations are similar or dissimilar. (See Chapter 12, Section B3, for the corresponding analysis of the law discussion as to this issue.)

In our client's case, the court will most likely find that our client, the bystander, gained a sensory perception of the negligent act and the resulting injuries to the direct victim. *See Ortiz; Spellman.* The court should reach this conclusion on the basis that our client arrived at the scene of his wife's accident immediately after she had been negligently struck by the Defendant's power lawnmower. *See Ortiz; Spellman.* Our client saw his wife's bloody face and gashed arms and legs as she lay moaning on the ground. He rushed over to hold her hand as he heard the sirens of the arriving ambulance and police. He watched the paramedics work to stabilize his wife's condition before they carried her into the ambulance. [*facts of client*] Given what he experienced, our client encountered the vivid injuries of the direct victim within an emergency context that captured the intensity of the event [*explanation*] in a similar manner to the bystander in the *Ortiz* case, whose experience was found sufficient by the court. *See Ortiz.* There, the child entered the scene immediately after a vicious attack had injured his mother and found her hog-tied, with knife-cuts all over her body, and struggling to breathe. *See Ortiz.* The child waited with his mother as she continued to choke until emergency services arrived. *See Ortiz.* [*facts of precedent*]

In contrast, our client's experience [*reference to client's facts above*] was very different from the experience of the bystander in *Freehold*, which did not satisfy the court, because the bystander reached the direct victim so long after the negligent event that the injuries were no longer vivid and the context no longer captured the intensity of the event. [*explanation*] *See Freehold.* In *Freehold*, two days after the negligent accident, the bystander encountered the direct victim at a funeral home where the atmosphere was calm and serene and the body had been prepared for the funeral. *See Freehold.* [*facts of precedent*]

For a more in-depth discussion of developing effective case comparisons, see Section D below. Chapter 10 explains situations where case comparisons may not be necessary in an application-prediction because the facts of precedent cases are not relevant in the courts' analysis of the particular issue.

4. Consider ending with a summary of how the courts' reasoning supports the predicted outcome

As Sections 2 and 3 above make clear, to support your predicted outcome by a future court on that component, you use your explanation of the courts' analysis to compare your client's facts as similar and dissimilar to the facts of precedent. By taking this step, you track the future court's decision-making process since it must justify its decision in your client's situation based on relevant precedent. Once you've done so, you should consider whether you should include the courts' reasoning for that component at the end of the prediction. While the reasoning is not the piece of analysis that the future court will use as it develops the comparisons, the reasoning does remind readers why the court chose its approach in the first place, as you first learned in Chapter 7.

> **Example of ending the application-prediction with the courts' reasoning**
>
> In the example below, a summary sentence reminding the reader of the courts' reasoning for the component is in bold.
>
> In our client's case, the court will most likely find that our client, the bystander, gained a sensory perception of the negligent act and the resulting injuries to the direct victim. *See Ortiz; Spellman.* The court should reach this conclusion on the basis that our client arrived at the scene of his wife's accident immediately after she had been negligently struck by the Defendant's power lawnmower. *See Ortiz; Spellman.* Our client saw his wife's bloody face and gashed arms and legs as she lay moaning on the ground. He rushed over to hold her hand as he heard the sirens of the arriving ambulance and police. He watched the paramedics work to stabilize his wife's condition before they carried her into the ambulance. Given what he experienced, our client encountered the vivid injuries of the direct victim within an emergency context that captured the intensity of the event in a similar manner to the bystander in the *Ortiz* case whose experience was found sufficient by the court. *See Ortiz.* In *Ortiz,* the child entered the scene immediately after a vicious attack had injured his mother and found her hog-tied, with knife-cuts all over her body, and struggling to breathe. *See Ortiz.* The child waited with his mother as she continued to choke until emergency services arrived. *See Ortiz.*
>
> In contrast, our client's experience was very different from the experience of the bystander in *Freehold,* which did not satisfy the court, because the bystander reached the direct victim so long after the negligent event that the injuries were no longer vivid and the

> context no longer captured the intensity of the event. *See Freehold.* In *Freehold,* two days after the negligent accident, the bystander encountered the direct victim's body at a funeral home where the atmosphere was calm and serene and the body had been prepared for the funeral. *See Freehold.* **In our client's situation, therefore, the future court would reason that our client's experience would objectively verify that he was directly reacting to the negligent injuries of the direct victim with resulting severe and genuine emotional distress.** *See Ortiz; Spellman; Freehold.*

5. Support the application-prediction with citation to legal authority

As Chapter 14 discusses, you should consider supporting your ideas in an application-prediction with citation to the relevant legal authority.

> **Example of using citation in an application-prediction**
>
> In the following example, the author supported the predicted outcome with citation to cases. The author used the citation "see," since the predicted outcome is an inference; no case directly discusses the client's situation.
>
> > In our client's case, the court will most likely find that our client, the bystander, gained a sensory perception of the negligent act and the resulting injuries of the direct victim. *See Ortiz; Spellman.*

6. Sample of an application-prediction in a memo

For an example of an application-prediction in a memo conveyed with the techniques described in this section, see Comments 15 through 18 to the Sample of a Formal Objective Memorandum in Appendix I.

D. EFFECTIVE CASE COMPARISONS

As you learned in Section C3 above, in most situations, you must compare your client's facts to the facts of precedent in application-predictions. To develop case comparisons effectively, you first need to select cases a future court likely would use to support its decision, which is explained in Section 1 below. In making that selection, you should consider including comparisons to similar and dissimilar precedent, as discussed in Section 2. For each comparison, you need to include the information a court would use when comparing the client's facts to precedent—that information is described in Section 3.

1. Choose precedent that a future court would likely use

To develop any individual comparison in an application-prediction, you must choose from the cases that were the foundation for the explanation you developed in the analysis of the law. In most situations, the future court will apply that abstract law to your client's situation and should therefore use these same cases as the basis for its decision, either viewing these cases as similar to your client's facts or not.

In some situations, however, you should choose one representative case from a group of potentially relevant cases to be concise. Especially when courts have decided a large number of cases in an area of law, you might have used many of them to develop the analysis of the law. While these cases might have provided a necessary range of factual situations to help your readers understand the analysis, they might not all be necessary to demonstrate how the future court would use that explanation in the corresponding application-prediction.

In choosing a representative case, you should consider the following, knowing that reasonable lawyers might reach somewhat different conclusions about the "best" case to use in any individual comparison. These considerations are generally the same as those that you used to choose relevant precedent to illustrate your explanation in the analysis of law, as you first learned in Chapter 12.

You would begin by evaluating the level of the court that had decided each case; all things being equal, the future court would rely more on the analysis of the highest appeals court of the jurisdiction than on that of an intermediate appeals court, and certainly than that of a trial court. You would also evaluate the depth and specificity of each case's analysis relevant to the issue under consideration. A better-developed decision of the intermediate appeals court might be more helpful for the comparison—and the future court would be more likely to use it—than a decision of the highest appeals court where the court failed to explain its analysis in much depth. Finally, you would give weight to whether the facts that supported each court's decision were very detailed and therefore would be the most helpful as a comparison to the facts of your client.

2. Include comparisons to similar and dissimilar precedent when possible

In general, you should include comparisons to similar and dissimilar precedent in any given prediction, assuming that you have relevant cases in both categories. In most instances, you should compare to similar precedent first and then compare to dissimilar second. Readers tend to understand comparisons in this order more easily.

3. Provide the information a court would use to compare the client's facts to precedent

You must compare the relevant facts of your client to the relevant facts of precedent. To demonstrate why the future court would view these two sets of facts as similar or dissimilar, you must use the courts' analysis from prior cases as you explained it in your analysis of the law for that issue.

> **Example of the basic parts of a case comparison**
>
> The future court will find that the [*facts of the client*] are similar to the [*facts of the relevant prior case*], which the court found sufficient [*decision in prior case*], since in both situations [*explanation from the analysis of the law relevant at this point in the application-prediction*].

> **Example of a case comparison based on specific analysis**
>
> Imagine that, in the analysis of the law, the author stated that the courts required a "short distance" between two structures. In analyzing the relevant cases, the author developed an explanation that a short distance was one that would allow a reasonable person to easily walk from one place to the other. The following example illustrates how to compare the client's facts to the facts of a case and to use this explanation to demonstrate why those facts are similar:
>
> > The future court will reason that the distance of one mile between the two locations in our client's situation [*client's facts*] is similar to the distance of half a mile that was found sufficient by the

> court in Case A [*facts of precedent*], because both distances would allow a reasonable person to easily walk from one place to the other [*explanation*].
>
> In the above example, the author has included the information that the court would use to make the comparison: The client's legally significant facts; the legally significant facts from the precedent; and the relevant analysis, as expressed in the explanation from the analysis of the law. All of these ideas are discussed in the sections below.

If you do not include all of the necessary information when providing case comparisons, your readers must stop reading the comparison, look elsewhere in the memo for the needed ideas, bring those ideas back to the comparison, and then reread the comparison to figure out the specific point being made. Busy law practice readers will be frustrated in this situation because it wastes their valuable time. More importantly, they may not fully understand why the comparison supports the predicted outcome.

a. The legally significant facts of the client's situation

In each comparison, you must begin with the legally significant facts of your client. Legally significant facts are ones that you predict the future court will use in deciding to view your client's situation as similar, or dissimilar, to the facts of precedent, given your explanation of the particular aspect of the analysis under consideration.

As you develop a comparison, therefore, be sure that you include all these facts and describe them clearly and accurately. Remember that your readers will likely be less conversant with your client's situation than you are as author. While they will have encountered the client's facts in the Facts Section at the beginning of the memo, in many memos that section will be pages before any application-prediction in the Discussion Section. More importantly, your readers will be relying on your decisions as to which facts are legally significant since you have analyzed the legal problem but they have likely not.

b. The legally significant facts of precedent

In each comparison, you must also include the legally significant facts from the precedent that you are using in the comparison. These facts are ones that the prior court used to reach its decision on the particular aspect of the analysis under consideration. They are therefore the facts that you predict the future court will use in deciding to view that opinion as similar, or dissimilar, to the client's situation.

As you develop the comparison, you must describe these facts accurately and clearly enough for your readers who likely will not be bringing the same working knowledge of the prior cases that you have as author. While your readers have just read the illustrations of precedent in the analysis of the law, they likely encountered these cases for the first time at that point. They will therefore not necessarily remember the facts of each case when they reach the application-prediction, which may be paragraphs or even pages further on in the memo.

c. Your explanation from the analysis of the law

To demonstrate why the future court would view facts as similar or not, you must use the explanation you developed in the analysis of the law for the issue. (For a discussion of the courts' "explanation," review Chapter 7, Section D2c, and Chapter 12, Section B3.) First-year law students often make the analytical mistake of comparing facts without making clear why the facts are similar or not. Encountering this type of comparison, readers have no idea as to why the future court would view the comparison of facts in a certain manner.

Example of unclear versus clear case comparisons

Again, using the example from above, imagine that you are working with one aspect of the courts' analysis that focuses on the distance between two locations. In your explanation of the courts' analysis, you make clear that the courts evaluate the distance to determine whether a reasonable person could easily walk from one location to the other.

Unclear comparison that compares two sets of facts without the explanation from the analysis of the law:

In the comparison below, your readers would not understand why a distance of one mile between two locations would be similar to the distance of half a mile that was found sufficient, because the comparison does not include the reason *why* these two facts are similar, based on the prior courts' analysis as you expressed it in your explanation in the analysis of the law.

> The future court would view the distance of one mile between the two locations in our client's situation [*client's facts*] as similar to the distance of half a mile that was found sufficient by the court in Case A [*facts of precedent*].

> ***Clear comparison that demonstrates why the two facts are similar, using the explanation from the analysis of the law:***
>
> In this comparison, your reader would understand why a distance of one mile between two locations would be similar to the distance of half a mile because the comparison includes the reason why the two facts are similar, based on the explanation in the analysis of law.
>
> > The future court would view the distance of one mile between the two locations in our client's situation [*client's facts*] as similar to the distance of half a mile found sufficient by the court in Case A [*facts of precedent*], because both distances would allow a reasonable person to easily walk from one place to the other [*explanation*].

You must use the same explanation — as to its content and phrasing — in both the analysis of the law and the application-prediction. If you discover that you have not, you must stop and think. Perhaps you have used the same content but just phrased that content inconsistently. If so, you'll need to choose the best phrasing and use it consistently so that your readers easily recognize the idea in both places. In the alternative, perhaps you have come to a more sophisticated understanding of your explanation as you applied it in the application-prediction. If so, go back and revise how you described that idea in the analysis of the law.

E. STRUCTURE OF APPLICATION-PREDICTIONS WITH PREDICTIONS AND COUNTER-PREDICTIONS

As you learned in Chapter 10, you will likely face legal questions where you won't be able to predict with a comfortable level of certainty what a future court would conclude on your client's facts since reasonable courts could reach different outcomes. When developing an application-prediction in this situation, you must fully explain the possible alternatives to your readers. To make the alternatives clear, you should develop your prediction of the more likely result in your client's situation and the necessary counter-predictions of potentially different results.

In many problems, you'll need to develop a prediction and just one counter-prediction because the court could decide either one way or the other. However, in more complex analyses, you may decide that several outcomes are reasonably possible. In that situation, you'll need to develop your prediction of the most likely outcome and then the other possible counter-predictions. In both these circumstances, you should begin with a statement that informs your readers of the lack of certainly in the outcome. You then need to explain each prediction and counter-prediction separately; fully develop each prediction and counter-prediction; and consider the order of how you present the prediction and possible counter-predictions.

1. Begin with a statement that the outcome is unclear

Whether you have a prediction and one or several counter-predictions, your busy law practice readers need to know at the very beginning of an application-prediction that you are not certain what outcome a future court will reach. You don't want to provide a prediction that suggests one outcome and then surprise your readers with a counter-prediction that supports another result later in the discussion. Thus, you should begin any application-prediction that includes counter-predictions with a statement that the result is uncertain.

> **Example of stating that the outcome before the future court is unclear**
>
> It is unclear whether the future court will decide that our client satisfies the requirement.

2. Develop the prediction and counter-predictions separately

Once you have explained that the outcome is uncertain, you must provide your readers with a cohesive analysis of each reasonable possibility separately. If you develop the prediction and each counter-prediction separately, you will help your readers quickly understand why reasonable courts could come to different conclusions. In contrast, merging the prediction with the possible counter-predictions will leave your readers with a fragmented analysis. They will need to spend their precious time piecing ideas together as they struggle to understand the future court's reasoning process in reaching each possible outcome.

As author, you will also find that you will develop a more thorough and accurate analysis for each potential outcome if you discuss the prediction and each possible counter-prediction separately. By separating out your discussion in this manner, you'll be less likely to miss critical steps in the future court's reasoning process in reaching each possible decision.

> **Example of presenting a prediction and corresponding counter-prediction separately**
>
> *Prediction:*
>
> The future court will probably conclude that our client does satisfy the requirement . . . . [Go on to apply the explanation of law to the client's facts to support why the court would probably reach this outcome.]
>
> *Corresponding counter-prediction:*
>
> The future court might conclude, however, that our client does not satisfy the requirement . . . . [Go on to apply the explanation of law to the client's facts to support why the court might reach this alternative outcome.]

3. Develop the prediction and counter-predictions fully

Generally, you should develop the prediction and any necessary counter-predictions with the same detail as a single prediction, which was explained in Section C above. Therefore, you should begin with a statement that makes the prediction or counter-prediction clear. You should go on and support that prediction or counter-prediction by applying to your client's facts the relevant explanation that you developed in the analysis of the law. In general, you then need to demonstrate how the future court would use that explanation to view the client's facts as similar to the facts of cases reaching the same outcome as predicted and dissimilar to the facts of cases that reached the opposite outcome, unless the issue doesn't require comparisons as discussed in Chapter 10.

4. Decide on the order of the prediction and counter-predictions

In an application-prediction section that requires one or more counter-predictions, you should consider the order of how you present the prediction and each counter-prediction. This order often depends on the logic of your analysis. Some analyses may allow you to begin with the prediction of the outcome that you think is most likely, and then move to relevant counter-predictions. However, other analyses may require you to begin by explaining a result that is not the most likely, moving to the most likely result later in the application-prediction. No matter what order you decide is necessary based on the analysis, you must clearly communicate to your readers at the beginning of the application-prediction that the result is uncertain so that the readers are prepared for the relevant counter-predictions, as explained in Section 1 above. You must also make clear which result you think is most likely. See Chapter 10, which discusses making that judgment.

> **Example of expressing uncertainty, the most likely result, and the alternative result**
>
> The language expressing the uncertainty of the result and the language identifying the most likely result and the possible result is in bold.
>
> *Language expressing uncertainty and introducing the most likely result:*
>
> > **It is unclear whether** our client will satisfy the requirement. The court **would most likely conclude** that our client does satisfy the requirement. . . . [Go on to fully develop the prediction.]
>
> *Language introducing the alternative result:*
>
> > **However, the future court could decide** that our client does not satisfy the requirement. . . . [Go on to fully develop this counter-prediction.]

5. Sample of an application-prediction based on a prediction and counter-prediction

For an example of an application-prediction based on a prediction and counter-prediction, see Comments 26 through 28 to the Sample of a Formal Objective Memorandum in Appendix I.

F. ADDITIONAL ORGANIZATIONAL TECHNIQUES

As you develop each application-prediction, you should use the same organizational techniques to help your readers that you used in the analysis of the law—techniques that were discussed in Chapter 12. In a relatively simple analysis, you may find organizing an application-prediction easy because you'll only need a few sentences to explain the important ideas. In a complex analysis, in contrast, you may need to develop paragraphs of analysis where you'll need to take extra care in organizing ideas for your readers in a prediction or counter-predictions.

1. Summaries

a. Beginning "roadmap" paragraph or sentence

After you set out the predicted outcome for the client in the first sentence, consider going on immediately to provide your readers with a "roadmap" paragraph or sentence that summarizes overall how a court would use all the parts of your explanation in the analysis of the law to reach that outcome. While in simple analyses you may be able to skip this step, in complex analyses readers need a cohesive overview that summarizes all the pieces of your explanation and how they fit together. With this overview, readers are then better able to follow the rest of the section as it moves from one piece of the explanation to the next.

For a summary to adequately prepare the readers, however, it must order and connect ideas consistently with how the rest of the discussion orders and connects those ideas. The whole point to the summary at the beginning is to prepare readers for the specific application of the different parts of your explanation that come afterward. If these two aspects of your discussion are inconsistent, readers will understandably be confused.

For an example, see Section G3 below.

b. Ending summary sentence or paragraph

When drafting a prediction or counter-prediction, once you've stated your predicted result, applied the explanation from your analysis of the law to support that predicted result, and included case comparisons, you might end with a summary sentence or brief paragraph. This summary might mirror the beginning of the prediction or counter-prediction where you set out the outcome the court would, or might, reach and why the court would reach that outcome.

When deciding to include such a summary, think about whether your readers need a synopsis at the end to "tie up" the preceding discussion. For complex analyses, a summary might help your readers. For simple analyses, it probably would not. In the middle, you'll have to make a judgment call—one that reasonable lawyers in the same situation might approach differently.

2. Transitions

Be sure that you use precise transitions throughout that connect ideas accurately between major pieces of the application-prediction, between paragraphs, between sentences, and within sentences. Doing so creates an application-prediction where all parts clearly join together to create a cohesive picture of why the court would reach the predicted outcome for the client based on your explanation from the analysis of the law. See the more complete discussion of transitions in Chapter 12.

3. Topic-transition sentences

Use strong topic-transition sentences at the beginning of each application-prediction and at the beginning of each paragraph. In an application-prediction, these topic-transition sentences will be a conclusion based on the law as applied to the client's situation instead of a discussion of abstract general principles as in the analysis of the law. In both places, however, the topic-transition sentences should provide readers with the same assistance by focusing on the precise topic of the next piece of the discussion and connecting back to the immediately preceding piece. In an application-prediction, these sentences must also be consistent with any initial summary as to both content and how that content is phrased, as was discussed in Section 1 above.

Near the end of your writing process, run a quick draft of all topic-transition sentences for each prediction and counter-prediction. Evaluate carefully—from your readers' point of view—whether you included all major ideas; whether you ordered those major ideas logically; and whether you connected them precisely.

4. Paragraph development

Be sure to develop paragraphs cohesively. The focus of each paragraph should be in the topic sentence, which in the application-prediction will be a statement of law as applied to the client's situation. The rest of the paragraph should build on and develop that focus, just as you learned for analyses of the law in Chapter 12.

G. STRUCTURE OF COMPLEX APPLICATION-PREDICTIONS

The sections below discuss some important organizational issues when you are applying more complex analysis in an application-prediction. Section 1 discusses placing an application-prediction in the Discussion Section when the analysis does not indicate a clear choice. Section 2 addresses structuring a prediction or counter-prediction based on complex analysis. Section 3 explains placing comparisons in a prediction that is based on complex analysis.

1. Placing an application-prediction when the analysis does not indicate a clear organizational choice

As you develop the Discussion Section, you must decide at what point or points to include an application-prediction. As was discussed in Section B above, you should begin by looking to the overall organization of the analysis because that organization will likely indicate the most effective placement.

However, you'll encounter more complex situations where your choice will not be so clear. In fact, in some circumstances, reasonable lawyers structuring the same analysis might reach different conclusions by balancing the relative strengths and weaknesses of several possible organizations.

> **Example of options for placing an application-prediction**
>
> Imagine that you are working with an analysis where the courts use a totality test based on a combination of several factors. Here, you might encounter competing considerations in choosing where to place an application-prediction.
>
> On the one hand, you might decide to develop the analysis of the law fully before applying any part of that analysis to your client's situation. Under this organization, in your explanation you would describe the totality test and go on to explain each factor in the combination in-depth, all of which you would do in the abstract, without applying any ideas to your client's facts. When that was complete, you would only then apply that entire analysis to the client's situation. On the other hand, you might decide to describe the overall totality test and then break down your analysis into components, each of which discussed a separate factor in the abstract and then immediately applied that individual factor to the client's situation.
>
> Both of these organizations would have strengths and weaknesses. The first would provide a more cohesive discussion of both the analysis of the law and what that analysis indicated for the client's situation. However, readers would wait a fairly long time to gain any sense of what the totality test indicated for the client's situation. In law practice, readers are going to be anxious to get to the result for the client.
>
> The second organization would provide readers with a quicker understanding of what the factors indicated on the client's situation. However, readers would need more summaries throughout so that they could understand how the combination of factors played out in the client's situation. Under this organization, therefore, you would have to balance avoiding excessive repetition on the one hand yet providing a cohesive analysis for readers on the other.

> One of these organizations might be "best," given your analysis from the cases and given the facts of the client. More likely, however, you would simply need to choose one organization, and then capitalize on its strengths and minimize its weaknesses

2. Structuring a prediction or counter-prediction based on complex analysis

How you break down and organize a prediction or counter-prediction in an application-prediction should generally be consistent with how you broke down and organized the ideas in the analysis of the law beforehand. Consistency of content and organization in both sections helps your readers easily understand the analysis quickly and accurately.

> **Example of structuring a prediction and a counter-prediction consistently**
>
> Imagine that you are working on an analysis with two separate pieces to your explanation of the courts' overall requirement. In developing an analysis of the law in your memo, you decide that you should organize around each of these pieces.
>
> *Analysis of the law:*
>
> The court's overall requirement includes two pieces:
>
> - Explanation of courts' analysis as to first piece.
> - Explanation of courts' analysis as to second piece.
>
> Assume further that the application-prediction that follows this analysis of the law is based on a single prediction that the future court would probably conclude that your client would satisfy the overall requirement because the client would satisfy both pieces of the courts' analysis. You would therefore organize the prediction in the same manner as you organized the corresponding analysis of the law:
>
> *Application-prediction:*
>
> The client will probably satisfy the court's overall requirement because:
>
> - Why the client would probably satisfy the first piece.
> - Why the client would probably satisfy the second piece.

3. Placing comparisons in a prediction or counter-prediction that is based on complex analysis

You need to incorporate any necessary comparisons of your client's situation to precedent at logical points as you develop each prediction or counter-prediction in an application-prediction. Just as with illustrations of precedent in the analysis of the law for a particular topic—see Chapter 12—comparisons in a prediction or counter-prediction should come at the precise place that they support a particular piece of the overall analysis. In simple analyses, you'll be able to immediately determine the best place for comparisons. In complex analyses, however, you may need to stop and think about placing them most effectively for your readers. In particular, you want to avoid leaving busy readers matching up parts of the analysis with the corresponding comparisons.

> **Example of comparing helpful versus unhelpful placement of case comparisons**
>
> Imagine that you are working on the same analysis as in the example in Section 2 above: A requirement that is based on two pieces of the courts' analysis with a single prediction that the client would probably satisfy both pieces of the analysis.
>
> In the prediction, you would need to incorporate comparisons to precedent in a manner that would help your readers easily grasp why the court would reach the predicted outcome on each piece of the courts' analysis. The outlines below, therefore, contrast a helpful and an unhelpful organization in this regard.
>
> *Helpful Organization*:
>
> In the organization below, readers would be able to understand immediately the predicted result that the client would satisfy the requirement; that the client would satisfy each of the two pieces of that analysis; and how the future court would reason to each of those conclusions, including how it would support its decision with case comparisons.
>
> - <u>Prediction that the future court will probably find that the client satisfies the overall requirement</u>
> - <u>Summary</u> of the future court's analysis as to why the client satisfies the overall requirement—see Section F1a above
>   - First Piece of the courts' analysis:
>   - Predicted result that client will satisfy the First Piece
>   - Application of explanation from the analysis of the law to support the predicted result as to the First Piece

- Comparisons of client's facts with cases supporting this predicted result as to the First Piece, including
  - a comparison to facts of similar precedent as to the First Piece
  - a comparison to facts of dissimilar precedent as to the First Piece
- Second Piece of the courts' analysis:
  - Predicted result that client will satisfy the Second Piece
  - Application of explanation from the analysis of the law to support the predicted result as to the Second Piece
  - Comparisons of client's facts with cases supporting this predicted result as to the Second Piece, including
    - a comparison to facts of similar precedent as to the Second Piece
    - a comparison to facts of dissimilar precedent as to the Second Piece

Unhelpful Organization:

In contrast, the organization below would be unhelpful since readers would encounter an analysis of each piece of the courts' analysis but would need to match up the overall analysis of each with the corresponding comparisons that came only at the very end of the prediction. These comparisons are highlighted in bold. This organization would waste readers' time and, even more importantly, make it more difficult for them to easily and quickly grasp why the future court would reach the predicted result.

- Prediction that the future court will probably find that the client satisfies the overall requirement
  - First Piece of the courts' analysis:
    - Predicted result that the client will satisfy the First Piece
    - Application of explanation from the analysis of the law to support the predicted result as to the First Piece
    - **Comparisons to precedent NOT INCLUDED HERE (see below)**
  - Second Piece of the courts' analysis:
    - Predicted result that the client will satisfy the Second Piece
    - Application of explanation from the analysis of the law to support the predicted result as to the Second Piece
    - **Comparisons to precedent NOT INCLUDED HERE (see below)**
  - Comparisons of client's facts to facts of precedent
    - Comparisons relevant to the First Piece
      - **Comparison to similar precedent**
      - **Comparison to dissimilar precedent**
    - Comparisons relevant to the Second Piece
      - Comparison to similar precedent
      - Comparison to dissimilar precedent

CHECKLIST

☐ Determine placement of application-predictions by considering the overall organization of the analysis of the law.

☐ Use a basic approach to structure a single prediction:
- Begin with the predicted outcome;
- Apply your explanation from the analysis of the law to demonstrate why the future court would reach the predicted outcome;
- Include comparisons of the client's facts to the facts of precedent;
- Consider ending with a sentence that reminds your readers of the courts' reasoning for that component; and
- Consider supporting your analysis with citation to legal authority.

☐ Make case comparisons effective:
- Choose precedent that would likely be the basis for the future court's decision;
- Include comparisons to both similar and dissimilar precedent; and
- Include information a court would use when comparing the client's facts to precedent:
  - The legally significant facts of the client;
  - The legally significant facts of precedent; and
  - Your explanation from the analysis of the law.

☐ Explain both predictions and any necessary counter-predictions:
- Identify the unclear outcome at the beginning of an application-prediction;
- Develop the prediction and any counter-predictions separately;
- Develop the prediction and any counter-predictions fully; and
- Consider the order of the prediction and any counter-predictions.

☐ Consider additional organizational techniques to help guide readers through a prediction:
- Consider using summary "roadmap" and ending paragraphs or sentences;
- Choose accurate transitions;
- Construct effective topic-transition sentences; and
- Develop paragraphs effectively.

☐ Organize application-predictions based on complex analysis:
- Decide where to place an application-prediction when the analysis does not indicate a clear organizational choice;
- Structure a prediction or counter-prediction consistently with the analysis; and
- Place case comparisons at logical points in a prediction or counter-prediction.

CHAPTER 14

Citation to Legal Authority

A. INTRODUCTION

In most objective writing, including formal objective memos to supervisors, you must cite to sufficient legal authority to support your analysis. These "cites" help convince your readers to accept your analysis of the law and what that law indicates for the client.

This chapter discusses important issues that you'll confront as you craft these citations. It does not discuss technical aspects of legal citation in any detail, since citation manuals, such as *The Bluebook* or the *ALWD Guide to Legal Citation,* fully explain these rules.

B. ANALYTICAL DECISIONS

In prior chapters, you learned how to analyze statutes and judicial opinions, both to develop an abstract analysis of the current status of the law and to apply that law to your client's situation and predict the result, or results, before a future court. As you communicate these steps of analysis in the Discussion Section of your memo, you must provide your readers with accurate and complete citation to the relevant sources of law.

1. Choosing the legal authority

You will be making an important analytical decision each time you choose the legal authority to cite in support of a particular assertion in your analysis.

a. Cite to mandatory primary authority

You must cite to the mandatory primary authority in the jurisdiction that is relevant to your client's issue. You would only cite to persuasive primary legal authority, or secondary authority based on an author's commentary on the law, when you decided that those additional references were necessary, given your particular analysis. For instance, citation to persuasive cases from another jurisdiction would be necessary if you had relied on these cases to fill in gaps in the law of your own jurisdiction, as was discussed in Chapters 8 and 9.

b. Cite to the "best" mandatory primary authority

In deciding the mandatory primary legal authority from your jurisdiction that you should include in your citations, you must choose the authority that "best" supports each individual assertion in your description of the analysis.

i. Constitutions, statutes, or regulations

In some legal problems, part or all of your analysis will be based on the ideas as set forth in a statute, as discussed in Chapters 4 and 5. In this situation, you would support each assertion of analysis with citation to the relevant part of the statute. The same would be true for analysis based on a constitution or regulation.

ii. Court decisions

In other legal problems, part or all of your analysis will be based on ideas as set forth in court decisions where the courts were interpreting a constitution, a statute, a regulation, or their own common law, as discussed in Chapters 6 through 8. When working with court decisions, you may encounter a situation where you legitimately have only one decision that supports a particular assertion of analysis. In that circumstance, you would cite only to that one decision.

More often, however, you'll be working with a group of relevant cases and will need to choose to cite to the "best" cases by considering some combination of the following:

- The level of the court deciding each opinion;
- The depth and explicit nature of each court's analysis;
- The date of decision for each opinion; and
- The consistency between the result in each opinion and your assertion of analysis.

You would begin by working with the decisions by the highest appeals court in your jurisdiction, since these cases would have the most authority. Within this group of decisions, you would evaluate the depth of each court's explicit analysis. A case will provide the best support for an assertion when that case fully develops those ideas explicitly. As part of your final decision as to the cases to cite, you would probably use more recent cases than older ones, although the strength of the reasoning would be your primary guide.

In some problems, however, the cases that developed the relevant analysis in the most helpful manner might be intermediate appeals court cases (or in rare instances even trial court decisions if the court issued a written opinion). In that circumstance, choosing a combination of highest and intermediate appeals court cases might provide the most effective foundation of support.

In some legal problems, you would be working with analysis that was in part based on the courts' explicit analysis and in part based on analysis that was implicit. When supporting implicit analysis, you would choose the cases where the implicit ideas tested back on the cases' facts, results, and explicit reasoning in the soundest manner, as was discussed in Chapter 7.

Finally, you would also, to some degree, base your choice of cases to cite on whether the result in any particular case was consistent with your assertion of analysis. Put another way, if you were analyzing how to satisfy a particular aspect of the analysis, you would initially consider citing to cases where the court found the situation before it to be sufficient as opposed to one where the court reached the opposite conclusion. Of course, here again, other considerations might come into play. If the case or cases that discussed the analysis in the most helpful manner were those that reached an opposite conclusion from your assertion, you would likely cite those cases as the best support.

Overall, therefore, choosing the cases to cite for any particular legal assertion will be an "art and not a science" because you will likely be working with a range of potentially competing analytical considerations. In many instances, therefore, even with an identical assertion of analysis, different lawyers could craft citations that sufficiently supported the analysis yet were based on somewhat different combinations of cases.

2. Citing sufficient legal authority

In general, you should cite to sufficient legal authority after each sentence in the analysis of the current status of the law portions of the Discussion Section of your memo, which is discussed in Section a below. You should strongly consider doing so also in the application-prediction sections in every instance where a sentence is applying law to the client's factual situation, which is discussed in Section b.

a. Analyses of the law

You must cite to the sources of law that support your analysis of the law portions of the Discussion Section after each sentence, whether describing your analysis or, if appropriate, illustrating that analysis with case descriptions.

i. Providing sufficient support for a description of analysis

Generally, as you develop analysis of the law portions of the Discussion Section, you must cite after each sentence to the sources of law that support your description of the analysis. Your law practice readers need to be confident that you based these ideas on a sufficient foundation of legal authority in the jurisdiction.

When you are working with analysis based on a constitution, statute, or regulation, you will simply cite to that piece of authority. When you are working with ideas based on a group of cases, you should cite to the two to three cases that best support your ideas, as discussed in Section 1bii above. Encountering two to three cases, your readers will feel confident that you have sufficient precedent to back up your assertion but will not be overwhelmed by too many citations.

You also must use "pinpoint" cites that identify the specific place, or places, where the authority supports the ideas in the text of the sentence. When citing a statute, you would include the relevant part of the statute. For a case, you would determine the specific page or pages where the court discussed the idea in its analysis.

Sometimes you'll choose a pinpoint cite easily. At other times, you will struggle to reach a decision as to the exact place in a piece of authority that supports your ideas in the most precise manner. Making this choice is very important for your law practice readers, though, since they need this information to easily locate where the authority supports your analysis.

ii. Providing sufficient support for case illustrations

When you include a case illustration, as discussed in Chapter 12, you must include pinpoint cites to the specific page or pages of the case that support each idea. When working with a case illustration of several sentences in the text, you must provide pinpoint cites for each sentence since in many situations the court's decision, analysis, and facts will all be located on different pages of the case. When illustrating a case with a parenthetical, you must provide pinpoint cites that include the specific page or pages that support all ideas included in the parenthetical.

b. Application-predictions

A difference of opinion exists in the legal profession concerning whether to cite to legal authority in application-prediction portions of a Discussion

Section in an objective memo. When you arrive at a new work place, therefore, be sure to determine the practice of the office in this regard.

Many lawyers reason that the same citation rules should apply in an application-prediction as in the preceding analysis of the law. These lawyers reason that, by encountering citations to legal authority in the application-prediction, law practice readers are more easily able to grasp exactly how the law applies to the client's situation and to go directly to the particular place in a piece of authority that supports the analysis. Therefore, these lawyers would expect citation to legal authority for any sentence that is "law as applied to" the client's situation, but would not expect citations for any sentence that simply describes the client's facts.

However, some lawyers don't see the need for citation in application-predictions. They reason that, since the preceding analysis of the law fully documents the ideas with sufficient citations to legal authority, readers don't need citations as support when authors apply their analysis to the client's situation. These lawyers believe that, not only are these citations unnecessary analytically, they also contribute to a memo that is less concise than is desirable for busy law practice readers.

3. Using citation signals

A citation signal is a word or phrase that is placed right before a citation to legal authority. These signals inform law practice readers about the precise relationship between assertion of analysis in the text of the sentence and the legal authority that is cited to support that assertion. Section a discusses the most commonly used signals for a citation in objective writing: No signal at all and the "see" signal. Three other potentially useful signals — "see also," "e.g.," and "compare . . . with . . ." — are discussed in Section b.

a. No signal as compared to the "see" signal

When you use no signal before a citation, you are informing your readers that the cited authority explicitly discusses the ideas from the preceding sentence of text. For instance, you would not use a signal if the text contains a quote, since a quote is verbatim language from the authority.

In contrast, you would use the "see" signal when you want to convey to readers that you have made an inference between the ideas in the sentence and what the legal authority actually says. For instance, you would always use the "see" signal when the ideas in the analysis are implicit in the case or cases being cited. The "see" signal informs readers that these ideas are supported by the cases in your judgment, but that they are not explicitly discussed on the page of any cited case.

Analogously, when you cite in an application-prediction, you would always use "see" before citation to legal authority. You would be making an inference in this situation because no piece of legal authority discusses how the law applies to a client's particular facts.

b. Some additional citation signals: "see also," "e.g.," and "compare . . . with . . . ."

You may also find a few other signals useful in conveying analysis in objective writing: "See also," "e.g.," and "compare . . . with . . . ."

"See also" tells a reader that the authority that is cited afterwards is "additional authority" and may be helpful. You would use this signal in the analysis of the law portions of the Discussion Section, for instance, when you illustrate one or more cases in several sentences in the text followed by one or more case illustrations in parentheticals, as is discussed in Chapter 12. Using this combination of case illustrations, you would first describe one case in the longer form of several sentences. At the end of that illustration, and after the citation to that case, you would use the citation signal "see also" and include an illustration of one or more additional cases in parentheticals. For an example of the use of "see also," see the Sample of a Formal Objective Memorandum in Appendix I.

The citation signal "e.g.," which means "for example," can play an important role when you are working with a large number of cases. At certain points, you might want to inform your law practice readers that many court decisions support an assertion in the text and that you've chosen to cite only two or three. This signal is useful when used at specific points to emphasize to readers the breadth of supporting authority; overused, however, it loses that impact. "See" and "see also" can be added in those instances where you are making an inference, or providing additional support, and then the signal becomes "see, e.g." or "see also, e.g." For an example of the use of "e.g.," see the Sample of a Formal Objective Memorandum in Appendix I.

The signal "compare . . . with . . ." may be useful to compare two or more legal authorities in parenthetical illustrations. For example, you could use this signal to contrast an illustration of a case in which the court reached one result with an illustration of a case in which the court came to a different result, as was discussed in Chapter 12, Section C6. For a specific example of "compare . . . with . . . ," see the Sample of a Formal Objective Memorandum in Appendix I.

C. TECHNIQUES TO INCORPORATE CITATION DURING DRAFTING

You need to consider when to incorporate citations during the different stages of drafting your memo that are discussed in Chapter 2. Everyone should confront the analytical decisions about working with citations, discussed in Section B above, beginning with the preliminary drafting stage and continuing through the final presentational stage.

However, you should consider when to stop and ensure that each citation is in correct form. On the one hand, you might be distracted during the preliminary drafting stage to focus on developing and structuring your analysis and at the same time inserting citations in correct form. If so, other than quickly noting sources that support your ideas, you would not address your citation in any complete manner until late in the preliminary drafting stage or during the final presentational stage.

On the other hand, you could benefit from focusing on more complete citation as you develop your analysis throughout the preliminary drafting stage. Some individuals like to change focus for a few minutes on citation and don't find it distracting. In fact, in some instances they discover that working on citation helps to develop ideas in the analysis. Such individuals only need to put finishing touches on their citation form during the final presentational stage.

D. PLAGIARISM CONSIDERATIONS

You will be aware from your prior work and academic experiences that you must not plagiarize when you express ideas in writing. In most nonlegal contexts, if you take unique ideas from another source, you must give credit to that source by citing to it. In addition, if you take actual language from another source, you must give credit by using quotation marks around the language in the text as well as citing to that source.

In expressing analysis in an objective memorandum, however, you should differentiate between taking ideas from primary authority — the "law" — and secondary sources that are commentaries on the law by specific authors, a distinction that you first learned about in Chapter 3.

1. Secondary authority

You must avoid plagiarizing from secondary authority sources that comment on the law, such as law reviews and treatises, because the ideas in these sources come from the authors. When you use paraphrased ideas from this type of source, you must cite to the place or places where you found the ideas. When you use verbatim language, you must use quote marks and cite to the place or places where you found those ideas.

2. Primary authority

As you know, primary authority is the "law"—e.g., a statute or a case. The legal community is divided as to whether a lawyer is plagiarizing in the following two situations:

- When the lawyer uses ideas from a piece of primary authority and does not cite to the authority; or
- When the lawyer uses verbatim language from primary authority but doesn't use quotation marks and doesn't include a citation to the specific place where that language is found.

a. Authors' viewpoint

The authors believe that you would *not* be plagiarizing if you used verbatim language from primary authority in a legal memorandum and didn't quote it or even attribute it to the particular primary authority source. They also believe that you would *not* be plagiarizing in this context if you used paraphrased ideas from primary authority and didn't cite to the authority where you found those ideas. Why? Because the law belongs to all citizens, and therefore ideas and language from sources of that law don't belong to the authors—for instance, judges or legislators.

Even though you would not be plagiarizing if you failed to cite in these situations, you must provide sufficient citation to the primary sources where you located your ideas—whether those ideas are summarized or used verbatim—for the reasons discussed above in Section B. Good lawyers know that they must support their ideas—their analysis—with sufficient citation in legal memoranda, whether written to a work supervisor or to a judge or to anyone else. Otherwise, the document will not effectively convince readers to accept and follow its recommendations.

In Chapter 4, you learned that you need to use quotation marks around verbatim language from a statute, based on general conventions in law practice as opposed to concerns about plagiarizing.

b. Contrary viewpoint

You could find, however, that you are writing an objective memo for someone in law practice who believes that taking ideas and language from primary authority is the same as taking ideas and language from secondary authority. In this situation, you must use the same rules you've always used to avoid plagiarism. While good citation practices would result in your citing sufficiently anyway, you would use quotation marks around all verbatim language from primary authority.

CHECKLIST

☐ **Provide accurate and complete citation in the Discussion Section:**
  - Choose the legal authority to cite:
    - Use mandatory primary legal authority over persuasive authority when possible; and
    - Determine the best primary authority;
  - Use sufficient legal authority to support all ideas in analysis of law portions;
  - Consider citing in application-predictions; and
  - Use appropriate citation signals to identify the precise relationship between an assertion in the text of the sentence and the cited legal authority.

☐ **Work with citations during the drafting process:**
  - Consider analytical choices about citation throughout the preliminary drafting stage and the final presentation stage; and
  - Consider timing of finalizing complete citation form.

☐ **Understand plagiarism in the context of objective memos:**
  - Think about the issues concerning citing and quoting ideas from secondary authority sources that comment on the law; and
  - Think about the issues concerning citing and quoting ideas from primary authority that are "the law."

PART IV

THE FINAL STEPS TO COMPLETE AN OBJECTIVE MEMO

CHAPTER 15

Beyond the Discussion Section: Adding the Facts, Conclusion, Question Presented, and Brief Answer Sections

A. INTRODUCTION

Chapter 1 provided you with an overview of the different sections of an objective memorandum. Chapters 2 through 13 discussed how to successfully draft the heart of an objective memo, the Discussion Section. This chapter will address how to finalize your memo, beginning with drafting the Facts Section, explained in Section B, and the Conclusion Section, discussed in Section C. Section D will then discuss two sections that some supervisors will want you to include: The Question Presented and Brief Answer. Finally, considerations regarding the order of drafting the Discussion Section and the other sections are presented in Section E.

For an example of the following sections in an objective memo, see the Sample Memo in Appendix I.

B. THE FACTS SECTION

As Chapter 1 discussed, your supervising attorney needs a Facts Section that describes the "story" of the client's situation objectively. To take this step, you need to understand the type of information that you should include in the Facts Section, which is discussed in Section 1. You also need to consider how to describe the different facts, as explained in Section 2, and how to organize the section to allow your readers to read it quickly, as discussed in Section 3.

For an example of a Facts Section in a memo, see the Sample of a Formal Objective Memorandum in Appendix I.

1. Understanding the information to include

Your supervising attorney needs a Facts Section that describes the "story" of the client's situation objectively and includes two kinds of facts. First, and most importantly, your supervisor needs to understand all legally significant facts in that "story," including those favorable for the client and those unfavorable. Second, your supervisor needs any facts that help her understand how the client's legal issue arose, including applicable background about the story and applicable procedural history. In addition, to be as concise as possible, you should exclude any information that is not legally significant or necessary background. You should also be careful to include only facts and to exclude legal conclusions based on those facts.

a. Include all legally significant facts

In drafting the Facts Section in an objective memo, you must include all legally significant facts, both those that are favorable to your client and those that are unfavorable. These are the facts that you predict the future court will use in deciding your client's situation. If you have already drafted the Discussion Section, you will be able to easily locate these facts in each application-prediction portion of the Discussion Section. Application-predictions neutrally predict what the law indicates for the client's situation and by their nature have to include any fact that a future court might use as a basis for its decision. For this reason, drafting the Discussion Section before the Facts Section is helpful.

b. Include necessary background facts

Once you identify the legally significant facts, you need to consider whether your readers need additional facts as background. To choose these facts, begin by thinking about the facts you needed to understand why you were asked to write the memo. While some of these facts may be legally significant, not all will be.

In addition, you may need to include facts relevant to the timing and location of any important events. Such information is important for a variety of reasons. For example, it could explain the law that applies to the situation—both the jurisdiction and the effective laws of that jurisdiction at the time of the event—and therefore justify your choice of legal authority. Additionally, the date of an event may trigger a relevant statute of limitations.

c. Include the procedural history of your client's case, if applicable

In many circumstances, you'll be writing an objective memo before your client's situation has arrived at court and therefore you'll have no procedural history to include in the Facts Section. In other circumstances, you'll be writing an objective memo after a complaint has been filed either by or against your client, after a pretrial motion has been filed, or after trial during an appeal. Here, you would include in the Facts Section any procedural steps that had occurred.

d. Exclude irrelevant facts

Given that your readers are very busy, you should exclude all facts that are irrelevant because they are neither legally significant nor arguably necessary as background. Of course, reasonable lawyers might differ to some degree as to whether any individual background fact might be helpful.

e. Exclude legal conclusions

The Facts Section should introduce your readers only to the facts of your client's situation and should not include legal conclusions based on those facts. You may find this a tricky distinction at times, but the choice may be easier if you think about the specific purpose of the Facts and Discussion sections. In the Facts Section, your goal is to inform your readers about the specific facts that make up your client's "story" and not to analyze whether those facts are sufficient under the relevant legal authority. That is the job of the Discussion Section.

Example of including facts but excluding legal conclusions

For instance, imagine that you are analyzing a group of cases to determine how the courts in your jurisdiction reach a conclusion as to whether a structure is "secured," which is a requirement of a particular claim. In the Facts Section, you would not include the legal conclusion of whether the structure was "secured" or not, but would include all the specific facts that might be relevant to that idea. Were the windows locked or barricaded in some way? Did the doors have locks or a key card system? Was an alarm system in place? And so forth, depending upon the relevant legal analysis. In the Discussion Section, however, you would apply your analysis of "secured" to the facts about locks or a key card system or an alarm system and predict whether these facts would result in a future court reaching the conclusion that the structure in your client's case was "secured" or not.

2. Describing the information

a. Describe facts accurately

You must describe the facts of your client's situation accurately. You must transcribe all facts from the client interview, investigator's report, or discovery information without making a mistake. You also must not "make up" facts that would be helpful for your client but that are untrue.

In addition, you must refrain from making assumptions about facts that aren't clear. When a question arises, you should either ask for clarification or identify this problem as you draft the Facts Section.

b. Make the relationship of all people or entities to the legal issue clear

Remember that your supervisor, and other individuals who read the memo, may not have any prior knowledge about the people or entitites that play a role in the events that gave rise to your client's legal issue. Encountering people or entities only by name, therefore, your readers may have to stop and figure out the particular role they played, thus wasting valuable time. As author, you can easily avoid this confusion by providing an appropriate phrase that describes the people or entities the first time they appear as you describe the facts. For instance, is the individual "your client"? The "property owner"? The "employee"? The "dog catcher"? The "mortgagee"? The "mortgagor"?

3. Organizing the section

Once you have identified the facts that are legally significant and that are necessary for background, you must decide how best to organize these facts. To begin with, remember that your supervisor probably does not have an in-depth understanding of the client's "story" or the analysis in the Discussion Section; she is depending on your memo to fully and accurately inform her. Given how little your supervisor may bring to the memo, therefore, you must choose an organization that helps her in two ways as she reads the Facts Section. That organization should present the facts in a manner that allows her to read the section quickly and still grasp the "story" easily and accurately. The organization also should present the facts in a manner that prepares her for the analysis in the Discussion Section.

To determine the best structure for a Facts Section, you should consider different organizational options, as discussed in Section a. You should also decide, depending on the organization that you choose, whether to begin the section with a statement of context, as explained in Section b.

a. Overall organization

Below are the three basic organizations to structure a client's "story" in a Facts Section. In any individual legal problem, you may find that one of these organizations is best or that you legitimately have a choice given that more than one could be successful.

i. Chronological organization

You may find that describing the chronology of what happened provides your supervising attorney with a clear understanding of the client's "story" and adequately prepares her for the analysis in the Discussion Section. Organizing in this manner may be helpful even if the facts relevant to the various components of analysis in the Discussion Section are dispersed throughout the chronology.

ii. Topical organization

In some legal problems, though, organizing the facts around topics based on the breakdown of the analysis in the Discussion Section best prepares your readers. If the Discussion Section addresses several separate components of a legal issue, for instance, and organizes around them, you should consider organizing the Facts Section in a similar manner. Here, you would arrange facts into clusters, each of which related to a separate component, and order these clusters in the same manner as the Discussion Section's analysis. Reading through these groups of facts, therefore, your supervising attorney would be intuitively prepared for the way in which the Discussion Section structures the analysis. Just check, however, that your story overall would make sense to readers who bring much less knowledge about the client's situation than you have as the author.

iii. Combination of chronological and topical organization

In some legal problems, organizing some of the facts in a chronology and some of the facts by topic will be most helpful for your readers. For instance, you might begin by describing the background facts in a chronology. You could then go on to group the legally significant facts by topic in the same manner as you grouped them in the Discussion Section.

b. Statement of context

You should always evaluate whether, given how you've organized your Facts Section, your readers would benefit from the section beginning or ending with a statement of context. For instance, a Facts Section might begin with the fact that the firm is evaluating filing a certain claim, which is the focus of the memo. Or, a Facts Section might end with the fact that the client has been charged under a particular criminal statute—the subject of the memo.

C. THE CONCLUSION SECTION

As you learned in Chapter 1, the Conclusion Section of an objective memo provides an executive summary of the analysis in the Discussion Section. Your supervising attorney will find this summary very helpful when she doesn't have time to read your entire memo right away, given the busy context of law practice.

Imagine that you hand your supervisor an objective memo just before she meets with the client or talks with the other side's attorney. In such a situation, your supervisor will likely skip the longer and more complicated analysis in the Discussion Section and instead get "up to speed" quickly by skimming the Conclusion's summary.

This summary, therefore, must provide her with a sufficient understanding of the memo's analysis but in a concise manner. To draft this kind of summary, you need to understand the type of information to include in the section, as explained in Section 1, and how to best organize the section to provide that information effectively, as explained in Section 2.

For an example of a Conclusion Section, see the Sample of a Formal Objective Memorandum in Appendix I.

1. Understanding the information to include

The Conclusion Section must include your overall prediction of the outcome for your client as well as a succinct summary of how you reasoned to that prediction in as few paragraphs as possible. In general, a Conclusion Section will be very short; it could be only one paragraph in a relatively simple problem or several paragraphs in a more complex problem.

a. Base the summary on the application-predictions

You should base the Conclusion Section's summary on the analysis in the application-prediction portions of the Discussion Section. To understand why, compare the purposes of these two sections. As you learned in Chapters 11 through 13, the Discussion Section should provide your reader with an in-depth analysis, including an analysis of law for the various issues, described in the abstract without regard to the client's facts. It should also include separate application-predictions, applying that law to the client's facts and predicting an outcome for those various issues. In contrast, the Conclusion Section simply provides an overview of that analysis. To do so very concisely, this section omits a summary of the law in the abstract and provides the supervisor only with what she is most interested in—the "bottom line" of your predictions for the client and a quick summary of how you reached those predictions.

b. Be sure the summary is consistent with the analysis in the Discussion Section

Because the Conclusion's summary is based on the Discussion Section's analysis, both sections must be consistent. Both sections must include the same content; they should order and connect all important ideas in that content consistently; and they should phrase all important ideas consistently. If these two sections conflict in any significant way, that conflict may cause problems for the supervisor. At a minimum, she might waste time trying to figure out the summary's analysis, which is a serious issue in the busy context of law practice. More importantly, your supervisor might reach a faulty conclusion, with dangerous consequences for the client.

c. Do not include new analysis that was not explored in the Discussion Section

In general, do not include new analysis in the Conclusion Section; this is a corollary to the rule that the Conclusion and Discussion sections must be consistent. When you have drafted both these sections, compare their content. If you find new ideas in the Conclusion, then ask yourself why you did not include these same ideas in the Discussion Section. On the one hand, perhaps you simply got off course and included an irrelevant idea in the Conclusion; if so, then delete it. On the other hand, as you summarized your analysis for the Conclusion, perhaps you only then understood the significance of an idea; if so, then go back and incorporate that new idea into the Discussion Section.

You might encounter an exception to this rule, however, if your supervisor asks you to briefly address in the Conclusion any future steps to be taken based on the memo's analysis. For instance, you might quickly discuss the next step of filing a complaint.

d. Communicate all ideas in a manner that adequately informs readers

As you draft the Conclusion, you must not assume that your supervising attorney has the same level of knowledge of the analysis that you have as author. As you learned in Chapter 1, your supervisor is a senior attorney with many responsibilities. To free up her time, she has asked you as the junior attorney to analyze the client's legal problem and then report that analysis in memo form. When she turns to the Conclusion Section, therefore, she will bring little knowledge herself to the summary and will rely completely on the analysis that she encounters on that page of the memo.

By the time you as author write the Conclusion, however, you will have a thorough understanding of the analysis and may forget that your readers have much less. You may phrase important ideas too vaguely or even skip important ideas that are "in your head" but never end up on the pages of the memo. You may refer to parties by name, but never make it clear who they are in relationship to the events. To avoid these problems, therefore, you must continually keep in mind that you are writing to your supervisor, and potentially a range of other readers, and not merely to someone like yourself.

e. Do not include citation to legal authority

In general, your supervisor will not need you to support the ideas in your Conclusion Section with citation to legal authority. The Conclusion is simply a summary of analysis in the Discussion Section, where, as you learned in Chapters 12, 13, and 14, you should have already supported all ideas with sufficient citation to relevant legal authority.

There are exceptions to this general rule, however. First, if you refer to a statute in the Conclusion, you must describe it sufficiently to differentiate it from other statutes, and you might need to include its citation to do so. Second, if a landmark decision of the United States Supreme Court governs the problem, you might refer to the case name and even include the citation in the summary.

2. Organizing the section

You should organize your Conclusion Section based on four important principles that will help your readers understand your analysis easily and quickly. To begin, be sure to organize the summary consistently with the Discussion Section. In addition, state your conclusion up front: Begin the summary with your overall prediction for your client and begin any subpart with your prediction as to that subpart. Then, summarize how you reached a prediction by ordering ideas from general to more specific. Finally, check to be sure you use precise transitions between paragraphs, sentences, and within sentences.

a. Organize the summary consistently with the Discussion Section

You should organize the Conclusion and Discussion sections consistently in the sense that you should provide the same content and present that content in the same order in both sections. If your supervising attorney reads the Conclusion first, she needs to be prepared for the content and structure of analysis in the Discussion Section. If she reads the Discussion Section and then the Conclusion, the Conclusion needs to adequately remind her of the analysis she just encountered in the Discussion Section.

> **Example of organizing the Conclusion Section consistently with the Discussion Section**
>
> For instance, if you organize the Discussion Section around two different possible causes of action, then you would organize the Conclusion Section in the same manner. If for one of those causes of action, the courts use three requirements and you organized around these in the Discussion Section, then the summary should organize around them also. Both sections should present the requirements in the same order.

In many legal analyses, you may be able to go to the application-predictions in the Discussion Section and pick out the beginning summary and topic-transition sentences used to organize the analysis there. You may then be able to use these as a beginning foundation for the Conclusion Section as long as you're careful to edit them into a cohesive summary.

b. Begin with your overall prediction for your client

Your supervising attorney will be most interested in your "bottom-line" assessment for the client and will therefore want your overall prediction at the very beginning of the Conclusion's summary. For instance, does your client's situation satisfy a term in a relevant statute or not? Or is it unclear?

For many of you, however, this idea of "conclusion up front" will be counterintuitive, based on writing that you may have done in other contexts before law school. It may also be uncomfortable for you, depending upon your own analytical and writing process. When this occurs, write a first draft where you reason *to* the conclusion; then simply move your conclusion to the beginning in the version you give your supervisor.

c. Summarize how you reached all predicted outcomes by ordering ideas from general to specific

After you state an overall prediction for your client, you must then summarize how you reached that prediction. To do so in a manner that helps your readers read fast, explain your analysis by moving from general ideas to less general ideas to more specific ideas, connected by very precise transitions.

d. Summarize all predictions and counter-predictions

You'll often analyze an issue where the future court might reach more than one outcome on your client's facts, and therefore you include predictions and counter-predictions in the Discussion Section. In the Conclusion Section in this situation, you must include all such possible outcomes and, consistently with the Discussion Section, summarize how a future court might reach each one.

e. Use precise transitions

You must use precise transitional words or phrases that connect ideas accurately throughout a Conclusion Section. Review the discussion of transitions in Chapter 12.

D. THE QUESTION PRESENTED AND BRIEF ANSWER SECTIONS

At the beginning of the memo after the Heading, your supervisor may want you to include two sections to provide her with an initial, quick overview of the memo's analysis: A Question Presented Section and a Brief Answer Section. The Question Presented identifies the legal issue in terms of the client's facts, framed as a question. The Brief Answer then "answers" this question in a very concise manner—usually one or two sentences that spell out the result for the client even more concisely than the Conclusion section. In complex memos, as is discussed in Section 3 below, you may need more than one Question Presented followed by a Brief Answer.

Increasingly lawyers are relying less on very formal objective memos, and even sometimes replacing them with emails that serve the same purpose, as is discussed in Chapter 17. For this reason, your supervisor may not ask you to include a Question Presented and a Brief Answer, given that these sections include essentially the same analysis as in the Discussion and Conclusion sections. In fact, even when supervisors do want a Question Presented Section, they may ask you to substitute the longer Conclusion Section for the Brief Answer in order to reduce redundancy in the memo.

1. The Question Presented Section

A Question Presented Section is placed right after the heading and is therefore the first section that readers encounter. It is a one-sentence question that identifies the overall focus of the memo—law as applied to client's facts—and therefore provides a context for all succeeding sections in the memo.

For an example of a Question Presented Section, see the Sample of a Formal Objective Memorandum in Appendix I.

a. Include the central issue and the client's facts relevant to that issue

The question should identify the central issue that is analyzed in-depth in the Discussion Section. It should also include the client's facts that are most likely to be the ones that govern the outcome of that issue as applied to the client's situation. If the legal problem is complex, you may have to make careful choices about which facts to include or not. You must keep the question a reasonable length; otherwise, it will not be easy enough to read quickly and grasp accurately.

b. Make the question consistent with the analysis in all other sections

So that the memo forms a coherent whole, the Question Presented Section must be consistent with the analysis in the Discussion Section as well as the Brief Answer and Conclusion sections. In particular, it must be consistent in content as well as how the ideas in that content are ordered, connected, and phrased.

c. Draft the question so it can be answered by a "yes" or "no" answer

Begin a Question Presented with a word like "does" or "is," instead of a word like "whether." Crafted in this manner, a Question allows the Brief Answer to begin with "yes" or "no" and therefore provide a more definitive answer.

d. Make the relationship of all people or entities to the legal issue clear

Especially if your Question Presented is placed before the Facts Section, you must make the relationship of all people or entities to the legal issue clear. For instance, if the legal issue revolves around your landlord-client's dispute with a tenant, then you would have a choice. You could just use the phrase "landlord-client" and not use a name. Or, you could use the client's name and include a descriptive phrase: Our client, Jane Smith, who is the property owner.

e. Order ideas from general to specific

Because the Question Presented Section is only one sentence, you must organize the ideas logically to make it easy to read and understand. Therefore, order the ideas in the question from general to more specific. Begin with the legal issue. If the legal issue includes a more general issue and a more specific aspect of that general issue, begin with the general and proceed to the more specific. End with the most specific ideas—the legally significant facts.

2. The Brief Answer Section

The Brief Answer Section provides a very quick "answer" to the question in the Question Presented Section. It is simply a more succinct version of the Conclusion Section.

For an example of a Brief Answer Section, see the Sample of a Formal Objective Memorandum in Appendix I.

a. Include a "yes" or "no" answer to the Question Presented and state how you reached that conclusion

In general, the Brief Answer should begin with a "yes" or "no" answer to the Question Presented to provide your supervisor with a clear sense of the outcome for the client. You may want to qualify this, however, as "probably yes" or "probably no." If your overall predicted outcome is unclear because you have included predictions and counter-predictions for some relevant issues in the Discussion Section, the Brief Answer should indicate that unclear result with "maybe" or "the result is unclear."

This section should then state why you came to that "yes," "no," or "maybe" answer. First, set out the overall prediction of the outcome for the client, just like the Conclusion Section. Second, summarize how you reached that conclusion in a very concise manner—usually one or two sentences. This summary should be even more concise than the Conclusion Section where you have a bit more leeway in adding detail.

b. Be sure the Brief Answer Section is consistent with the analysis in all other sections

This section, like the Conclusion Section, must be consistent with all other sections of the memo. First, it must obviously "answer" the question in the prior Question Presented Section in a manner that shows the intimate analytical connection between the two sections. Second, it must be consistent with the Conclusion Section since it is simply a more concise version of that section's summary. Third, it must be consistent with the Discussion Section since it is summarizing very concisely that section's more in-depth analysis.

Thus, when you have final versions of all these sections begin by comparing their content. Go on to check whether you have ordered, connected, and phrased all significant ideas in a consistent manner.

c. Do not include citation to legal authority

For the same reasons as with the Conclusion Section, you do not in general need to cite to legal authority to support your ideas in the Brief Answer Section. Here, too, however, you should adequately describe a statute if one governs the analysis.

d. Organizing this section

You should organize the Brief Answer Section based essentially on the same principles you used for the Conclusion Section.

i. Organize this summary consistently with the Question Presented

Organize the Brief Answer summary consistently with the way in which you organized the ideas in the Question Presented. That parallel structure will help your supervisor read both sections quickly and grasp their overall import easily and accurately.

> *ii. Begin this summary with your overall prediction for your client*

Just as in the Conclusion Section, your supervising attorney will be most interested in your "bottom-line" assessment for the client. She will therefore want your overall prediction at the very beginning of the Brief Answer. Again, this will include first your "yes" or "no" answer and then the substantive overall prediction for the client that supports that answer.

> *iii. Summarize how you reached that prediction by ordering ideas from general to specific*

Even more succinctly than the Conclusion, you must summarize how you reached your overall prediction for your client in a logical manner by ordering ideas from general to more specific. Structured in this manner, the Brief Answer will provide a summary that your supervisor will be able to read quickly and understand easily and accurately.

3. More than one Question Presented and Brief Answer

In very complicated legal problems, your memo might need to address more than one major legal issue in the Discussion Section. For instance, you might need to explore whether your client would be able to state successfully alternative causes of action or whether your client could be successfully prosecuted under more than one criminal statute. In this situation, you would include more than one Question Presented with its corresponding Brief Answer, focusing each on one of the major issues analyzed in the Discussion Section.

E. THE TIMING TO DRAFT THE DISCUSSION SECTION AND THE OTHER SECTIONS

To complete your memo efficiently, you should consider when to draft the different sections. You may be someone who prefers to begin with the Discussion Section, as explained in Section 1. However, you might find that your drafting process would be more effective if you started with another section, as discussed in Section 2. Wherever you begin, however, you need to be sure that the entire memo is consistent. This idea is explained in Section 3.

1. Try beginning with the Discussion Section

You might consider drafting the Discussion Section first. As you already know, the Discussion Section includes an in-depth objective analysis of the current status of the law and what that law neutrally indicates for the client. Having already developed that analysis, you are likely to find drafting other sections of the memo easier and more economical. For instance, you might draft the Conclusion Section after the Discussion Section. Summarizing analysis accurately and succinctly is likely to be easier after having explained that analysis in depth in the Discussion Section.

2. Consider starting with sections other than the Discussion Section

You might draft the sections in a different order, however. To make this determination, you should be sensitive to your own analytical and drafting process that may require you to vary from the norm. For instance, some lawyers understand ideas best when dealing with legal abstractions, but others understand ideas best when thinking about these abstractions in terms of their client's "story." For those in the latter category, drafting a version of the Facts Section first might prove helpful in developing the Discussion Section's analysis.

You also should be sensitive to the fact that different legal problems may require somewhat different approaches to drafting an objective memo. For instance, in a situation where the client's facts are very complex and detailed, you might benefit from drafting a Facts Section early in your analytical process simply to ensure that you understand what happened. This understanding, even if it changes as your analysis progresses, might help you as you develop the Discussion Section.

3. Ensure consistency among all sections

Whatever order you choose to draft the different sections, you must ensure consistency among all sections of a memo's final version; only in this way will the memo as a whole provide your readers with a coherent analysis. If you begin with the Discussion Section and move on to other sections, you must revisit the Discussion Section afterwards. However, if you draft other sections first, you must then spend sufficient time revising those sections after you have developed a good draft of the Discussion Section.

Use the following checklist, therefore, to ensure that all sections of the memo are consistent with each other:

- Do the Facts Section and application-prediction portions of the Discussion Section include the same legally significant facts?
- Is the Conclusion Section's executive summary of analysis consistent with the Discussion Section's analysis?
- Is the Question Presented Section's identification of the legal issue and significant facts consistent with the analysis in the Discussion Section and the executive summary in the Conclusion Section?

- Is the Brief Answer Section's summary consistent with the Discussion Section's analysis and the executive summary in the Conclusion Section?

CHECKLIST

☐ Draft the Facts Section:
  - Include all necessary facts:
    - Include all legally significant facts, whether favorable or unfavorable to your client;
    - Include any necessary background facts;
    - Include the procedural history of your client's case, if applicable;
    - Exclude irrelevant facts; and
    - Include only facts and exclude legal conclusions;
  - Provide the information effectively:
    - Describe facts accurately; and
    - Clearly identify any individual's relationship to the legal issue;
  - Choose an overall organization carefully:
    - Chronological organization;
    - Topical organization; or
    - Combination of chronological and topical organization; and
  - Consider beginning or ending the section with a statement of context.

☐ Draft the Conclusion Section:
  - Summarize your predictions effectively:
    - Base the summary on the law as applied to the client's situation;
    - Verify that the summary is consistent with the analysis in the Discussion Section;
    - Do not include new analysis that was not explored in the Discussion Section;
    - Communicate all ideas in a manner that adequately informs readers who may not have specific knowledge of the situation; and
    - Exclude citation to legal authority; and
  - Choose an overall organization carefully:
    - Organize the summary consistently with the Discussion Section;
    - Begin the summary with the overall prediction for your client;
    - Order ideas from general to more specific;
    - Summarize all predictions and counterpredictions; and
    - Use precise transitions.

☐ Draft the Question Presented:
  - State the question effectively:
    - Include the central legal issue and the client's facts relevant to that issue;

- Make the question consistent with the analysis in all other sections;
- Draft the question so it can be answered by a "yes," "no," or "maybe" answer; and
- Clearly identify any individual's relationship to the legal issue; and
- Organize the section logically by ordering ideas from general to more specific.

☐ **Draft the Brief Answer:**
- State the answer effectively:
  - Include a "yes," "no," or "maybe" answer to the Question Presented and state how you reached that conclusion;
  - Make the content of the answer consistent with the analysis in all other sections; and
  - Do not include citation to legal authority; and
- Choose an organization carefully:
  - Organize the section consistently with the Question Presented;
  - Begin with the overall prediction for your client; and
  - Summarize how you reached that prediction by ordering ideas from general to specific.

☐ **Consider the timing of drafting the Discussion Section and the other sections:**
- Try beginning with the Discussion Section;
- Experiment with starting with sections other than the Discussion Section;
- Check the consistency among all sections:
  - Do the Facts Section and application-predictions portions of the Discussion Section include the same legally significant facts?
  - Is the Conclusion Section's summary consistent with the Discussion Section's analysis?
  - Is the Question Presented Section consistent with the analysis in the Discussion Section and the Conclusion Section?
  - Is the Brief Answer consistent with the Discussion Section and the Conclusion Section?

CHAPTER 16

Presentational Considerations

A. INTRODUCTION

In prior chapters, you've learned how to analyze a legal problem and structure your analysis well for your readers in the Discussion Section. In this chapter, you'll learn some specific ways to convey your ideas clearly. By this point, you should fully understand why your readers—your supervising attorney and other members of your team—need to understand your analysis easily and accurately.

B. DECIDE BETWEEN QUOTING OR PARAPHRASING LEGAL AUTHORITY

As discussed in Chapter 4 as to statutes and in Chapter 7 as to judicial opinions, you need to confront the following question as you describe your analysis: Should you use the verbatim language of a piece of legal authority, paraphrase those ideas, or, as to judicial opinions, use your own words to describe ideas that were only implicit in a group of cases? While you will first confront this question as you work out your analysis early on in your process, you should also revisit this question as you refine the presentation of analysis to your readers.

C. PRECISION

You must express your analysis precisely. Unfortunately, no formula will ensure that you do so. Instead, you must simply challenge yourself to answer the following questions as you edit for precision. First, do you fully understand the analysis yourself? Second, if you do, have you conveyed it well enough for your law practice readers?

You must understand all aspects of the analysis yourself. No one can convey analysis well if they are still struggling with the underlying ideas. Therefore, when you are having difficulty expressing an idea precisely, stop and work through the analysis again.

In addition, you must train yourself to read what you've written from the point of view of your readers, who will have to understand the analysis as expressed on the page. Readers who are confused by what is written on the page will have no access to ideas in your head, and you will likely not be there in person to answer their questions.

> **Example of imprecise language creating ambiguity for the reader**
>
> Imagine that you are analyzing a cause of action that is based on a plaintiff satisfying two requirements. In your introductory paragraph of the Discussion Section, you identify the cause of action and the fact that it is based on two requirements. As you describe the two requirements in that paragraph, you use the transitional word "and." With that transition, you accurately convey to your readers the precise analytical relationship between the two requirements because both must be satisfied.
>
> But, instead of using the word "requirement" or "require," you go on to use the following phrase to express the idea of "requirement": "The courts **look** at . . . ." In your own mind, you knew that you were discussing something that a plaintiff must satisfy. However, that precise idea is not what you communicated to your readers since "looking at" something is not equivalent to "requiring that it be satisfied." When your readers encounter your phrasing, therefore, they will have had to stop and ask the question, "Well, what do the courts do after they 'look at' this"?

> **Example of imprecise language creating contradictory ideas in the analysis**
>
> Imagine that you are working with an analysis that is based on a totality test. As you know from Chapter 7, a totality test is one where the court must evaluate several factors and then reach a

conclusion about whether the overall combination of those factors is sufficient. To describe this test to your readers, you write the following:

> The courts use a totality test where they **evaluate the overall combination of the following three factors** that measure one structure's relationship to another. First, the distance between the two structures **must be** sufficient. Second, the route between the two structures **must be** direct. Third, the two structures **must be** physically connected to each other.

You began well by identifying the overall totality test and by conveying the sense of that test with the phrase "evaluate the overall combination of the following three factors." But, as you went on to set out each factor, your use of "must" contradicted the idea of "combination," since your choice of words suggested that the court uses three bright-line tests, each of which must be sufficient in and of itself.

To describe this test more precisely, you would need to redraft this portion of your analysis as follows:

> The courts use a totality test where they **evaluate the overall combination of the three factors** that measure one structure's relationship to another. **These factors include** the distance and directness of route between the two structures and whether they are physically connected to each other.

As you wrote the first example above, you may have completely understood that the courts were using a totality test and exactly how the court evaluated the three factors. The way in which you described in writing the entire test, including the factors, however, would have raised a question for your readers as to whether the courts were using a totality test or whether they were instead using a series of requirements, each of which was based on a bright-line test.

D. CONSISTENCY

You should also describe ideas consistently in your analysis. In other words, you should use exactly the same word or phrasing for the same idea all the way through the memo.

Reading the above paragraph, you may well have been thinking, "But I thought it was a good thing to vary how I phrased my ideas in order to keep my readers interested? I've always used a thesaurus extensively."

While not an absolute rule, you should generally avoid using a thesaurus simply to vary your language when writing an objective memo in law practice.

And this is especially true when you are first learning how to write in this new context. Your supervising attorney is much less concerned about being kept interested than in reading quickly and never having a question about what you are communicating. She will be able to understand the analysis much more easily when you convey the ideas consistently. Of course, you might use a thesaurus effectively when you are struggling to figure out a precise term for a particular idea.

To ensure consistency, you must train yourself to read what you've written from the point of view of your supervisor and other readers. Begin by working through your memo and looking for places where you've expressed the same idea in different ways. When you find what appears to be an inconsistency, ask yourself the following questions. First, are *you* completely clear about this aspect of the analysis? Sometimes writers use different wording because they are still struggling with the ideas and their relationship. If so, you must stop and think through that issue before proceeding to convey those ideas to your readers.

Second, if you do completely understand the analysis, ask yourself whether you've just been careless or used a thesaurus in a manner that will undermine ease of reading for your readers. If so, choose the best way to express the idea and then edit through the memo to ensure you've expressed that idea in the same way each time.

The sections below highlight some of the most likely places in a memo where you may find inconsistencies as to how you've expressed your analysis.

1. The introductory paragraphs and the rest of the Discussion Section

The analysis in your introductory paragraphs must be entirely consistent with the analysis in the rest of the Discussion Section. As you learned in Chapter 11, the Discussion Section begins with introductory paragraphs that acquaint readers with the overall analytical structure of the legal problem and therefore prepare readers for the development of the analysis in the rest of the section. Therefore, the ideas introduced in these beginning paragraphs must be consistent with the content and phrasing of ideas developed in more depth afterwards in the rest of the Discussion Section. In particular, check that the content and phrasing of ideas in the introductory paragraphs is consistent with the same ideas in the topic-transition sentences of later paragraphs.

2. Descriptions of the courts' analysis and case illustrations

In a Discussion Section, you must be sure that your description of the courts' analysis stated in general principles is consistent with any corresponding case illustrations, as was first discussed in Chapter 12. To craft an effective illustration, therefore, you must demonstrate how the court used the same analysis — with the same content and phrased in the same manner — to reach a result on the facts before it.

3. Analysis of the law and the corresponding application-prediction

The law that you apply to your client's situation in an application-prediction must be completely consistent in content and phrasing with the ideas in the analysis of the law beforehand, as was discussed in Chapter 13. The analytical purpose of these two aspects of your analysis requires this consistency. The analysis of the law informs readers about a reasonable interpretation of the current status of the law. The application-prediction then demonstrates how the future court will use that same law to reach a conclusion on your client's situation. Therefore, the content and phrasing of that "law" must be entirely consistent in both places to convey a cohesive analysis.

If these two aspects of your analysis are inconsistent in any important respect, your readers will be confused, with the result that they will not be confident in your ideas. They may therefore question the validity of your analysis of the law or of what that law indicates about the future court's reaction to your client's situation.

4. The Discussion Section and other sections of the memo

Chapter 15 discusses consistency among the different parts of an objective memo, including the Facts Section, the Discussion Section, the Question Presented Section, the Brief Answer Section, and the Conclusion Section.

E. CONCISION

You should also express analysis concisely. While some writers naturally express ideas in as few words as is necessary, most of us need to spend significant time editing to achieve a sufficient level of concision. The sections below will help you with this process.

1. Evaluate the organization

You should always evaluate whether your organization at any point unnecessarily requires repeating ideas. If so, you'll need to stop and rethink how to organize the pieces of analysis so you can convey your ideas more concisely.

Understanding the issues discussed in Chapters 11 through 13 will assist you in this process.

2. Consider all summaries

You should also evaluate any place where you have summarized your ideas, whether to provide readers with a roadmap for ideas that follow or to sum up the prior discussion, as you learned in Chapters 12 and 13. Keep summaries that sufficiently help your readers despite the fact that they repeat ideas, but delete the rest. In many instances, this decision will be a judgment call where reasonable lawyers might reach different conclusions.

3. Revise passages with unnecessary repetition

You must also determine when you have unnecessarily repeated ideas in the same or different words as you explain your analysis. If you are developing your descriptions of the analysis of the law, for example, look for phrasing or sentences that appear to express the same idea. When you've used the same words, you'll be able to find these places without much effort. When you've used different words, you'll need to challenge yourself to answer the following questions. Are you saying the same thing in different words? Or does the difference in phrasing indicate different aspects of the analysis and you just haven't made that clear? Editing your writing for concision, then, may identify places where you are still struggling with the analysis.

However, you must distinguish between times that you are repeating ideas when you have no reason to do so and times when a natural repetitiousness in the memo may be helpful to your readers. For instance, if you set out and describe your analysis and then use a case example to illustrate that description, you will have to use some repetition so your readers fully understand why the case illustrates the analysis, as was discussed in Section D2 above. When you move from the analysis of the law to the application-prediction, you'll have to repeat the law to some extent in order to make clear how that law applies to the client's situation and supports your prediction of the future court's conclusion. The bottom line is that you must distinguish between times when repeating an idea reminds readers of an idea that they need right at that point to understand the analysis, and times when repeating an idea is simply distracting.

4. Reduce use of repetitive transitions

When you are first drafting your analysis sentence by sentence, you may find transitions that simply repeat ideas from the prior sentence to be helpful. By doing so, you force yourself to connect ideas, point by point, precisely and accurately.

However, a "repeating" transition, if used too often, is not helpful for readers in a final version of a memo. This type of transition is precise; however, it is also repetitious and therefore slows readers down—something that busy law practice readers will find distracting. Therefore, try to rephrase some of the "repeating transitions" during a final edit of a memo so that the resulting transitions are equally precise but more concise.

> **Example of shortening transitions that repeat ideas**
>
> The two examples below illustrate how to make transitions more concise.
>
> *Early draft using a "repeating transition" between two sentences:*
>
> > The courts require a bystander to have a close relationship with the direct victim. To date, immediate family members satisfy **the requirement that a bystander have a close relationship with the direct victim.**
>
> *Final draft revising the repeating transition:*
>
> By using the transitional word "this" instead of "the" in the second sentence below, the author precisely connects the two sentences and therefore can delete "that a bystander must have a close relationship with the direct victim." This simple change in the transition makes the second sentence more readable and concise, yet the transition still provides readers with a precise connection between the ideas in the two sentences.
>
> > The courts require a bystander to have a close relationship with the direct victim. To date, immediate family members satisfy **this requirement.**

5. Delete unnecessary statements

In addition, delete statements that do not help your readers understand your analysis.

First, rephrase statements that have insufficient substance because they focus on identifying what you are going to do next in the memo. This type of statement will distract your readers from understanding the analysis.

> **Example of rephrasing a statement that provides insufficient substance**
>
> ~~I will now discuss the next topic of relationship, whether~~ The courts first require that a bystander ~~has~~ have a sufficient relationship with the direct victim.

Second, delete statements that describe your own process of determining analysis. In the context of law practice, your readers will depend upon you to follow a correct process. What they need from you is the result of that process—the substance of your analysis.

> **Example of removing a statement that describes the author's analytical process**
>
> ~~I synthesized the ideas in the four cases to determine that the~~ The court requires that the bystander have a sufficient relationship with the direct victim.

If you are a writer who uses writing to think out ideas, you may include such statements in early drafts because they are part of your focus on your *own process*. In a later draft, however, you must delete these statements as you fine-tune a memo so that it will be helpful for law practice readers.

6. Remove unnecessary introductory phrases

You should evaluate whether introductory phrases are necessary because they state the obvious. In many instances, you can either delete the idea completely or replace the phrase with only one word later in the sentence.

> **Examples of removing unnecessary introductory phrases**
>
> ~~It is clear that a~~ A plaintiff must satisfy the requirement that . . . .
>
> ~~It is important to note that a~~ A plaintiff must satisfy the requirement that . . . .

> **Example of replacing an introductory phrase with one word later in the sentence**
>
> ~~It is necessary that a~~ A plaintiff must satisfy the requirement that . . . .

F. CLARITY

The following sections describe some of the most important ways to ensure your memo is expressing ideas clearly enough for your readers.

1. Evaluate paragraph length

Paragraphs that are a reasonable length will help your readers to understand the analysis more easily. While you can't apply any formula to determine the appropriate length to any given paragraph, you should skim your draft memo during the presentational stage and simply look at the length of your paragraphs. When you encounter one that is very long—three-fourths of a page to over a page—stop and decide if you should shorten it.

Begin by determining whether the paragraph's central idea is clearly set out in the first sentence and whether the rest of the paragraph develops that idea. If not, you need to ask yourself whether you are still struggling with the analysis or you just haven't structured the ideas well in the paragraph. In rethinking the analysis or how it's structured, you may find that you are able to shorten the paragraph considerably.

If the paragraph is still too long, evaluate whether you logically could divide the focus of the paragraph into two or more paragraphs to provide your readers with smaller pieces of the analysis each time. Then, assess whether the paragraph contains unnecessary ideas or is repetitious. You might be able to shorten the paragraph simply by rephrasing ideas more concisely or deleting ones that are unnecessary to developing the analysis. Finally, delete any final sentence that simply summarizes the point of the paragraph unless your readers need that reiteration because the analysis is complex and difficult to grasp easily.

2. Consider sentence length

You will also make your analysis easier for readers to understand if your sentences are a reasonable length. While here, too, you can't apply any formula to determine the appropriate length, you should skim your draft memo during the presentational stage and just look at the length of your sentences. When you encounter one that is very long—two or more lines—stop and read it aloud. If you have trouble doing so and understanding what you've written, then evaluate whether the sentence is attempting to convey too many ideas. If so, try dividing the sentence at logical places. Next, evaluate whether the sentence contains ideas that are unnecessary and could be deleted, or ideas that could be rephrased more concisely. Finally, check whether you could revise the sentence construction to present ideas more economically.

3. Clarify "who does what to whom"

In legal writing, your readers often need to easily grasp "who does what to whom" in order to fully understand the analysis. The following sections address some major ways to ensure that your sentence structure clearly conveys these ideas.

a. Consider using active verbs instead of passive verbs

i. Using an active verb when the analysis focuses on the actor

To help your readers understand "who does what to whom," you should always try to make the subject of your sentence the main actor in the analysis and use an active verb that makes clear what that actor must or must not do. An active verb makes clear what the subject of the sentence is doing—it's an "action" word. In contrast, a passive verb does not.

Example that compares active and passive verbs

Sentence with active verb:

In the sentence below, the author clearly identifies who the actor is—the girl. And the author makes clear what she did—ate something. And the author clearly identifies what she ate—the apple.

> The girl [*subject of sentence*] ate [*active verb*] the apple.

Sentence with passive verb:

In the sentence below, "who is doing what" is much less clear because the author uses a passive verb. The apple is the subject of the sentence and the verb is a passive one. If the author wished to emphasize the apple, then use of the passive would be appropriate, as is discussed in the section below. But if the author wished to make clear who ate the apple, then use of the passive obscured that to some degree.

> The apple [*subject of sentence*] was eaten [*passive verb*] by the girl.

Example that compares active and passive verbs in legal analysis

Imagine that, in one aspect of an analysis, the courts require that a bystander witness the negligent act.

> *Sentence with active verb:*
>
> The sentence below communicates clearly that the analysis is about the main actor, who is "the bystander." It also makes completely clear what that bystander must do, which is to "witness the negligent act."
>
> > The bystander [*subject of sentence; main actor in the analysis*] **must witness** [*active verb*] the negligent act.
>
> *Sentence with passive verb:*
>
> In the version of this sentence below, readers will have a difficult time focusing on the main actor—the bystander—and what that bystander must or must not do. The use of the passive verb obscures to some degree "who does what to whom."
>
> > The negligent act [*subject of sentence*] **must be witnessed** [*passive verb*] by the bystander.

ii. Using passive verbs when the analysis focuses on the action

Of course, you should use passive verbs when you want readers to focus not on the actor but on the action itself. In fact, some analyses don't focus on any actor but on the object of an action.

> **Example of appropriate use of passive voice**
>
> In the sentence below, the use of a passive verb is appropriate because the analysis focuses on what must be secured—the "structure"—and not about "who had to secure it."
>
> > The structure **must be secured**.

b. Question use of "there is"

You should always question sentences that begin with variations of "there is." By beginning a sentence with this phrase, you may not make clear enough "who did what to whom." In addition, the phrase may make your sentence too wordy.

> **Example of rephrasing a sentence to avoid "there is"**
>
> > ~~There must be a~~ A bystander ~~who witnesses~~ must witness the negligent act.

c. Avoid turning active verbs into nouns

In general, avoid sentences where you have changed active verbs into nouns. Often this kind of sentence joins two of these nouns with a "to be" verb. Analogously to passive voice, this type of sentence makes less clear "who does what to whom" because the "action" is hidden and often so are the actors.

> **Example of using active verbs rather than verbs turned into nouns**
>
> *Sentences based on active verbs turned into nouns:*
>
> In the sentence below, the author turns two active verbs into nouns. First, the author turns the active verb "witness" into the noun "witnessing." Second, the author turns the active verb "require" into the noun phrase "what the courts require." By constructing the sentence in this manner, the author has obscured "who must witness" and "who must require." The result is a sentence that does not spell out clearly "who is doing what to whom."
>
> > **Witnessing** [*noun*] the negligent act **is** [*"to be" verb*] **what the courts require** [*noun phrase*].
>
> *Revised sentences using active verbs:*
>
> In the revised sentences below, the actor—who is doing the act of "requiring"—and the actor—who must do the act of "witnessing"—are both easily apparent.
>
> > The **courts require** [*active verb*] that the **bystander witness** [*active verb*] the negligent act.
> >
> > The **bystander must witness** [*active verb*] the negligent act.

d. Modify the correct idea in the sentence

You will hinder your readers' ability to understand "who is doing what to whom" when you fail to place phrases in a manner that makes precisely clear what they modify or that results in their modifying the wrong idea.

> **Example of moving a phrase so that it modifies the correct idea**
>
> *Sentence in which a phrase modifies the wrong idea:*
>
> In the following sentence, the phrase "witnessing the negligent act" is placed in the sentence so that it modifies the subject of the sentence, which is "the court." In fact, however, this idea should modify "the bystander."

> Witnessing the negligent act, the court requires the bystander to encounter the injuries of the direct victim firsthand.
>
> *Revised sentence with the correct modification:*
>
> In the revised sentence below, the phrase "witnessing the negligent act" clearly relates to the "bystander" and not to the "court."
>
> > The court requires that **the bystander** encounter the injuries of the direct victim first-hand by **witnessing the negligent act.**

e. Correct problems with pronouns

Avoid using a singular noun and then a plural pronoun afterward that refers back to the noun. While this practice is becoming commonplace in our language, you should avoid it when writing to your busy law practice readers. Encountering this inconsistency, your readers will have to stop and think about whether the plural pronoun really does refer back to the antecedent noun that is singular.

> **Example of revising a sentence to correct misuse of a plural pronoun**
>
> *Sentence with incorrect use of a plural pronoun:*
>
> In the following sentence, "their," a plural pronoun, refers to "bystander," a singular noun.
>
> > **A bystander** must encounter through **their** own senses the serious injuries of the direct victim.
>
> *Revised sentence to correct misuse of a plural pronoun:*
>
> In the following revised sentence, the author changes the singular noun "bystander" to a plural noun so that both the noun and pronoun are plural.
>
> > **Bystanders** must encounter through **their** own senses the serious injuries of the direct victim.

Similarly, be careful not to create ambiguity with the vague use of variations of the pronoun "this," including "that," "these," and "those." These pronouns can confuse readers if you use them in a manner that can refer back to more than one previous idea.

> **Example of editing to avoid vague use of "this"**
>
> *Sentence in which use of the pronoun "this" creates ambiguity:*
>
> The pronoun "this" in the second sentence below is vague because readers would be unsure exactly what it referred back to in the previous sentence.
>
> > The court requires that bystanders encounter through their own senses the injuries of the direct victim and the general environment of the accident scene. **This** helps the court determine whether the bystander's reaction is reasonable.
>
> *Revision that avoids the ambiguity by identifying the relevant idea after "this":*
>
> In the sentences below, by repeating "encounter" after "this," the author clearly identifies the specific idea to which "this" refers. Often, you can simply repeat the previous idea in this fashion. However, to avoid excessive repetition, you may describe the previous idea with a synonym or other phrasing.
>
> > The court requires that bystanders encounter through their own senses the injuries of the direct victim and the general environment of the accident scene. **This encounter** helps the court determine whether the bystander's reaction is reasonable.

f. Avoid too much separation between a subject and its verb

As you edit, look for sentences with too much information between the subject and verb. When this occurs, your readers will struggle to figure out "who does what to whom" and how all the ideas in the sentence fit together.

To solve this problem, you can either restructure the sentence or divide the sentence into two.

> **Example of too much separation between subject and verb**
>
> *Original sentence with too much separation*:
>
> > **Bystanders** [*subject*] who encounter through their own senses the serious injuries of the direct victim **will react** [*verb*] with serious and genuine emotional distress.

> *Revised sentence placing the subject and verb closer together:*
>
> **Bystanders** [*subject*] **will react** [*verb*] with serious and genuine emotional distress when they encounter through their own senses the serious injuries of the direct victim.

4. Edit and proofread

While this book generally does not cover basic grammar, using proper grammar and punctuation is important in legal writing. You should therefore consult whatever tools available to you to avoid grammatical and punctuation errors in your writing.

In addition, before turning in your memo to your supervising attorney, always run a spell-check on your computer and read your memo to be sure that you've used words correctly since a spell-check will not identify all errors. For instance, a spell-checking program will not identify the misuse of words like "there" and "their," "discreet" and "discrete," or "its" and "it's." Finally, be sure to proofread your memo very carefully to correct any other errors in formatting.

Failure to use correct grammar and punctuation, to spell correctly, or to proofread your memo may result in adverse consequences to your career. If you submit a writing sample with these errors, you may not be hired in the first place. These errors in memos submitted to your work supervisor may result in an unfavorable review of your work or even termination of your employment.

G. A PROFESSIONAL TONE

In general, you should use a professional, formal tone in an objective memo unless you are writing to a supervising attorney who is comfortable with more informal writing. The following are some simple rules to achieve this goal.

1. Use third-party neutral tone

Use a third-party neutral tone and in general avoid referring to yourself in first person.

> **Example of editing a sentence to avoid using first person**
>
> ~~My opinion~~ [*first person*] ~~is that the~~ The future court [*third person*] would probably conclude that our client satisfies the first requirement.

There are, of course, exceptions. If you are including instructions from your supervising attorney in the introductory paragraphs of a Discussion Section, for example, you might use something like the following:

> **Example of appropriate use of first person**
>
> I have been asked to focus on the following issue . . . .

2. Avoid archaic and informal language

a. Avoid "legalese"

You want to express ideas simply and straightforwardly, and one important way to do so is avoiding "legalese," which tends to express ideas in archaic words and phrases. You may encounter examples of legalese in different kinds of legal writing, including court opinions, but this kind of phrasing never expresses ideas as clearly as ordinary English.

> **Examples of avoiding legalese when referring to cases**
>
> *Examples of sentences in which the author uses legalese to refer to a particular judicial opinion:*
>
> > In the instant case, the court should . . . .
> >
> > In the case at bar, the court should . . . .
>
> *Revised sentences with no legalese:*
>
> To correct this problem, you should avoid terms like "said case," "instant case," or "case at bar." Instead, use a clear transitional reference. If you are referring to a court opinion, then use something like "that case" or "this case" or refer to the name of the case.
>
> > In Johnson, the court decided that . . . .
> >
> > In that case, the court found that . . . .

> **Example of revising a sentence to replace antiquated phrasing with simple terms**
>
> The court's goal should be to reach a decision that ~~is meet and just~~ will create a just result between the parties.

b. Avoid informal language

You should always revise places where you've used colloquial words or phrases that are conversational and therefore more like talking or texting with a friend. Instead, always strive to use a formal, professional tone in a law practice document.

To avoid being too conversational, for instance, think twice about using contractions, like "you're," "it's," and "wasn't." Note that the authors of this textbook use contractions throughout to help you feel as if they are speaking personally to you as the reader. In contrast, contractions are generally not desirable in a formal document to a work supervisor.

In addition, you should avoid colloquial expressions.

> **Example of rephrasing a sentence to remove colloquialism**
>
> In the sentence below, the colloquial term "kids" is replaced with the more formal term, "child":
>
> The court failed to address any of the ~~kid's~~ child's problems.

3. Describe parties with appropriate formality

Take care in describing and referring to the parties. While you may not need to be overly formal, using "Mr.," "Mrs.," or "Ms.," you should describe the parties with sufficient formality to be respectful. In general, therefore, do not refer to parties by only their first names. Instead, use a party's full name, the party's last name only, or the party's relationship to the analysis, like "our client" or the "Defendant."

> **Example of revising an informal reference**
>
> *Reference to client that is too informal:*
>
> > The court would conclude that **our client, Jane,** satisfies the first requirement.
>
> *Rephrasing the references to more appropriate formality:*
>
> > The court would conclude that **our client, Jane Delgardo,** satisfies the first requirement.
> >
> > The court would conclude that **our client** satisfies the first requirement.

H. GENDER-NEUTRAL LANGUAGE

Always consider using gender-neutral language. Gender-neutral language has become the norm in our society, and you may be writing to a supervising attorney or others who will be offended if you fail to use it as you convey your analysis.

In general, this issue is most important as you set out your analysis of the law and are conveying ideas in general principles. In contrast, when you describe a specific case in illustration of those principles or you apply the law to your client's situation, you will know what gender to use since you'll be describing specific individuals or entities.

1. Use plurals

To avoid sexist language, you might choose to use plurals. Using plurals avoids the very awkward "he/she" or "he or she" or "his or her." It also avoids the confusion of a plural pronoun referring back to a singular noun, as is discussed above in Section F.

Examples of using gender-neutral references

Less desirable because pronoun is not gender-neutral:

A **bystander** must witness the negligent act so that **he** encounters the injuries of the direct victim.

Better because of gender-neutral pronouns, but awkward because of "he or she":

A **bystander** must witness the negligent act so that **he or she** encounters the injuries of the direct victim.

More desirable because it uses gender-neutral language with plurals:

Bystanders must witness the negligent act so that **they** encounter the injuries of the direct victim.

---

2. Repeat nouns

You might also repeat the noun instead of using a pronoun.

> **Example of repeating nouns to avoid sexist language**
>
> *Less desirable because no gender-neutral pronoun or because "he or she" is used:*
>
> > A bystander must witness the negligent act so that he encounters the injuries of the direct victim.
> >
> > A bystander must witness the negligent act so that he or she encounters the injuries of the direct victim.
>
> *More desirable because the author repeats the noun to avoid "he or she":*
>
> > A bystander must witness the negligent act so that the bystander encounters the injuries of the direct victim.

CHECKLIST

☐ Reevaluate using verbatim language or paraphrasing ideas from legal authority.
☐ Be precise.
☐ Be consistent:
  - Between the introductory paragraphs and the rest of the Discussion Section;
  - Between descriptions of the courts' analysis and case illustrations in the analysis of the law;
  - Between an analysis of the law and corresponding application-prediction; and
  - Between the Discussion Section and other sections of the memo.

☐ Be concise:
  - Evaluate the organization;
  - Consider all summaries;
  - Revise passages with unnecessary repetition;
  - Reduce use of transitions that repeat ideas;
  - Delete unnecessary statements; and
  - Remove unnecessary introductory phrases.

☐ **Be clear:**
- Evaluate paragraph length;
- Evaluate sentence length;
- Make action and the actors clear:
  - Consider using active verbs rather than passive verbs;
  - Always consider using an active verb when the analysis focuses on a main actor;
  - Use passive verbs when the analysis does not focus on the actor but on the action itself;
  - Question sentences that begin with variations of "there is"; and
  - Question making active verbs into nouns;
- Modify the correct idea in the sentence;
- Avoid problems with pronouns;
- Avoid too much separation between a subject and its verb; and
- Do basic editing as to:
  - Correct grammar, punctuation and spelling; and
  - Proofreading.

☐ **Use a professional tone:**
- Use third-party neutral tone;
- Express ideas in a manner that is neither archaic nor too informal;
- Avoid using "legalese";
- Avoid expressing ideas in an informal manner; and
- Describe parties in a relatively formal manner.

☐ **Consider using gender-neutral language:**
- Use plurals; and
- Repeat nouns.

PART V

OTHER FORMS OF OBJECTIVE WRITING

CHAPTER 17

Informal Internal Office Communications: Shorthand Memos and Emails

A. INTRODUCTION

When you are a summer employee or junior lawyer in law practice, you'll often be assigned projects requiring a neutral analysis of the current status of the law and what that law indicates about a client's facts. As part of the project, you may be asked to draft a formal objective memo where you explain your analysis in detail to your supervising attorney and other colleagues — the kind of memo that you've learned about in prior chapters.

In that busy environment, however, you might be asked instead to present that analysis in a more "short-hand" written form. You might be asked for a summary of analysis in a brief informal memo or email. You might even be asked to provide copies of the relevant legal authority with only a quick written answer to the question posed by your supervising attorney. The sections below, therefore, address some important concepts about drafting documents that are more summary in nature than formal objective memos.

For an example of such a summary document, see the Sample Email to Supervisor in Appendix II, which is based on the Sample Formal Objective Memorandum in Appendix I.

B. ANALYTICAL FOUNDATION

Your readers in law practice will need an accurate and complete analysis of the law and what it means for the client regardless of how they request that analysis to be reported back to them. Whether they request a formal memo that spells all important ideas out in detail or a more informal format that summarizes the high points to varying degrees, you'll need to determine all necessary steps in the analysis. If you skip these steps, except for the simplest legal problems, you'll likely end up conveying an analysis that is incomplete or even inaccurate.

In fact, you'll likely find drafting a summary analysis more challenging than drafting one spelled out in more detail. To summarize effectively, you must first understand the analysis to the same degree as needed for a formal memo. You must then make a variety of difficult choices concerning the amount of detail necessary to capture in as few words as possible all important nuances of the analysis.

C. FORMAT

In an informal memo or email that summarizes the analysis, you should usually begin with a clear answer to the question posed by the supervising attorney and then go on to include a concise version of all the analytical steps that you would have discussed in a formal memo. How concise that summary of analysis needs to be, however, will vary with the specific assignment and the needs of the reader.

In some informal memos or emails, you might need to provide only a summary of analysis that would be slightly more detailed than that included in a formal memo's Conclusion Section, which is discussed in Chapter 15. In this type of informal memo or email, you would simply summarize the law as applied to the client's facts, assuming you had been provided with those facts.

In other informal memos or emails, you would provide an analysis in a bit more detail by separating your summary of the abstract analysis of the current status of the law from the summary of the application of that law to the client's facts. Under this approach, you would follow the organization of the Discussion Section in a formal memo. You would begin by providing a succinct introduction to the overall analytical structure of the analysis. You would go on with an abstract analysis of the current status of the law that would include a quick analysis of each component but would likely not include complete explanations, illustrations of the relevant authority, or as complete citation to legal authority. Once you had finished the summary of the abstract law, you would summarize concisely how that law applied to your client's situation and what the facts indicated as the outcome.

Instead of an informal memo or email that summarized the analysis, you might be asked instead to research a specific question and simply submit copies of, or citation to, the relevant legal authority, without including much analysis of that authority and what it indicated for the client. In this situation, you would begin by working through the analysis yourself during your research process. Once you had located the relevant authority, you would draft a brief cover memo or email that would identify the question you were asked to research and would explain that you were instructed to locate relevant authority without fully analyzing the question. You might then end with a statement to the effect that you could submit a complete analysis if that were necessary.

Regardless of the format in which you submit your analysis to your supervising attorney, remember to keep all your notes and copies of the relevant legal authority. You might be asked as a next step to submit a more formal memo that developed some or all of your analysis in more depth.

D. STRUCTURE

You should structure informal memos and emails in a manner that helps busy law practice readers grasp the analysis easily, quickly, and accurately. Therefore, you must use many of the organizational concepts that you learned in Chapters 11 through 13. In particular, for summaries of more than one sentence, pay special attention to:

- Organizing around the logic of the analysis itself;
- Using strong topic-transition sentences to introduce the different parts and paragraphs of the summary;
- Developing each paragraph around the ideas in the first "topic-transition" sentence; and
- Crafting transitions that connect ideas precisely and accurately between sentences and within sentences.

E. PROFESSIONALISM

When preparing these types of informal internal-office written communications, you'll be writing to your supervisor or other colleagues about professional matters in a work environment. Therefore, informal memos or emails must have the same professional quality as more formal memoranda. In particular, remember that written analysis, no matter how succinct, will likely be used to evaluate your performance.

Before you submit any written assignment, therefore, you should always carefully proofread to check for grammatical mistakes, punctuation problems, incorrect spelling, typos, and formatting issues. In addition, as you summarize your analysis, you should use a professional, formal tone unless you are writing to someone who is comfortable with informality, as was discussed in Chapter 16.

F. EMAIL—SOME SPECIAL ISSUES

Email allows lawyers in an office to communicate quickly and easily, which is very important in the fast-paced environment of law practice. That very ease and quickness of communication, however, creates some risks. The sections below discuss some additional common sense rules to use when drafting emails internally within your workplace that discuss analysis, sensitive or confidential information, and important logistical issues.

1. Draft emails off-line

In a work environment, you should usually draft off-line emails that discuss analysis, sensitive or confidential information, or important logistical issues. You might either draft off-line on your email system or create a new document using your word processing program. Drafting off-line, you will be more likely to work through several versions to ensure that the content is complete, accurate, and proofread. In addition, you will be less likely to inadvertently send an email that is unfinished.

2. Keep emails at an appropriate length

You should always evaluate whether the information that you are communicating is too long and complex to be included in the body of an email. Emails that are multiple screens are quite difficult to read and understand quickly. When an email is very long, therefore, include a very short summary in the body of the email and attach a longer summary in a separate document.

3. Use a precise subject-matter reference

When you draft an email, you should identify the subject matter of the memo in the "re" ("regarding") line. In that part of the heading, you should identify the client involved, if relevant, and the general content of the email in a succinct phrase. Well-crafted subject-matter references allow recipients to manage their email economically, an objective that is important in the busy environment of law practice.

4. Use an appropriately formal tone

To draft emails in law practice, you must make the shift from the kinds of informal emails that we all write to our friends and family to those that communicate information in a professional environment. First, take care not to use abbreviations and acronyms. Many are inappropriately informal, like the "laugh out loud" acronym of "lol." In addition, you cannot assume that your readers, especially more senior attorneys, will have knowledge of the myriad abbreviations and acronyms used in emails, instant text messaging, and so forth. For instance, a senior colleague might not understand that the acronym "btw" stands for "by the way," and would consequently struggle to figure out what you were trying to convey.

Second, you should use a salutation that is formal enough to show respect but not so formal that it's stilted. For instance, when writing to your supervisor, you should probably not begin with "Hi, Joe," unless you knew that "Joe" likes this kind of informality. In contrast, you would also not address him as "Dear Mr. Jones" when he was someone you had worked for and had known for a while.

5. Consider waiting to react to email about important matters

The very ease and quickness of email, its great strength in law practice, also presents one of its greatest disadvantages: It's much too easy to quickly respond to an email in a manner that doesn't clearly communicate your ideas or that is inappropriate in a professional environment. Therefore, whenever you are responding to an email about analytical issues or ones that are sensitive or emotionally charged, try to wait before responding. This "waiting time" gives you the ability to be sure what you've written is clear and that its tone and content are appropriate.

First, if you respond too quickly, you may articulate your response in a manner that doesn't clearly communicate what you intended. Always remember that your recipient only has the words as you write them in the email and not as you thought about them in your mind. While this concept is just as important in a formal memo, we all tend to remember that formal memos require several drafts but forget that emails may need to go through the same drafting process—usually offline, as discussed in Section 1 above.

Second, if you respond too quickly to an email about emotionally charged or sensitive issues, you may express your response in a manner that is inappropriate in a professional environment. Especially when you're tired, you may quickly send an angry or emotional message that will be unprofessional in tone and content. Such an email may damage your reputation and relationship with supervisors or other colleagues. In this kind of situation, therefore, always try to draft a response off-line and wait a substantial amount of time before sending the message. Waiting allows you time to calm down and redraft the email. It may also allow you to show the message to someone you trust so that you are able to get their opinion about whether its tone and content are appropriate under the circumstances.

6. Pay special attention to confidential emails

You often will be writing emails that convey confidential and sensitive information concerning a client or other matters in your work place. When you use a message in this manner, you must be sure that you send it only to the intended individuals and that you include a confidentiality disclaimer.

You must be careful to send emails only to the intended recipient or recipients. When you are initiating an email communication, always double-check that you have inserted correct email addresses. When you are responding to an email, always stop and think. Remember that choosing "reply all" will send your response to everyone included in the prior email—both the sender and anyone that was copied on the original email—which may not be what you intend, especially if individuals outside the firm were copied on the original email. To avoid this mistake, you might forward the email to the intended recipient instead of choosing to reply.

You should also always include at the bottom of an email a statement of confidentiality.

> **Example of email statement of confidentiality**
>
> The information contained in this electronic message may be legally privileged and confidential under applicable law and is intended only for the use of the individual or entity named above. If you are not the above-named intended recipient, you are hereby notified that you are strictly prohibited from disseminating, copying, or disclosing this communication. If you have received this communication in error, please notify [*insert appropriate name of firm and phone number*] and purge the communication immediately without making or distributing any copy.

Remember that, once an email has been sent, that message is easy to forward to an infinite number of additional people. While a confidentiality disclaimer isn't foolproof, it does provide some protection if an email is forwarded to recipients who have no right to the information.

CHECKLIST

☐ Understand that informal memos and other writings should include all important steps of the analysis in a summary manner.

☐ Change the format to correspond to the specific assignment and the needs of readers.

- ☐ Use an effective structure:
  - Help busy law practice readers grasp the analysis easily, quickly, and accurately; and
  - Consider many of the same organizational concepts discussed in Chapters 11 through 13.

- ☐ Check that the writing has the same professional quality as more formal memos.

- ☐ Pay particular attention to email correspondence:
  - Draft emails off-line;
  - Keep emails at an appropriate length;
  - Use a "Re" line that identifies the content clearly;
  - Use an appropriately formal tone;
  - Wait before replying to any email about important matters; and
  - Pay special attention to emails that contain confidential information.

APPENDIX I

Sample of a Formal Objective Memorandum

> 1. For a general discussion of a formal objective memorandum, see Ch. 1.

Memorandum

To: Senior Attorney
From: Junior Colleague
Date: September 1, 20XX
Re: Mike Long: Enforceability of Noncompetition Clause

Question Presented

> 2. Question Presented. See Ch. 15, D1.

In Minnesota, can an employer enforce a noncompetition clause in an employment agreement against a departing employee who had contacts with former customers if the clause restricts the employee from working in a similar position for a competitor for one year in any state where the employer does business?

Brief Answer

> 3. Brief Answer. See Ch. 15, D2.

Probably not. A Minnesota court probably would not enforce the noncompetition clause as written. Although a court likely would find that the employer has a legitimate interest to restrict the departing employee because of his relationships with its customers, a court probably would find that the clause itself is too broad to reasonably protect those relationships. While the time and subject matter restrictions are reasonable, the territory provision is not. Therefore, a court probably would revise the clause with the "Blue Pencil Doctrine" to make it reasonable. However, what modifications a court would make are unclear.

A court could revise the clause so that it restricts the employee from contacting any of his former customers on behalf of a competitor in the northern part of Minnesota for the one-year period. On the other hand, a court could modify the clause so that it restricts the employee from working in a similar position for a competitor in the northern part of Minnesota for one year.

283

> **4. Facts Section.** See Ch. 15B.

Facts

Our client, Mike Long, has sought advice about whether Energy Resources, Inc. ("Energy") can enforce the following noncompetition clause that was included in his original employment agreement with Energy:

> [E]mployee will not, for a period of 12 months after Termination, enter into employment as a service representative or salesperson with any Business that sells or markets Generator Equipment in any state where Employer sells or markets Generator Equipment.

Energy, a Minnesota corporation, provides large energy generators to commercial enterprises, such as hotels, hospitals, military installations, law enforcement offices, and shopping malls. Energy sells and services its equipment throughout the Midwest.

Energy uses a team approach to market and service its equipment. It assigns a team of four employees for each region. Although all team members are trained and competent to deal with all the servicing needs of the customers, each member is mainly responsible for one of four areas: Mechanical upkeep of generators; ongoing customer training; maintenance of computer equipment; and updating the computer software. Long was the team member responsible for customer training.

Before a sale, the teams meet with customers as a group several times a week for about six months to evaluate equipment selection, installation, and long-term servicing options. Once a sale is completed, the team works with the customers for regular upkeep and servicing. Each team member meets with the customers for approximately the same amount of time, which typically includes a regular quarterly meeting and additional meetings about once a month.

Energy assigned Long to the team in the northern region of Minnesota, which is approximately the northern half of the state. He was a member of that team for the approximately six years he was employed with Energy. Long did not become friends with any of his customers during his time at Energy. The team did not contact all potential customers in its territory.

Energy trained Long for about a year to fully familiarize him with the equipment and technical information. Energy provides the same training to all team members. For purposes of the memorandum, I have been asked to assume that Energy did not disclose any of its confidential information to Long.

Several months ago, Long left Energy and began working as a salesperson for a competitor, Bright Lights Unlimited, Inc. ("Bright Lights"). His territory is all of Minnesota. Since leaving Energy, Long has not solicited or contacted any of Energy's customers.

Long has sought our advice about the noncompetition clause because his new employer, Bright Lights, has expressed concern about his ability to continue working as one of its sales representatives if Energy attempts to enforce the clause against him.

Discussion

Introduction

Minnesota has not enacted a statute regarding the enforceability of noncompetition provisions in employment agreements. When evaluating such clauses, Minnesota courts disfavor them because they restrict employees' right to work and earn a livelihood. *See, e.g., Davies & Davies Agency, Inc. v. Davies*, 298 N.W.2d 127, 131; *Bennett v. Storz Broad. Co.*, 134 N.W.2d 892, 899 (Minn. 1965); *Webb Publ'g Co. v. Fosshage*, 426 N.W.2d 445, 450 (Minn. Ct. App. 1988). However, the courts recognize that employers need to be able to protect their businesses from departing employees using advantages they gained during employment to compete against the employers. *See Davies*, 298 N.W.2d at 131; *Bennett*, 134 N.W.2d at 898. To balance these competing concerns, a court will enforce a noncompetition clause only if the employer has a legitimate interest to restrict the departing employee and the terms of the clause reasonably protect that interest. *See, e.g., Davies*, 298 N.W.2d at 131; *Bennett*, 134 N.W.2d at 898.

Legitimate Interest Analysis

The courts first require that the employer have a legitimate interest in restricting the departing employee from competing against it. *E.g., Bennett*, 134 N.W.2d at 898–99; *Webb*, 426 N.W.2d at 450. An employer has such an interest when the employee acquired the employer's confidential information or developed close relationships with the employer's customers. *See Eutectic Welding Alloys Corp. v. West*, 160 N.W.2d 566, 569 (Minn. 1968); *Webb*, 426 N.W.2d at 450. The courts protect these interests because employers need the ability to defend themselves from unfair competition that would result if employees were allowed to use their confidential information or client relationships to compete against them. *See Bennett*, 134 N.W.2d at 898; *Webb*, 426 N.W.2d at 450. For purposes of this memo, I have been asked to assume that Long did not receive Energy's confidential information. Therefore, the discussion will focus only on Long's relationships with Energy's customers.

An employer has a legitimate interest when the departing employee has such close contacts with its customers that the strength of those relationships could draw the customers to the employee's new employer. *See, e.g., Davies*, 298 N.W.2d at 131; *Menter Co. v. Brock*, 180 N.W. 553, 555 (Minn. 1920); *Webb*, 426 N.W.2d at 450. To make this determination, the courts evaluate the totality of the relationships, including exclusivity, length, regularity, and the level of friendship between the employee and customers. *See, e.g., Davies*, 298 N.W.2d at 131; *Menter,* 180 N.W. at 555; *Webb*, 426 N.W.2d at 450. In addition, if the departing employee has begun working for a competitor and some customers have already followed the employee to that competitor, the court usually finds that the relationships were sufficiently close that more customers could be drawn to the new employer. *See Webb*, 426 N.W.2d at 450; *see also Davies*, 298 N.W.2d at 129-31.

> **12. Totality test.**
> See Ch. 7, C3.

For example, in *Davies*, the court found that the relationships between the employee and his clients were sufficiently close because the employee worked for the employer for eleven years, eventually taking over the employer's bond business and becoming the exclusive contact for many of those clients. 298 N.W.2d at 129. The court found that customers could follow the employee due to the strength of their relationships with him because he had exclusive contact with the clients for a significant length of time. *See id.* at 131.

> **13. Case illustrations in the text.**
> See Ch. 12, B5 and C.

The court also found sufficient relationships in *Webb*, where the departing employee, an account executive, was the exclusive contact with his clients for about seven years and became a friend with several of them during that time. 426 N.W.2d at 449. After the employee began working for a competitor, almost half of his customers canceled their contracts with the employer and followed him to the new employer. *Id.* at 450. The court reasoned that, because the employee had worked exclusively with the clients over seven years, and the employee developed friendships with some customers, the relationships between the employee and the clients were such that customers would likely follow the employee to the competitor. *See id.* Furthermore, because two of the clients actually had followed the employee to his new employment, the court found that more customers would likely do the same. *See id.*

> **14. Organizing case illustrations by court's result.**
> See Ch.12, C6.

On the other hand, the relationships are not sufficiently close if clients are unlikely to follow the departing employee to a competitor. *See Davies*, 298 N.W.2d at 131; *Menter,* 180 N.W. at 555. For example, in *Menter*, the court determined that the store manager of a retail-clothing store did not have sufficiently close relationships because he had only irregular and brief contacts with walk-in customers. *See* 180 N.W. at 554–55. Since these contacts were not regular and consistent, the court found that customers were unlikely to be drawn to a competitor by the employee. *See id.*; *see also Klick v. Crosstown State, Inc.*, 372 N.W.2d 85, 87–89 (Minn. Ct. App. 1985) (finding bank vice-president's eight-month employment too short to form close client relationships, even though relationships might have been regular and exclusive).

Energy probably has a legitimate interest

A court would probably find that Long has a close relationship with Energy's customers because he met with them frequently and regularly over a long period. *See Davies*, 298 N.W.2d at 131; *Webb*, 426 N.W.2d at 450. While he was not the only contact with the customers, he had fairly exclusive contact with them as a member of a small team of four that had the only interaction the customers experienced on behalf of Energy. *See Davies*, 298 N.W.2d at 131; *Webb*, 426 N.W.2d at 450. Furthermore, he was the sole representative responsible for working with the customers on equipment training. *See Webb*, 426 N.W.2d at 450. Thus, a court would probably find that his client relationships were close enough that they could draw those customers to his new employer. *See Davies*, 298 N.W.2d at 131; *Webb*, 426 N.W.2d at 450.

The court could consider the relationships in Long's case as similar to the close relationships found in *Webb*, where the employee worked for the business seven years, and during that time he developed regular, exclusive, and personal relationships with the clients, 426 N.W.2d at 447, 449. In that case, the totality of the relationships between the employee and the clients indicated that the relationships were sufficiently close that they could draw the clients to the departing employee's new employer. *See id.* The relationships in Long's case are similar in that he worked with his clients regularly and frequently for a period of six years. *See id.* Although the relationships are not exclusive or personal, the totality of Long's relationship with his clients is similar to the totality of the relationship in *Webb*. *See id.*

Furthermore, Long met with his customers regularly at least once a month for the past six years and therefore these customers would be much more likely drawn to his new employer than the customers in *Menter*. *See* 180 N.W. at 555. There, the employee only had infrequent, inconsistent, and brief contacts with clients. *See Menter*, 180 N.W. at 555.

---

15. Application-prediction. The next three paragraphs discuss how a future court would apply the analysis of the law for the legitimate interest component to the client's facts and reach a result. For a discussion of an application-prediction, see Ch. 10 (analytical foundation) and Ch. 13 (structure).

16. Prediction of likely result. See Ch. 10C and Ch. 13C.

17. Citation in an application-prediction. See Ch. 14, B2b.

18. Case comparisons. See Ch. 10D, and Ch. 13, C3 and D.

Reasonableness Analysis

If an employer has a legitimate interest in the departing employee's customer relationships, the court next requires that the clause reasonably protect those relationships in terms of time, subject matter, and territory. *See, e.g., Davies,* 298 N.W.2d at 131; *Overholt v. Bredeson,* 437 N.W.2d 698, 703–04 (Minn. Ct. App. 1989); *Dean Van Horn v. Wold,* 395 N.W.2d 405, 409 (Minn. Ct. App. 1986). If the relationships are close but the clause is unreasonable, the court has the discretion to refuse to enforce the clause or modify it to make it reasonable with the "Blue Pencil Doctrine." *See Davies,* 298 N.W.2d at 131; *Overholt,* 437 N.W.2d at 703–04; *Dean Van Horn,* 395 N.W.2d at 409.

Time Restriction

To be enforceable, the clause must include a reasonable time limit. *See, e.g., Davies,* 298 N.W.2d at 131; *Overholt,* 437 N.W.2d at 703–04; *Dean Van Horn,* 395 N.W.2d at 409. To be reasonable, the clause cannot restrict the departing employee any longer than approximately the time that the employer trained the departing employee, with a maximum limit of about two years. *See Davies,* 298 N.W.2d at 131; *Overholt,* 437 N.W.2d. at 703–04; *Dean Van Horn,* 395 N.W.2d at 409. The departing employee's training time is a reasonable period because it is enough time for the employer to train a replacement and for the customers to adjust to the change in company representation. *Compare Overholt,* 437 N.W.2d. at 703–04 (finding two-year restraint reasonable because departing employee received about that much training), *with Davies,* 298 N.W.2d at 131 (finding five-year restriction unreasonable and revising it to one year, the estimated time to train replacement); *Dean Van Horn,* 395 N.W.2d at 409 (finding three-year restriction unreasonable and revising it to one year, about the departing employee's training period).

Subject Matter Restriction

The courts also require that the clause include a reasonable subject matter restriction. *See, e.g., Davies,* 298 N.W.2d at 131–32; *Eutectic,* 160 N.W.2d at 570; *Overholt,* 437 N.W.2d. at 703. Courts originally seemed to require that the subject matter be no broader than restricting the employee from working for a competitor in a position that could put the employee in contact with the potential customers, usually the same position the employee held with the former employer. *See Eutectic,* 160 N.W.2d at 570; *Overholt,* 437

N.W.2d. at 703. This type of restriction protects employers' client relationships because it restricts departing employees from exploiting those relationships on behalf of competitors by prohibiting them from working in positions that could put them in contact with those customers. *See Eutectic*, 160 N.W.2d at 570 (finding subject matter unreasonable because it should have limited departing employee to similar position with competitor that he had with former employer).

More recently, courts seem to favor subject matter restrictions that only prohibit departing employees from contacting their former customers on behalf of a competitor. *See Davies*, 298 N.W.2d at 131–32; *Dean Van Horn*, 395 N.W.2d at 406; *Overholt*, 437 N.W.2d. at 703. Such nonsolicitation provisions more narrowly protect the client relationships than position-based restrictions. *See Dynamic Air v. Bloch*, 502 N.W.2d 796, 797–800 (Minn. Ct. App. 1993). When a job restriction is used, the employee is restricted from taking a position that might put the employee in contact with former customers. *See Davies*, 298 N.W.2d at 131–32; *Dynamic,* 502 N.W.2d at 797–800. Such a restriction effectively prevents the employee from working with any potential customers, even though the employee may not have had any contact with many of those customers while working with the former employer. *See Davies*, 298 N.W.2d at 131–32; *Dynamic,* 502 N.W.2d at 797–800. A nonsolicitation restriction, on the other hand, only restricts the employee from contacting former customers, which leaves the employee free to contact other potential customers who did not have a connection with the former employer through the departing employee. *Compare Dynamic,* 502 N.W.2d at 797–800 (finding subject matter reasonable because it only restricted departing employee from contacting his former customers on behalf of competitor); *Overholt*, 437 N.W.2d. at 703 (finding subject matter reasonable because it was interpreted to only restrict departing employee from contacting his former customers on behalf of competitor), *with Davies*, 298 N.W.2d at 131–32 (suggesting that appropriate revision to subject matter would be to restrict departing employee from only contacting his former customers on behalf of competitor).

Territory Restriction

The court also requires that the territory of the clause be reasonable. *See, e.g.*, *Walker v. Parkhurst,* 219 N.W.2d 437, 441 (Minn. 1974); *Eutectic*, 160 N.W.2d at 570; *Overholt*, 437 N.W.2d. at 703. The courts generally require that, to be reasonable, the territory restriction be no broader than limiting the departing employee from working in the same geographic area where the employee had worked for the employer. *See Walker*, 219 N.W.2d at 441; *Eutectic*, 160 N.W.2d at 570; *Overholt*, 437 N.W.2d. at 703. This type of restriction protects the employers' client relationships because it prohibits departing employees from working in areas where they could exploit their relationships with the former employers' customers to the benefit of the new employers. *Compare Walker*, 219 N.W.2d at 441 (finding territory reasonable because it limited departing employee from working in the county where he had worked for former employer); *Overholt*, 437 N.W.2d. at 703 (finding territory reasonable because it limited departing employee from competing in his former sales territory), *with Eutectic*, 160 N.W.2d at 570 (finding territory unreasonable because it limited departing employee from competing in 50-mile radius of former territory, which included areas in which employee had not worked for former employer).

Recently, however, courts seem willing to allow employers to include an unlimited territory restriction if they use a subject matter provision that only prohibits the departing employee from contacting former customers, rather than one that restricts the employee from working in a particular position. *See Dynamic,* 502 N.W.2d at 797–800. Limiting the employee from contacting former customers — wherever they are located — reasonably protects the employer's client relationships. *See id.* That limitation, the courts reason, would still allow the former employee to contact other potential customers who had no previous connection with the former employer through the employee. *See id.* (finding territory restriction unnecessary because the subject matter limited departing employee from contacting all former customers).

Blue Pencil Modifications of Unreasonable Restrictions

24. Topic-transition sentence. See Ch. 12, D2.

If the noncompetition clause is not reasonable, the court may refuse to enforce the clause entirely or modify it with the "Blue Pencil Doctrine" to make it reasonable. *See Davies*, 298 N.W.2d at 131; *Klick*, 372 N.W.2d at 88–89; *Dean Van Horn*, 395 N.W.2d at 409. Although the use of the doctrine is discretionary, the courts favor its application unless the clause suggests that the employer fashioned it to discourage competition generally, rather than tailoring a clause that would reasonably protect its legitimate interest. *See Dynamic,* 502 N.W.2d at 800 (reminding trial court of discretion to "blue pencil" a clause that it remanded for reconsideration). To make this determination, courts examine the terms of the clause as a whole to decide if they are so burdensome on the departing employee that the clause makes finding work elsewhere effectively impossible, even though much less burdensome restrictions would adequately protect the employer's legitimate interest. *See Davies*, 298 N.W.2d at 129–32 (revising clause even though all provisions were unreasonable because overall effect of clause did not seem to suggest that employer was trying to make finding work effectively impossible for employee).

Energy's clause probably is unreasonable, but will be enforced with "Blue Pencil" modifications

> 25. Separation of an analysis of the law from the corresponding application-prediction. See Ch. 11, C2c.

A Minnesota court probably would find that Long's noncompetition clause is unreasonable, but enforce it with modifications. *See Davies*, 298 N.W.2d at 131; *Overholt*, 437 N.W.2d at 703–04; *Dean Van Horn* at 409. Although a court likely would determine the time and subject matter restrictions are reasonable, it probably would decide that the territory restriction does not reasonably protect Long's relationships with his former customers at Energy. *See Davies*, 298 N.W.2d at 131; *Overholt*, 437 N.W.2d. at 703–04; *Dean Van Horn* 395 N.W.2d at 409. Instead of refusing to enforce the unreasonable clause, a court likely would revise it with the "Blue Pencil Doctrine." However, the specific modifications a court would make are unclear. *See Davies*, 298 N.W.2d at 131; *Klick*, 372 N.W.2d at 88–89; *Dean Van Horn*, 395 N.W.2d at 409.

Time restriction will likely be enforced as written

A court probably would find the time restriction is reasonable because it restricts Long for 12 months and his training period was about a year. *See Davies*, 298 N.W.2d at 131; *Overholt*, 437 N.W.2d. at 703–04; *Dean Van Horn*, 395 N.W.2d at 409. The court likely would consider this one-year restriction similar to the one-year restriction the court enforced in *Dean Van Horn*, because they are both equivalent to the departing employees' training period. *See* 395 N.W.2d at 409.

Subject matter and territory will likely be enforced with Blue Pencil revisions

A court would also probably find that the subject matter restriction is reasonable because it restricts Long from working as "a service representative or salesperson with any Business that sells or markets Generator Equipment." *See Eutectic*, 160 N.W.2d at 570; *Dynamic*, 502 N.W.2d at 797–800. This provision is reasonable because it only restricts Long working for a competitor in a position that would put him in contact with his former customers on behalf of a competitor. *See Eutectic*, 160 N.W.2d at 570 (finding a reasonable subject matter would limit departing employee to similar position he held with former employer).

However, a court probably would find that the territory of the clause to be unreasonable because it restricts Long from working "in any state" where Energy does business. *See Davies*, 298 N.W.2d at 131–32; *Walker*,

219 N.W.2d at 441 *Eutectic*, 160 N.W.2d at 570. This provision is unreasonable because it is not limited to restricting Long from working in the geographic area where Long worked with Energy's clients. *See Eutectic,* 160 N.W.2d at 570; *Overholt,* 437 N.W.2d. at 703. The territory restricts Long from working in any state where Energy sells its equipment, even though his customers were located in only part of Minnesota. *See Eutectic,* 160 N.W.2d at 570; *Overholt,* 437 N.W.2d. at 703. Therefore, a court likely would find this provision unreasonable because it restricts Long more than is necessary to protect Energy's interest in his relationships with its clients. *See Eutectic,* 160 N.W.2d at 570; *Overholt,* 437 N.W.2d. at 703. Long's territorial restriction is similar to the unreasonable restriction in *Eutectic* because they both restrict the departing employee from geographic areas where the employees had not worked for the former employer. *See* 160 N.W.2d at 570. Thus, it is unlike the reasonable restriction in *Overholt*, which limited the departing employee only from working for a competitor in his former sales territory. *See* 437 N.W.2d. at 703.

Even though a court likely would find the noncompetition clause unreasonable, it would probably exercise its discretion to enforce the clause with modified terms, using the "Blue Pencil Doctrine." *See Davies*, 298 N.W.2d at 131; *Klick*, 372 N.W.2d at 88–89; *Dean Van Horn*, 395 N.W.2d at 409. Since both the time and subject matter provisions are reasonable, a court would likely decide that the provisions of the clause are not so excessive to suggest that Energy was simply trying to prevent any possible competition rather than tailoring a clause that would narrowly protect its interest. *See Davies*, 298 N.W.2d at 131; *Klick*, 372 N.W.2d at 88–89; *Dean Van Horn*, 395 N.W.2d at 409. A court probably would decide that the overall impact of the clause is similar to the covenant that the court revised with the "Blue Pencil Doctrine" in *Davies,* because even though both clauses had unreasonable terms, the clause overall was not so broad as to suggest that the employer was trying to make finding work effectively impossible for the employees. *See* 298 N.W.2d at 131.

> **26. Application-prediction based on a prediction and a counter prediction.** See Ch. 10C and Ch. 13E.

Although the court will likely enforce a modified clause, the modifications a court would make are unclear because the court would have two options. *See id.* at 131; *Klick*, 372 N.W.2d at 88–89; *Dean Van Horn*, 395 N.W.2d at 409. A court could decide that, even though the subject matter seems reasonable, since the territory is more burdensome than necessary, the best way to improve the clause would be to make both the subject matter and territory narrower. *See Davies*, 298 N.W.2d at 131–32; *Eutectic*, 160 N.W.2d at 570; *Overholt*, 437 N.W.2d. at 703. In this situation, the court could

> **27. Prediction.** In this paragraph, the author sets out the prediction of one possible result. For the counter prediction, see Comment 28.

modify the clause so it restricts Long only from contacting his former customers on behalf of a competitor in the northern region of Minnesota, his former sales territory. *See Davies*, 298 N.W.2d at 131–32; *Eutectic*, 160 N.W.2d at 570; *Overholt*, 437 N.W.2d at 703. This change would make the clause similar to the reasonable clause in *Overholt* and the revised clause in *Davies* because they would all only limit the departing employee from contacting former customers on behalf of a competitor in the territory where they worked for the former employer. *See Overholt*, 437 N.W.2d. at 703; *Davies*, 298 N.W.2d at 131–32.

However, a court could leave the subject matter alone, revising only the territory clause. *See Eutectic*, 160 N.W.2d at 570; *Overholt*, 437 N.W.2d. at 703. Taking this approach, the court would modify the clause so it restricts Long from working as a sales representative for a competitor in his former territory, the northern part of Minnesota. *See Eutectic*, 160 N.W.2d at 570; *Overholt*, 437 N.W.2d. at 703. With this modification, the clause would be similar to the covenant the court suggested would have been reasonable in *Eutectic* because they would be restricting the departing employees only from working for a competitor in a similar position and territory as they had worked for the former employers. *See* 160 N.W.2d at 570; *see also Dynamic*, 502 N.W.2d at 797–800 (suggesting that non-competition clause can be reasonable if it includes reasonable job-based subject matter and territorial restrictions).

28. Counter prediction. In this paragraph, the author sets out the counterprediction of another possible result.

Conclusion

29. Conclusion Section. See Ch.15C.

A Minnesota court probably would not enforce Mike Long's non-competition clause as written. Although a court would probably find that Energy has a legitimate interest to restrict Long because of his close relationships with its customers, it would also find that the clause itself is too broad to reasonably protect those relationships. While a court likely would find that the time and subject matter restrictions are reasonable, it probably would decide that the territory provision is not and revise the clause with the "Blue Pencil Doctrine." However, the specific modifications a court would make are unclear.

A court could revise the clause so that it restricts Long from contacting any of his former customers on behalf of a competitor in the northern part of Minnesota, his former territory with Energy, for the one-year period. However, a court could modify the clause so it restricts Long from working as a service or sales representative, his former position with Energy, for a competitor in the northern part of Minnesota for one year.

APPENDIX II

Sample Email to Supervisor

Email to:	Senior Colleague
From:	Junior Colleague
Re:	Long: Noncompete Clause — Memo Summary
Attachments:	Memo on Long Noncompete Clause

After our meeting about my memo on Mike Long's noncompete clause, I thought you might like a quick synopsis of the memo to help prepare for your meeting with Mike and Barbara Trujillo, his new boss at Bright Lights. I have attached a copy of the memo to this message.

I understand that Ms. Trujillo has told Mike that she is worried about his ability to continue working with Bright Lights because of the noncompete clause. Specifically, she is not sure if Bright Lights should invest in Mike's training if Energy will be able to use the clause to enjoin him from working for Bright Lights for the one-year limit. Based on my analysis, I do not think that a court would likely enforce the clause as written — in particular the territory restriction — although it probably would enforce the clause with modified terms. Here are the bottom-line predictions (explained in detail in my memo) if we challenged the clause in court:

- *Most likely result: Mike Long can work for Bright Lights anywhere, including northern Minnesota, but he will be restricted from contacting his former Energy customers for one year.* The court will revise the clause to restrict Mike from contacting his former Energy customers on behalf of Bright Lights in northern Minnesota for the one-year period in the clause.
- *Worst-case scenario: Mike Long will be restricted from working for Bright Lights in northern Minnesota for one year.* The court could revise the clause to restrict Mike from working as a service representative or salesperson for Bright Lights in northern Minnesota for the one-year period in the clause.

After your meeting, please let me know if you would like me to begin working on a summary of potential arguments or to get started on drafting a brief.

---

1. This Sample Email is an example of a message transmitting a complete memo to a supervising attorney, based on the Formal Objective Memorandum in Appendix I. For a discussion of informal internal office communications, including use of different formatting and style options, see Ch. 17.

Index

Active verbs
  nouns, questioning turning active verbs into, 264
  passive verbs versus, 262–263
Addendum
  checklist, 10
  inclusion of statutes, regulations, or constitutional provisions, 8–9
  overview, 8–9
Alternative application-predictions, 147–150
ALWD Guide to Legal Citation, 225
Analysis
  by courts. *See* Court's analysis
  of judicial opinions. *See* Judicial opinion analysis
  legal analysis in discussion section. *See* Legal analysis in discussion section
  of statutes. *See* Statutory analysis
Analysis of the current status of the law in discussion section. *See* Legal analysis in discussion section
Annotated codes, 43
Application-predictions
  alternative versus single predictions, 147–150
  analytical foundation of, 145–154
  arguments, moving from predictions to, 153–154
  brief answer section and
    inclusion of, 249
    summarization of, 249
  case comparisons, 209–214
    analytical foundation of, 150–153
    choice of precedent, 210
    complex analysis, based on, 222–223
    explanation from legal analysis, 213–214
    information court would use, inclusion of, 211–214
    legally significant facts of client, 212
    legally significant facts of precedent, 212–213
    similar and dissimilar precedent, 211
  checklists, 154, 224
  citation to legal authority in, 228–229
  comparison of precedent
    necessary, 150–151
    unnecessary, 152–153
  complex analysis, based on, 219–223
    analysis not indicating clear organizational choice, 220–221
    case comparisons, 222–223
    structuring, 221
  consistency between analysis of the law and application-predictions, 257
  counter-predictions, 214–217
    discussion section, summarization in, 245–246
    full development of, 216
    lack of clarity of law, due to, 149
    order of predictions and counter-predictions, 216–217
    separate development of predictions and counter-predictions, 215–216
    statement regarding lack of clarity of outcome, 215
    uncertainty of result, due to, 149–150
  discussion section and
    inclusion in, 245
    summarization in, 245–246
  effective structure, 203–224
  in judicial opinion synthesis, 129–130
    consistency between analysis of the law and application-predictions, 257
    organization of discussion section, separation of analysis of the law from application-predictions, 166–167
  organization of discussion section, separation of analysis of the law from application-predictions, 166–167
  overview, 145, 203
  paragraph development in, 219
  placement of, 204
  preliminary drafting stage and, 16–17
  purpose of, 146–147

relationship to analysis of law
single predictions, 205–209
   alternative predictions versus, 147–149
   citation to legal authority, inclusion of, 209
   comparison of facts, inclusion of, 206–207
   legal analysis, application of, 206
   predicted outcome, beginning with, 205–206
   summary sentence, 208–209
  summary paragraphs or sentences, use of, 218
   at end of prediction, 218
   "roadmap" paragraphs or sentences, 218
  topic-transition sentences, use of, 219
  transitions, use in, 218–219
Audience for memo, 4–5
  attorneys with little prior knowledge of content, 4
  busy attorneys, 4
  checklist, 9
  persons evaluating work for hiring or promotion, 5
  persons taking action on analysis, 4–5

Balancing tests, 97–98
Bill of Rights, 29
The Bluebook, 225
Brainstorming stage, 12–15
  checklist, 24
  judicial opinion synthesis, use of brainstorming in, 110–111
  legal issues, preparation for, 14–15
   clear answer provided by relevant legal authority, 14
   interpretation of relevant legal authority required, 14
   questions of first impression, 14–15
  note-taking, development of techniques, 13
  overview, 12
  relevant law, determination of, 13
Brief answer section, 247–249
  application-predictions and
   inclusion of, 249
   summarization of, 249
  checklists, 9, 252
  citation to legal authority, exclusion of, 248

consistency with question presented section, ensuring, 248–249
  example, 283
  multiple answers, 249
  ordering ideas from general to specific, 249
  organization of, 249
  overview, 7, 246
  "yes" or "no" answer, inclusion of, 248
Bright-line tests, 97

Canons of statutory construction
  definitions and, 139
  ejusdem generis, 139
  noscitur a sociis, 139
  ordinary usage of terms, 139
  punctuation, 139
  questions of first impression, 137–140
  statutory analysis, consultation in, 50
Case briefs, 79
Case comparisons in application-predictions, 209–214
  analytical foundation of, 150–153
  choice of precedent, 210
  complex analysis, based on, 222–223
  explanation from analysis of the law, 213–214
  information court would use, inclusion of, 211–214
  legally significant facts of client, 212
  legally significant facts of precedent, 212–213
  similar and dissimilar precedent, 211
Charts
  judicial opinion synthesis, use in, 115–117
   basic information, inclusion of, 115
   decision, inclusion of, 115–116
   explicit language, inclusion of, 116
   facts, inclusion of, 115
   implicit analysis, inclusion of, 116
   overview, 114
   setting up, 115–116
   synthesis of ideas, use in, 116–117
  preliminary drafting stage, use in, 19–20
Checklists
  analysis of the law, content and structure, 201–202
  application-predictions, 154, 224
  audience for memo, 9
  brainstorming stage, 24

brief answer section, 252
citation to legal authority, 233
codes, 51
conclusion section, 251–252
discussion section, 252, 265–266
email, 281
facts section, 251–252
final presentation stage, 25
informal internal office communications, 280–281
judicial opinion analysis, 92–93
judicial opinion synthesis, 122–123, 136
objective writing, 24–25
parts of memo, 9–10
   addendum, 10
   brief answer section, 9
   conclusion section, 10
   discussion section, 9–10
   facts section, 9
   heading, 9
   question presented section, 9
preliminary drafting stage, 25
presentation, 271–272
purpose of memo, 9
question presented section, 251–252
questions of first impression, 143
sources of law, 38
statutes, 51
statutory analysis, 51–52, 70–71
as tests, 99
Citation to legal authority, 225–233
   analytical decisions, 225–230
   application-predictions, inclusion in, 209
   in application-predictions, 228–229
   appropriate citation signals, 229–230
      "compare . . . with . . . ," 230
      "e.g.," 230
      no signal, 229–230
      "see," 229–230
      "see also," 230
   brief answer section, exclusion from, 248
   checklist, 233
   choice of authority, 225–227
   conclusion section, exclusion from, 244
   in discussion section, 228
      description of legal analysis, 228
      legal analysis, use in, 178
   overview, 225
   plagiarism in, 231–232
      author's viewpoint, 232
      contrary view, 232

   primary legal authority, 232
   secondary legal authority, 231
   preliminary drafting stage, during, 230–231
   primary legal authority
      "best" mandatory authority, 226–227
      constitutional provisions, 226
      judicial opinions, 226–227
      own jurisdiction, 226
      plagiarism in, 232
      regulations, 226
      statutes, 226
   secondary legal authority, plagiarism in, 231
   sufficiency of authority, 227–229
Clarity in presentation, 261–267
   active verbs versus passive verbs, 262–263
   editing, 267
   excessive separation between subject and verb, avoidance of, 266
   modifying phrases, 264
   nouns, questioning turning active verbs into, 264
   paragraph length, evaluation of, 261
   pronouns, avoiding problems with, 265–266
   sentence length, evaluation of, 261
   "there is," questioning sentences beginning with, 263
   "who does what to whom," 262–266
Codes, 40–43
   checklist, 51
   context, use of topical organization for, 42–43
   editorial features in annotated codes, 43
   location of complete statute using, 40–42
Common law
   discussion section, introduction in, 161
   judicial opinion synthesis, illustrations, 119–122
   questions of first impression
      consideration in, 140–141
      new approach to, 141–143
Components. *See* Judicial opinion synthesis
Concision in presentation, 257–260
   legal analysis, use of parenthetical case illustrations in, 189–190
   organization, evaluation of, 257–258
   passages including repetition, revision of, 258

Index

summaries, evaluation of, 258
transitions using repetition, reducing use of, 258–259
unnecessary introductory phrases, deletion of, 260
unnecessary statements, deletion of, 259–260
Conclusion section, 242–246
  checklists, 10, 251–252
  discussion section and
    consistency with, ensuring, 243–245
    legal analysis not included in, exclusion of, 243
  example, 293
  informal internal office communications compared, 276
  information included in, 242–244
    adequately informing readers without specific knowledge of situation, 243–244
    citation to legal authority, exclusion of, 244
    consistency with discussion section, ensuring, 243
    law as applied to client's situation, based on, 242
    legal analysis not included in discussion section, exclusion of, 243
  organization of, 244–246
    application-predictions, inclusion of, 245
    consistency with discussion section, ensuring, 244–245
    ordering ideas from general to specific, 245
    precise transitions, use of, 246
    summarization of application-predictions, 245–246
  overview, 8, 242
Confidential information in email, 280
Consistency in presentation, 255–257
  between discussion section and other sections, 257
  between introductory paragraphs and remainder of discussion section, 256
  between legal analysis and application-predictions, 257
Constitutions
  addendum, inclusion of provisions in, 8–9
  citation to legal authority, 226
  discussion section, introduction in, 160–161
  organization of discussion section around discussion following introductory paragraphs, 164–165
  introductory paragraphs, 160–161
  questions of first impression and. *See* First impression, questions of
  as source of law, 29–32
  state constitutions, 30–32
  United States Constitution, 29–32
Counter-predictions, 214–217
  discussion section, summarization in, 245–246
  full development of, 216
  lack of clarity of law, due to, 149
  order of predictions and counter-predictions, 216–217
  separate development of predictions and counter-predictions, 215–216
  statement regarding lack of clarity of outcome, 215
  uncertainty of result, due to, 149–150
Court's analysis
  explanation, development of, 174
  judicial opinion analysis
    important aspects of court's analysis, 81–89
    tracking court's analysis, 85–87
  organization of discussion section around discussion following introductory paragraphs, 164–167
  introductory paragraphs, 162–163
  tests
    explanation of court's analysis of components, determination of, 105–106
    identification of court's analysis, 100–107

Definitions
  canons of statutory construction and, 139
  statutory analysis, consultation in, 49–50
Diagrams
  judicial opinion analysis using, 78–79
  preliminary drafting stage, use in, 19–20
  statutory analysis, use in, 48–49
Dicta, 88–89
Discussion section, 157–235

application-predictions and. *See also* Application-predictions
  inclusion of, 245
  summarization of, 245–246
checklists, 9–10, 252, 265–266
citation to legal authority in, 228
  description of legal analysis, 228
  legal analysis, use in, 178
conclusion section and
  consistency with, ensuring, 243–245
  legal analysis not included in, exclusion of, 243
consistency in
  between discussion section and other sections, 257
  between introductory paragraphs and remainder of discussion section, 256
example, 285–293
informal internal office communications compared, 276
legal analysis in. *See* Legal analysis in discussion section
organization of. *See* Organization of discussion section
overview, 8
timing considerations, 249–251
  beginning with discussion section, 250
  beginning with other sections, 250
  consistency with other sections, ensuring, 249–251
Dissenting opinion analysis, 91
Drafting memo. *See* Preliminary drafting stage

Editorial features
  in annotated codes, 43
  distinguishing from text, 75–76
Ejusdem generis, 139
Email, 278–280
  appropriate length, 278
  checklist, 281
  confidential information in, 280
  drafting off-line, 278
  example, 295–296
  formal tone, 278–279
  replying to, 279
  subject matter reference, clear identification of content in, 278
Examples
  brief answer section, 283
  conclusion section, 293
  discussion section, 285–293
  email, 295–296
  facts section, 284–285
  memo, 283–293
  problem, 297–313
  question presented section, 283
Explanation of court's analysis
  Analysis of component, 105–106
  Analysis of the law, use in, 174
  Application-prediction, use in, 206
Executive branch, 30

Facts section, 237–241
  checklists, 9, 251
  description of information in, 240
    accurate description of facts, 240
    relationships of individuals to legal issues, 240
  example, 284–285
  information included in, 238–239
    all legally significant facts, 238
    irrelevant facts, exclusion of, 239
    legal conclusions, exclusion of, 239
    necessary background facts, 238
    procedural history, 239
  organization of, 240–241
    chronological organization, 241
    combination of chronological and topical organization, 241
    statement of context, 241
    topical organization, 241
  overview, 7–8, 237
Federalism, 29
Final presentation stage, 23–24
  checklist, 25
  overview, 23
  timing considerations, 24
  two-step process, 24
First impression, questions of, 137–143
  brainstorming stage, 14–15
  checklist, 143
  common law, new approach to, 141–143
    analogous law in same jurisdiction, consideration of, 142
    other jurisdictions, consideration of law from, 142
    secondary legal authority, consideration of, 142–143
  constitutional or statutory provision not previously interpreted, 137–141

canons of statutory construction,
consideration of, 137–140
common law, consideration of, 141
external sources, consideration of,
140–141
historical context, consideration
of, 141
legislative history, consideration of, 140
other jurisdictions, consideration of
law from, 141
secondary legal authority,
consideration of, 141
textual context, 139–140
textual evaluation, 138–139
organization of discussion section, 169
overview, 137
plain meaning doctrine, 138

Gender-neutral language in presentation,
270–271
nouns, repetition of, 271
plurals, use of, 270
Grammar. *See* Presentation
General principles.
Analysis of the law, importance of
using in, 172
Distinguished from case illustrations, 172
Expressing all important ideas in, 117–118
Introductory paragraphs in discussion
section, use in, 163

Heading
checklist, 9
legal analysis in discussion section, use
in, 201
overview, 7
Highest appeals courts
judicial opinion synthesis
contradictory approaches with
unresolved conflicts, 127–130
incorrectly decided cases, exclusion
of, 133–135
as source of law, 33–34
statutory analysis and, 40

Illustrations, in general. *See* Examples
Illustrations, cases. *See* Legal analysis in
discussion section
Informal internal office communications,
275–281
analytical foundation, 275–276
checklist, 280–281

email, 278–280
appropriate length, 278
confidential information in, 280
drafting off-line, 278
example, 295–296
formal tone, 278–279
replying to, 279
subject matter reference, clear
identification of content in, 278
format of, 276–277
overview, 275
professionalism in, 277
structure of, 277
Intermediate appeals courts
judicial opinion synthesis
contradictory approaches with
unresolved conflicts, 130–131
incorrectly decided cases, exclusion
of, 133
as source of law, 33–34

Judicial branch, 30
Judicial opinion analysis, 73–93
actively reading cases, 75–79
active engagement with content, 76–79
diagrams or pictures, use of, 78–79
editorial features, distinguishing from
text, 75–76
narrative writing, use of, 77–78
outlines, use of, 78
skimming for sense of content, 75
summarization, 79
checklist, 92–93
court's language, use of, 91–92
dissenting opinions, 91
majority opinions
accurate description of facts, 84
application of law, determination of,
86–87
background facts, locating, 83–84
court's analysis, tracking, 85–87
dicta, evaluation of, 88–89
important aspects of court's analysis,
81–89
interpretation of law, determination
of, 85–86
legally significant facts, locating, 83–84
procedural history, determination of, 80
procedural results, 81
relevant versus irrelevant issues,
distinguishing, 80–81
reliance on court's discussion, 87–88

substantive decisions, 82–83
thorough analysis, 79–81
overview, 73
own personal opinion, distinguishing, 89–91
purposes, distinguishing between, 74–75
doctrine, learning, 74–75
law of jurisdiction, determination of, 74
statutory analysis compared, 73–74
Judicial opinions
analysis of. *See* Judicial opinion analysis
application-predictions from. *See* Application-predictions
legal analysis in discussion section. *See* Legal analysis in discussion section
overview, 36–37
as source of law, 36–37
statutory analysis, consultation in, 50
synthesis of. *See* Judicial opinion synthesis
Judicial opinion synthesis, 95–136
overview, 95–96
charts, use of, 115–117
basic information, inclusion of, 115
decision, inclusion of, 115–116
explicit language, inclusion of, 116
facts, inclusion of, 115
implicit analysis, inclusion of, 116
overview, 115
setting up, 115–116
synthesis of ideas, use in, 116–117
checklists, 122–123, 136
Components. *See below* Tests, analysis of
client's facts, use of, 113–114
common law, illustrations, 120–122
in complex analyses, 125–136
consistent approach but undeveloped law, 126
contradictory approaches with unresolved conflicts, 127–131
application-predictions, 129–130
highest appeals courts using, 127–130
identification and description of contradictory approaches, 128–129
intermediate appeals courts using, 130–131
description of results, 117–119
general principles, use of, 116–117
paraphrasing, 118–119

quotation marks, use of, 119
verbatim language, use of, 118–119
diagrams, use of, 114
explicit ideas, use of, 107–109
ideas explicit in all relevant cases, 108
ideas explicit in some relevant cases but implicit in others, 109
implicit ideas, use of, 109–113
brainstorming, 110–111
repetition of process, 113
revision or discarding of inconsistent descriptions, 112
testing descriptions on cases, 111–112
incorrectly decided cases, exclusion of, 133–135
highest appeals courts reaching, 133–135
intermediate appeals courts reaching, 133
keeping track of ideas, 114–117
charts, use of, 115–117
diagrams, use of, 114
other jurisdictions, use of cases from, 135–136
overview, 125–126
Tests, analysis of
choice of additional cases, 103–104
choice of first case, 102–103
components of
analysis of each component, development of, 104–107
court's reasoning for, 106–107
explanation of court's analysis of, 105–106
label of components, 104–105
organization of discussion section around, 165–166
role in court's overall test, 101, 105
court's analysis, identification of, 100–107
legal issues, determination for, 101
organization of discussion section around, 163–164
overall test of court,
components of, identifying, 101
court's reasons for, identifying, 101
reevaluation of, 104
Tests, kind of
balancing tests, 97–98
bright-line tests, 97
checklists of requirements, 99

303

sliding scale tests, 98
threshold tests, 100
totality tests, 98-99
unique facts, exclusion of cases decided on, 131-133
Jurisdiction, 30-31

Language. *See* Presentation
Legal analysis in discussion section
  Analysis of current status of the law, 145, 157
    Basic structure based on judicial interpretations, 171-178
    Relationship to application-predictions, 145, 157
    Separation from application-predictions, 166-167
  application-predictions and
    case comparisons, explanation of, 213-214
    consistency between analysis of the law and application-predictions, 257
    organization of discussion section, separation of analysis of the law from application-predictions, 166-167
    single predictions, application in, 206
  case illustrations in the analysis of the law, 178-196
    choice between text and parenthetical illustrations, 193-194
    choice of cases, 179
    combination of text and parenthetical illustrations, 192-193
    explicit versus implicit court analysis, 184
    legal convention, description of court's actions consistently with, 184
    legal interpretations, structuring based on, 175-178
    organization by result, 195-196
    parenthetical illustrations, use of, 185-192
    relationship between parties and legal analysis, 185
    tailoring to description of analysis, 180-184
    text, use in, 179-185
  checklist
    Analysis of the law, 201-202
    application-prediction, 224
    citation to legal authority, description of legal analysis, 228
  conclusion section, exclusion of legal analysis not included in discussion section, 243
  heading, use of, 201
  legal interpretations, structuring based on, 171-178
    case examples, use of, 175-178
    citation to legal authority, use of, 178
    court's analysis, development of explanation of, 174
    court's reasoning, description of, 175
    example, 178
    facts of cases not providing helpful illustrations of court's analysis, 177-178
    facts of cases providing helpful illustrations of court's analysis, 175-176
    general principles, use of, 172
    "label" and role of component in test, beginning with, 173
  overview, 171
  paragraph development in, 200
  parenthetical case illustrations, use of, 185-192
    choice between text and parenthetical illustrations, 193-194
    combination of text and parenthetical illustrations, 192-193
    concision, 189-190
    consistent construction of, 191-192
    ease of reading, 190-191
    placement of, 186
    tailoring to description of analysis, 186-189
  summary paragraphs or sentences, use of, 200-201
  text, use of cases in, 179-185
    choice between text and parenthetical illustrations, 193-194
    combination of text and parenthetical illustrations, 192-193
    consistent content and phrasing, use of, 183-184
    necessary aspects, description of, 180-181
    placement of, 180
    relationship with description of legal analysis, beginning with, 181-182

Index

topic-transition sentences, use of, 173, 199–200
transitions, use of, 196–199
  double-checking, 198–199
  precise connection of ideas based on underlying analysis, 196–198
Legal authority
  citation to. *See* Citation to legal authority
  legal issues, preparation for
    clear answer provided by relevant legal authority, 14
    interpretation of relevant legal authority required, 14
  primary legal authority
    citation to legal authority, 226–227. *See also* Citation to legal authority
    overview, 37
    plagiarism in, 232
  secondary legal authority
    citation to legal authority, plagiarism in, 231
    overview, 37
    questions of first impression, consideration in, 142–143
"Legalese," avoidance of, 268
Legislative branch, 30
Legislative history
  historical context and, 141
  questions of first impression, consideration in, 52, 140

Majority opinions. *See* Judicial opinion analysis

Narrative writing
  judicial opinion analysis, use in, 77–78
  statutory analysis, use in, 48
Noscitur a sociis, 139
Note-taking
  brainstorming stage, development of techniques in, 13
  judicial opinion analysis, use in, 79
  statutory analysis, use in, 63
Nouns
  questioning turning active verbs into, 264
  repetition of, 271

Objective writing. *See also specific section of memo*
  audience for memo, 4–5. *See also* Audience for memo
  brainstorming stage, 12–15. *See also* Brainstorming stage
  checklist, 24–25
  final presentation stage, 23–24. *See also* Final presentation stage
  Necessity of objectivity, 5–6
  overview, 11–12
  preliminary drafting stage, 15–23. *See also* Preliminary drafting stage
  purpose of memo, 5–6
Opinions. *See* Judicial opinions
Ordinary usage of terms, 139
Organization of conclusion section, 244–246
  application-predictions, inclusion of, 245
  consistency with discussion section, ensuring, 244–245
  ordering ideas from general to specific, 245
  precise transitions, use of, 246
  summarization of application-predictions, 245–246
Organization of discussion section, 157–170
  checklist, 169–170
  discussion following introductory paragraphs, 164–167
    application-predictions, separation of legal analysis from, 166–167
    court's analysis, organization around, 164–167
    order, experimentation with, 168
    statutes, regulations, or constitutional provisions, organization around, 164–165
    tests, organization around, 165–166
  introductory paragraphs, 159–163
    common law, introduction of, 161
    court's analysis, introduction of, 162–163
    guidelines, 163
    order, experimentation with, 168
    relevant legal authority, introduction of, 160–162
    statutes, regulations, or constitutional provisions, introduction of, 160–161
  multiple issues, 158–159
  order, experimentation with, 168–169
    abstract legal analysis, 168–169
    application of law to client's situation, 168–169

discussion following introductory
paragraphs, 168
introductory paragraphs, 168
other than questions of first impression,
159–169
questions of first impression, 169
Organization of facts section, 240–241
chronological organization, 241
combination of chronological and topical
organization, 241
statement of context, 241
topical organization, 241
Outlines
judicial opinion analysis using, 78
preliminary drafting stage, use in, 19–20
statutory analysis, use in, 48

Paragraph development
in application-predictions, 219
legal analysis in discussion section, 200
Paragraph length, evaluation of, 261
Paraphrasing
judicial opinion synthesis, use in,
118–119
presentation, use in, 253
Parties
description of in formal manner, 269
legal analysis, relationship with, 185
Parts of memo
addendum
checklist, 10
inclusion of statutes, regulations, or
constitutional provisions, 8–9
overview, 8–9
brief answer section. *See* Brief answer
section
checklist, 9–10
conclusion section. *See* Conclusion
section
discussion section. *See* Discussion section
facts section. *See* Facts section
heading
checklist, 9
overview, 7
question presented section. *See* Question
presented section
Passive verbs, 262–263
Pictures
judicial opinion analysis using, 78–79
preliminary drafting stage, use in,
19–20

statutory analysis, use in, 48–49
Plagiarism in citation to legal authority,
231–232
author's viewpoint, 232
contrary view, 232
primary legal authority, 232
secondary legal authority, 231
Precedent
application-predictions from. *See also*
Application-predictions
comparison necessary, 150–151
comparison unnecessary, 152–153
legal analysis in discussion section. *See*
Legal analysis in discussion section
stare decisis. *See* Stare decisis
Precision in presentation, 253–255
Predictions. *See* Application-predictions
Preliminary drafting stage, 15–23
checklist, 25
citation to legal authority during,
230–231
further explanation, keeping track of
issues needing, 21
overview, 15
shift of analysis to practitioners, 17–18
understanding process of writing, 18–20
combination of techniques, use of, 20
diagrams, pictures, or charts, use
of, 20
outlines, use of, 19–20
process of writing, use of, 18–19
unresolved problems, keeping track
of, 21
"writer's block," 21–23
"free writing," 22
paper copies, use of, 23
unnatural methods, use of, 23
verbal explanation of ideas, 23
writing to self as author, 15–17
analysis of current state of law,
development of, 16
application-predictions, 16–17
Presentation, 253–272
checklist, 271–272
clarity in, 261–267
active verbs versus passive verbs,
262–263
editing, 267
excessive separation between subject
and verb, avoidance of, 266
modifying phrases, 264

nouns, questioning turning active verbs into, 264
paragraph length, evaluation of, 261
pronouns, avoiding problems with, 265–266
sentence length, evaluation of, 261
"there is," questioning sentences beginning with, 263
"who does what to whom," 262–266
concision in, 257–260
legal analysis, use of parenthetical case illustrations in, 189–190
organization, evaluation of, 257–258
passages including repetition, revision of, 258
summaries, evaluation of, 258
transitions using repetition, reducing use of, 258–259
unnecessary introductory phrases, deletion of, 260
unnecessary statements, deletion of, 259–260
consistency in, 255–257
between discussion section and other sections, 257
between introductory paragraphs and remainder of discussion section, 256
between legal analysis and application-predictions, 257
gender-neutral language in, 270–271
nouns, repetition of, 271
plurals, use of, 270
overview, 253
paraphrasing, 253
precision in, 253–255
professional tone in, 267–269
informal language, avoidance of, 269
"legalese," avoidance of, 268
parties, description of in formal manner, 269
third-party neutral tone, use of, 267–268
verbatim language, use of, 253
Primary legal authority
citation to legal authority
"best" mandatory authority, 226–227
constitutional provisions, 226
judicial opinions, 226–227
own jurisdiction, 226
plagiarism in, 232

regulations, 226
statutes, 226
overview, 37
plagiarism in, 232
Professional tone in presentation, 267–269
informal language, avoidance of, 269
"legalese," avoidance of, 268
parties, description of in formal manner, 269
third-party neutral tone, use of, 267–268
Pronouns, avoiding problems with, 265–266
Purpose of memo, 5–6
checklist, 9

Question presented section, 247–248
central issue, inclusion of, 246–247
checklists, 9, 251–252
consistency with other sections, ensuring, 247
example, 283
multiple questions, 249
ordering ideas from general to specific, 247
overview, 7, 246
relationships of individuals to issues, inclusion of, 247
relevant facts, inclusion of, 247
"yes" or "no" answer, amenability to, 247
Questions of first impression. *See* First impression, questions of
Quotation marks, use of, 119

Regulations
addendum, inclusion in, 8–9
citation to legal authority, 226
discussion section, introduction in, 160–161
organization of discussion section around discussion following introductory paragraphs, 164–165
introductory paragraphs, 160–161
as source of law, 32
statutory analysis, consultation in, 50
Replying to email, 279
Requirements
Check-list tests, series of requirements, 99
Expressing precisely, Example of imprecise language, 254

307

Figuring out, Example, 119–120
"Roadmap" paragraphs or sentences, 218

Samples. *See* Examples
Secondary legal authority
   citation to legal authority, plagiarism in, 231
   overview, 37
   plagiarism in, 231
   questions of first impression, consideration in
      common law, new approach to, 142
      constitutional or statutory provision not previously interpreted, 141
Sentence length, evaluation of, 261
Separation of powers, 30
Session laws, 41–42
Shorthand Memos
   Analytical foundation, 275–276
   Format, 276–277
   Professionalism, 277
   Structure, 277
Signals. *See* Citation to legal authority
Single application-predictions, 205–209
   alternative predictions versus, 147–150
   citation to legal authority, inclusion of, 209
   comparison of facts, inclusion of, 206–207
   legal analysis, application of, 206
   predicted outcome, beginning with, 205–206
   summary sentence, 208–209
Skimming
   judicial opinion analysis, use in, 75
   statutory analysis, use in, 45
Sliding scale tests, 98
Sources of law, 29–38
   Bill of Rights, 29
   checklist, 38
   executive branch, 30
   hierarchy of, 31–32
   judicial branch, 30
   judicial opinions, 36–37
   jurisdiction and, 30–31
   legislative branch, 30
   primary legal authority, 37
   regulations, 32
   relationship among, 30–32
   secondary legal authority, 37
   stare decisis and, 32–36
      court following decision of court from other jurisdiction, 35–36
      court following decision of court from same jurisdiction, 33–34
      highest appeals court following own decision, 34
      overview, 32–33
   state constitutions, 30–32
   statutes, 32, 39–40
   United States Constitution, 29–32
Stages of memo writing
   brainstorming stage, 12–15. *See also* Brainstorming stage
   final presentation stage, 23–24. *See also* Final presentation stage
   preliminary drafting stage, 15–23. *See also* Preliminary drafting stage
Stare decisis, 32–36
   court following decision of court from other jurisdiction, 35–36
   court following decision of court from same jurisdiction, 33–34
   highest appeals court following own decision, 34
   overview, 32–33
State constitutions, 30–32
Statutes
   addendum, inclusion in, 8–9
   analysis of. *See* Statutory analysis
   checklist, 51
   citation to legal authority, 226
   discussion section, introduction in, 160–161
   organization of discussion section around
      discussion following introductory paragraphs, 164–165
      introductory paragraphs, 160–161
   questions of first impression and. *See* First impression, questions of
   relationship with courts, 40
   role of, 39–40
   as source of law, 32, 39–40
Statutory analysis, 39–71
   active exploration, 47–49
      diagrams or pictures, use of, 48–49
      narrative writing and, 48
      outlines, use of, 48
   applicability to situation, confirmation of, 43–45
      effective date, checking, 43–44
      verification of relevance, 44–45
   basic process, 39–52

Index

breaking down statute, 55–63
canons of statutory construction
   consultation of, 50
   definitions and, 139
   ejusdem generis, 139
   noscitur a sociis, 139
   ordinary usage of terms, 139
   punctuation, 139
   questions of first impression, 137–140
cause and result, identification of, 58
checklists, 51–52, 70–71
codes, use of, 40–43
   checklist, 51
   context, use of topical organization for, 42–43
   editorial features in annotated codes, 43
   location of complete statute, 40–42
common transitions, identification of, 60–61
comparison of similar statutes, 46–47
definitions, consultation of, 49–50
exceptions, creation of, 58
expression in memo, 51
further development, 49–50, 70
individual terms
   breaking down specific pieces into, 64–67
   distinct role of, determination of, 65–66
   relationship among, determination of, 66–67
   separation of, 64–65
judicial opinion analysis compared, 73–74
judicial opinions, consultation of, 50
note-taking, use of, 62–63
overview, 39, 53
reevaluation of organization of statute, 53–67
regulations, consultation of, 50
rereading statute to break down content, 45–47
restriction, provision of, 58–59
skimming statute for content, 45
specific pieces
   distinct role, determination of, 56–60
   individual terms, breaking down into, 64–67
   relationship among, determination of, 60–62
   separation of, 55–56
   understanding how pieces fit together, 68–70
structure used by legislature, identification of, 54–55
substantive focus of statute, addressing, 57
summarization, 49
test, identification of, 59–60
transitions, use of
   common transitions, identification of, 60–61
   transitions referring to prior ideas, 62
understanding how pieces fit together, 68–70
Summary paragraphs or sentences
   application-predictions, use of, 218
      at end of prediction, 218
      "roadmap" paragraphs or sentences, 218
   legal analysis in discussion section, use in, 200–201
Synthesis. *See* Judicial opinion synthesis

Tests. *See* Judicial opinion synthesis
Threshold tests, 100
Topic-transition sentences
   application-predictions, use in, 219
   legal analysis in discussion section, use in, 173, 199–200
Totality tests, 98–99
Transitions
   application-predictions, use in, 218–219
   conclusion section, use of precise transitions in, 246
   legal analysis in discussion section, use in, 196–199
      double-checking, 198–199
      precise connection of ideas based on underlying analysis, 196–198
   statutory analysis, use in
      common transitions, identification of, 60–61
      transitions referring to prior ideas, 62
      transitions using repetition, reducing use of, 258–259
Trial courts, 33–34

United States Constitution, 29–32
United States Courts of Appeals, 34
United States District Courts, 34
United States Supreme Court, 34, 40

Verbatim language
    judicial opinion synthesis, use in, 118–119
    presentation, use in, 253
Verbs
    active verbs versus passive verbs, 262–263
    excessive separation between subject and verb, avoidance of, 266
    nouns, questioning turning active verbs into, 264

"Writer's block," 21–23
    "free writing," 22
    paper copies, use of, 23
    unnatural methods, use of, 23
    verbal explanation of ideas, 23